ANSYS® Workbench

Software
Tutorial with Multimedia CD
Release 11

Fereydoon
Dadkhah
and
Jack
Zecher

ISBN: 978-1-58503-426-0

PUBLICATIONS

Schroff Development Corporation

www.schroff.com
www.schroff-europe.com

Preface

There are many good textbooks that cover the theory of finite element analysis, and several tutorials that illustrate the steps that must be followed to operate a finite element program. However, there is a lack of material that integrates both basic finite element modeling concepts with a tutorial approach of learning how to operate a finite element program. This book and the accompanying CD are aimed at filling this void. The tutorials are presented in both written and multimedia formats to accommodate different learning styles. The book is directed to using finite element analysis to solve engineering problems. In several chapters, the finite element tutorial problem is compared with manual calculations so that the reader can compare and contrast the finite element results with the manual solution.

The primary purpose of this tutorial is to introduce new users to the ANSYS® Workbench™ software, by illustrating how it can be used to solve a variety of problems. This book and CD do not contain an in depth treatment of the theoretical basis of finite element analysis (FEA), but instead, are aimed at the practitioner who wishes to begin making use of the software.

Because of the "applied" sense of this book it can be used in combination with other textbooks, to cover the "laboratory" portion of courses that are theoretically based. In cases where the course is application based, it can serve as the primary text. In addition to the step by step tutorials, introductory material is provided that covers the capabilities and limitations of the different element and solution types. The majority of topics and examples presented are oriented to stress analysis, with the exception of natural frequency analysis (chapter 12) and heat transfer (chapter 13). It is expected that the reader has a background in engineering mechanics and mechanics of materials and for chapter 13, heat transfer.

This tutorial takes the approach that the reader should always compare their FEA results with other data; obtained from either manual calculations or experimental test data. Most of the examples and some of the exercises make reference to existing analytical solutions. The authors feel that only through this process will new users be able to begin understanding how good finite element models are built.

Finite element analysis has become a widely accepted powerful tool in both today's engineering offices as well as being taught in most engineering related programs. The ANSYS Workbench software discussed in this tutorial represents a powerful tool that can be used to solve many types of engineering problems. However, without appropriate training on how to use this powerful software, its benefits cannot be fully realized. It is the goal of this tutorial to provide both written and multimedia material that will assist users of this software to begin learning some of its capabilities.

DISCLAIMER

The material contained in this tutorial, including the discussions, examples and exercises, are intended to only demonstrate the functionally of the software, and are not to be construed as full engineering design solutions for any particular problem. Use of any of the methods and procedures described herein are for instructional purposes only and are not warranted or guaranteed to provide satisfactory solutions in any specific problem. The authors and publisher assume no responsibility or liability for any errors or inaccuracies contained in this tutorial, or for any results or solutions obtained using the methods and procedures described herein.

This book and accompanying CD are not endorsed or sponsored by ANSYS, Inc. or Delphi Corporation.

Acknowledgements

We would like to express our appreciation to Rob Wolter for his excellent narration work of the audio portion of the CD-Rom.

We would like to thank Professor Dan Baldwin for his efforts and artistic talent in creating the book's cover.

Acknowledgement is due to Stephen Schroff of SDC Publications for his encouragement and willingness to distribute this book and CD-Rom to a larger audience.

Special thanks to Mary Schmidt of SDC for her skilful assistance in preparation of the manuscript.

To Dr. Paul Lethbridge and Dr. Shane Moeykens of ANSYS, Inc., we are most appreciative for their assistance. Our thanks also go to John Ferens and Al Hancq for their concise technical answers.

Jack Zecher writes:

I would like to thank the many students who have used various forms of course notes and the preliminary version of the text. Your input has helped mold this book and CD-Rom into its present form.

Finally, a very sincere thanks to my wife, Karen, for her continued love, understanding and tolerance of my schedule during the past year when the preparation of this book and accompanying CD-Rom preempted time that belonged, by all reasonable standards, to important family and social activities.

Fereydoon Dadkhah writes:

I am grateful to my family for their patience while I worked on completing this book. I am particularly grateful to my wife Barbara and my daughter Shireen whose love, support and encouragement kept me going.

About the CD-Rom

The files contained on the CD-Rom were developed on a PC compatible machine running under the Windows XP operating system. However, they should be usable on most windows based operating systems.

The folders contained in the top level of the CD-Rom are: **Tutorials** and **Student Files**. These are described below:

Tutorials-

> This folder contains the audio-video version of each tutorial in *avi* format. They can be viewed using a number of different Windows utilities, such as Windows Media Player. The resolution of these audio-video files is 1020 x 732 pixels, therefore, they are most effectively viewed on systems running at a resolution of 1024 x 768 or higher.

> You can adjust the volume on the speakers or use the Windows utility's adjustment (if it provides this feature). If you are using headphones, make sure to plug them into the sound card and not the headphone jack located on the CD-Rom drive. Also, if you are using headphones, be aware that excessive sound volumes for even short periods of time can be dangerous – check the volume level before you put the headphones on.

Student Files-

> This folder contains two sub-folders: **Models** and **Tutorial Material Database**.

> **Models**-

>> This folder contains geometry files that are used in some of the tutorials and exercises.

> **Tutorial Material Database**-

>> This folder contains data files that describe material properties for some of the tutorials.

Contents

5   Using DesignModeler to Create Surface and Line Geometry

6   Introduction to Finite Element Simulation

7   Using the Wizards

8   Modeling Techniques

9   3D Solid Element Modeling & Simulation Techniques

1

Introduction

Finite element analysis is a computer-based numerical technique that is used to solve stress analysis, heat transfer, fluid flow and other types of engineering problems. It was first used to solve stress analysis problems (which is also the focus of this book), but is now used in the solution of many other types of problems. It is based on solving a system of equations that describe some parameter (such as displacement) over the domain of a continuous physical system, (such as a part's surface).

The real power of the finite element method lies in its ability to solve problems that do not fit any standard formula. Prior to the use of the finite element method, stress analysis problems were usually matched to a handbook's formula, which was derived for a standard shaped part. If the shape of the part being analyzed did not fit any standard formula, the analyst would approximate it, best he could. This was done by envisioning some simplified shape or loading system that approximated the actual case at hand. In contrast, the finite element method is able to analyze physical parts that are of any shape or size having arbitrarily located loads and supports.

As the name implies, finite element analysis involves the partitioning (also called discretizing) of a structure into a finite number of elements. Elements are connected to one another at their corner points. These corner points are called nodes or nodal points. Each element is a simple geometric shape, such as a triangle or quadrilateral. Being a standard shape (triangle, quadrilateral...) facilitates the development of the governing equations that relate the displacement and stress behavior within the element.

In order to completely define a finite element model, nodal points, elements, loads, supports and element related data (such as material properties) must be defined. Once this data has been defined, it is submitted to a finite element program for the actual computational process. The program then formulates a set of simultaneous equations, which are the equilibrium equations corresponding to each degree of freedom (directions in which movement can occur) at each nodal point. A nodal point can have up to six degrees of freedom - translation in the x, y, and z directions and rotation about each of these axes. As the finite element model is loaded and begins to deform, the force at each nodal point depends on the force at every other node. The finite element model, therefore, acts like a large system of springs - deflecting until all forces balance. Since there are usually hundreds or thousands of equilibrium equations generated to represent a typical finite element model, the use of a computer for the solution process is mandatory.

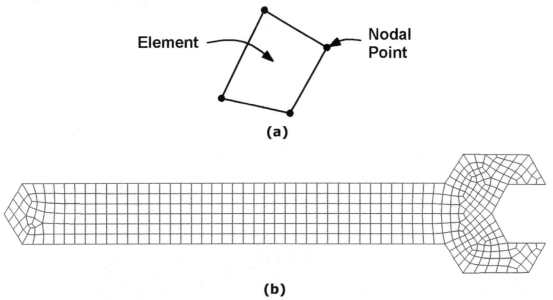

(a)

(b)

Figure 1.1 Typical individual finite element (a) and a sample model (b).

In stress analysis problems, the numerous simultaneous equilibrium equations are solved for the displacements at each nodal point. These displacements are then used to determine the stresses within each element. In order to define a model that accurately represents the physical part being modeled, a sufficiently fine mesh of elements must be defined. This will ensure that the deflection of the finite element model closely resembles that of the actual part. In addition, the type of element and appropriate boundary conditions must be applied to correctly represent the physical behavior of the part. As we will discuss throughout the remainder of this book, different element types (having up to six different degrees of freedom per nodal point) can be used to build finite element models.

Because finite element models usually involve the preparation of a large number of nodal points and elements, the process of data preparation and data analysis has developed into a specialty area of finite element analysis. These steps are referred to as Pre-processing and Post-processing. Since both of these steps involve a large amount of user interaction, computer graphic techniques and the ability to interface with CAD databases have done much to automate both the pre- and post-processing phases. In contrast, the analysis process (solving the simultaneous equations) is done entirely by the computer. Typical computer graphic displays of the resulting deflected shape and stress contours of an example part are shown in Figure 1.2.

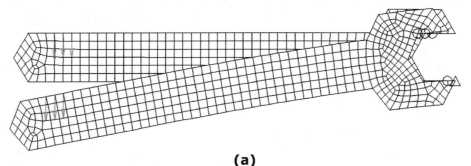

(a)

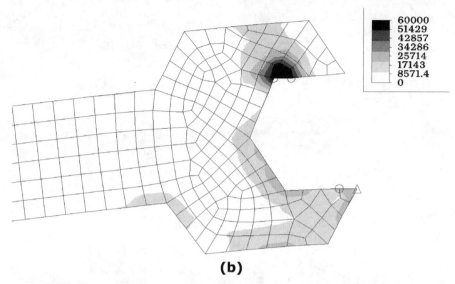

(b)

Figure 1.2 Example displays of the deformed shape (a) and stress contours (b) of the finite element model shown in Figure 1.1.

1.1 Steps in the Finite Element Analysis Process

The first step in preparing a finite element model involves defining the input data and is referred to as the Pre-processing phase. It consists of the following:

- Discretize the part by defining nodal points (*x, y, z* coordinates) and elements (connectivity).

- Define the elements' material properties, such as: modulus of elasticity, Poisson's ratio, density, and thermal expansion coefficient.

- Specify the supports, also called boundary conditions (locations where the part is attached to ground or an adjacent part).

- Specify the loads (forces, centrifugal loading, thermal expansion, deflections).

The actual analysis process does not require any user interaction and is frequently quite time consuming. Users often times start the analysis phase and let it run in the "background" while they continue to work on other tasks in the foreground environment. During this analysis phase, the program performs the following steps:

- Formulates equations that describe each element's stiffness and then assembles all of the elements' equations so that they form a set of simultaneous equations that represent the total structure's stiffness.

- Solves the system of equations for the displacements at each nodal point.

- Uses the nodal point displacements to solve for stress within each element.

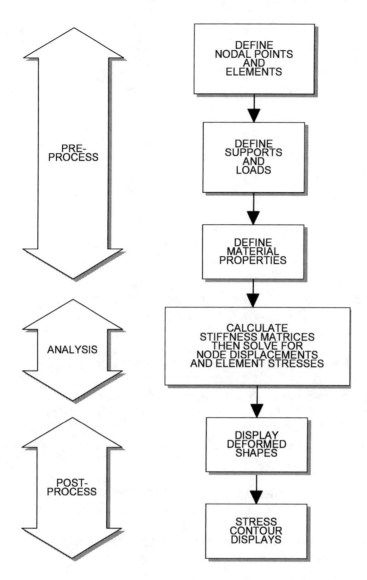

Figure 1.3 Flowchart of the Finite Element Analysis Process

The final phase is referred to as post-processing. The primary goal of this phase is to make sense out of the large amount of data that is generated during the analysis phase. Since there is usually a large number of nodal points and elements, the process of manually examining page after page of computer printouts has been replaced by reviewing computer graphic displays. These displays usually show: displacements at nodal points, stresses within each element, deformed shapes and various stress contour plots.

1.2 Library of Element types

Most commercially available FEA programs allow models to be build using a number of different types of finite elements. The figure shown below illustrates several different types of elements usually included in most finite element programs.

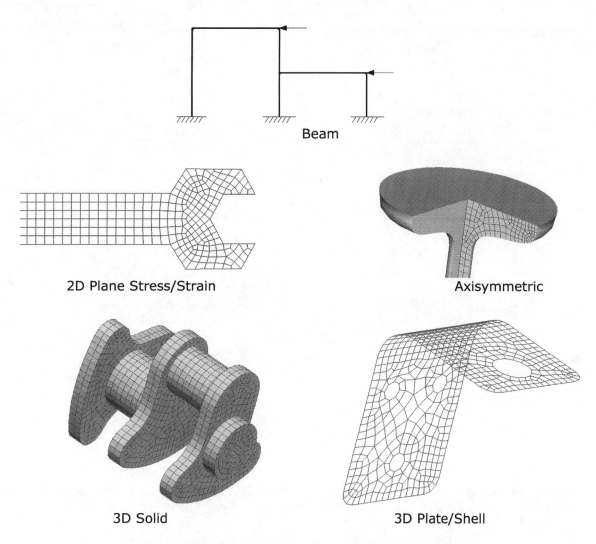

Beam

2D Plane Stress/Strain   Axisymmetric

3D Solid   3D Plate/Shell

Figure 1.4 Typical Element types usually available in finite element programs

1.3 Overview of ANSYS Workbench

Workbench can be thought of as a software platform or framework where you perform your analysis (Finite Element Analysis) activities. In other words, Workbench allows you to organize all your related analysis files and databases under the same framework.   Among other things, this means that you can use the same solid model file to perform a number of different analyses or use the same material property set for all your analyses. If this description still seems abstract, don't worry, it will become clearer as you learn to use Workbench.

The applications that fit into the Workbench framework are:

- DesignModeler
- Simulation
- DesignXplorer
- DesignXplorer VT
- CFX Mesh
- FE Modeler

The individual applications are briefly described below.

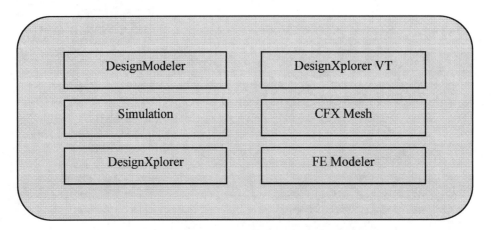

Figure 1.5 The Workbench Environment

DesignModeler – Use this application to create CAD geometry or modify geometry created in third party applications and use the geometry in the other Workbench applications.

Simulation – Use this application to perform Finite Element Analysis including structural, thermal and modal analysis. The main focus of this book is the Simulation application.

DesignXplorer – Use this application to optimize a design using Design of Experiments (DOE) methodology.

DesignXplorer VT – Use this application to optimize a design using Variational Technology (VT). This application differs from the standard DesignXplorer in that it uses a mathematical technique to drastically decrease the number of runs made to find the optimized design.

CFX Mesh – Use this application to generate a mesh that is used by the CFX program. CFX performs Computational Fluid Dynamics (CFD).

FE Modeler – Use this application to import a finite element model that was generated using the FEA program Nastran into Workbench.

In this book, our focus is on Simulation which is where you perform FEA of mechanical components and systems. DesignModeler, which is the solid modeling application, will also be introduced and its major features and workings explained because we will need to use it to build some of the models that are used in Simulation.

1.4 Advantages of using Finite Element Analysis

Use of the finite element method provides several advantages over conventional stress analysis and experimental techniques. Several of these advantages are listed below:

- Allows irregularly shaped parts to easily be analyzed.
- Allows parts which are made from a combination of several different types of materials to be analyzed, since each element's equations are formulated separately.
- Allows irregular loads to be placed on the part being analyzed.
- Allows a large number of locations on the part to be supported.
- Provides results of deflections and stresses throughout the entire part, rather than at just the location where strain gages are placed, as in the case of experimental evaluations.
- Easily allows changes to be made to the model, so that alternative designs can be evaluated. This reduces the number of physical prototypes that need to be built.

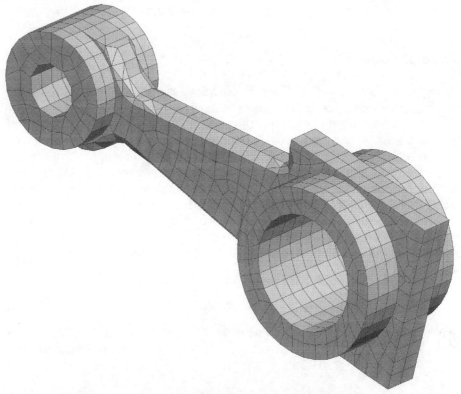

Figure 1.6 Typical finite element model

1.5 Historical Development

Development of the finite element method closely parallels the time table of the development of the digital computer. Prior to the advent of the digital computer, work during the 1940's involved the approximation of continuous solids as a collection of line elements (bars and beams). However, due to the lack of computation tools, the number of line elements had to be kept to a minimum. The first appearance of two-dimensional elements appeared in a paper published in 1956 by Turner, Clough, Martin, and Topp[1]. However, the term *finite element* was not used until 1960 in a paper by Clough. The 1960's were an era in which most large corporations began installing mainframe computers. However, most finite element analysis work was done as a research exercise, rather than being part of the normal product design cycle. During the 1970's, several large general purpose finite element programs running on mainframe computers began to appear. However, due to the dependence on large computing facilities, finite element analysis was generally used by only large corporations.

Computer graphic displays were not prevalent until the late 1970's. This forced the pre- and post-processing steps to rely on hardcopy graphical displays produced on plotters. This greatly increased the time required to perform the steps required in pre- and post-processing phases. During the 1980's, many finite element software packages were running on minicomputers along with highly interactive graphically oriented pre- and post-processors. The late 1980's and 1990's found many of these finite element packages being moved onto personal computers. However, even today, some finite element analysis is still done on large scale computers for problems which involve very large models, such as fluid flow computations, casting solidification and some non-linear structural analysis.

1.6 Scope of book

The goal of this book is to focus on introductory modeling techniques used in finite element analysis, specifically the Ansys Workbench finite element program. Both the capabilities and limitations of the finite element analysis for the solution of stress analysis problems will be addressed. This will hopefully help the reader to become a *responsible user* of the finite element method. Unfortunately, some people believe that finite element analysis is just another add-on feature to a CAD program, and therefore does not require any additional expertise to use. Several situations will be illustrated throughout this book in which very impressive finite element meshes can produce incorrect results. Hopefully, after reading this book and working through the exercises, the reader will gain a better understanding of how to build finite element models that correctly represent the corresponding physical part.

Reference

[1] Turner, M. J., Clough, R. W., Martin, H. C., and Topp, L. J., "Stiffness and Deflection Analysis of Complex Structures," Journal of Aeronautical Sciences, Vol. 23, No. 9, pp 805-824, Sept. 1956.

Exercises

1. Define the terms: ***nodal point, element,*** *and* ***degree of freedom***.
2. What does the term ***discretization*** mean in the finite element method?
3. List three different material properties that must be defined for each element.
4. Explain why the computer is necessary in the use of the finite element method.
5. Explain why computer graphic techniques are used during the post-processing phase of a finite element analysis. What is the alternative to using these graphical displays?
6. What advantage would a company derive by performing a finite element analysis of an existing part, which can be strain gaged and tested in a lab?

NOTES:

2

Stiffness Matrices

As discussed in Chapter 1, the process of calculating the displacements at each nodal point within a finite element model requires that a set of simultaneous equations be solved. In order to both assemble and then solve the resulting simultaneous equations, matrix concepts are used. Appendix A presents a summary of matrix algebra operations, and should be reviewed by readers not familiar with these techniques. In this chapter matrix techniques will be used to present the basic concepts of the *direct stiffness method*. Although other methods can be used to formulate element stiffness matrices, the direct method provides a straightforward technique when working with spring, bar (truss), and beam elements, and therefore, will be used in this chapter.

2.1 One-dimensional Spring Element

Although structural parts are actually three dimensional in shape, two-dimensional and sometimes one-dimensional models often times yield results that adequately represent the physical behavior of some parts. This simplification yields the advantage that a smaller number of equations have to be developed and then subsequently solved. We will likewise, take advantage of this simplification process in order to illustrate the fundamental principles of the finite element method.

The discussion in this chapter will be limited to the simplest type of structural element: the one-dimensional spring. While being simple, it still serves as a good instructive tool to illustrate basic concepts. The spring obeys Hooke's law (which states that the amount of deflection of the spring is linearly proportional to the force within the spring divided by its spring rate) and it only resists forces that are applied along the axis of the spring. Each spring has a nodal point at both of its ends and is restricted to lie along the *x-axis*. Each nodal point, therefore, has just one degree of freedom - translation in the *x*-direction.

A structural system modeled with two spring elements is shown below in Figure 2.1. The number enclosed in parentheses identifies each spring element's number. The numbers above the heavy dot identifies the nodal points numbers. The ***u*** values represent the displacement at the corresponding nodal point. Notice that these displacements concur with the degree-of-freedom of the node, which in this case is restricted to one direction (along the *x-axis*). The symbol ***F***, represents an applied force. We will begin by illustrating how to develop the stiffness matrix for each element as well as the entire model, and then explain how to solve for the displacement at each nodal point and the force within each spring element.

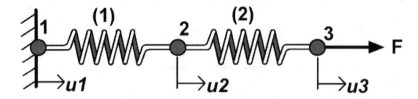

Figure 2.1 Structure modeled by two spring elements

2.2 A Single Spring Element

We will begin by developing the stiffness matrix of a single spring element. Figure 2.2 shows the general configuration of a spring element. Its spring rate will be defined as **k**, and its nodal points are indicated as **i** and **j**. The resulting displacements at nodes **i** and **j**, will be assumed to be positive (to the right) and will have the magnitudes u_i and u_j, as shown below. Nodal point forces at each nodal point, are defined by Hooke's law as: $f = k \cdot u$, and are represented as f_i and f_j, to indicate the force that this particular spring element is producing at end **i** and end **j**.

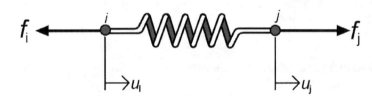

Figure 2.2 General configuration of the One-Dimensional Spring Element

Writing the equilibrium equations at each end of the spring in terms of the spring's relationship, yields:

$$k(u_j - u_i) = -k \cdot u_i + k \cdot u_j = f_i$$
$$k(u_i - u_j) = k \cdot u_i - k \cdot u_j = f_j$$

eq. 2.1

These equations can be written in matrix form (after multiplying both sides by -1) as shown below:

$$\begin{bmatrix} k & -k \\ -k & k \end{bmatrix} \begin{Bmatrix} u_i \\ u_j \end{Bmatrix} = \begin{Bmatrix} -f_i \\ -f_j \end{Bmatrix}$$

eq. 2.2

Or more compactly as:

$$[k]\{u\} = \{f\}$$

eq. 2.3

where, $[k]$ is referred to as the element stiffness matrix, $\{u\}$ is the element's nodal points displacement vector, and $\{f\}$ is the element's internal force vector.

EXAMPLE 2.1

In this example, we will examine a single spring element that is part of a finite element model that contains several elements. The spring rate is $k = 10$ lb/in., and the spring is producing two unknown internal forces: f_i and f_j which we assume to be positive, as shown below. The displacements are as shown below.

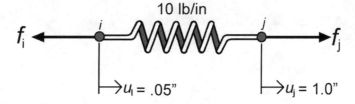

Using eq. 2.2, we can write:

$$\begin{bmatrix} 10 & -10 \\ -10 & 10 \end{bmatrix} \begin{Bmatrix} 0.5 \\ 1.0 \end{Bmatrix} = \begin{Bmatrix} -f_i \\ -f_j \end{Bmatrix}$$

multiplying the matrices yields:

$$5 \quad -10 \quad = \quad -f_i \quad \therefore \quad f_i \quad = \quad 5 \rightarrow$$
$$-5 \quad +10 \quad = \quad -f_j \quad \therefore \quad f_j \quad = \quad 5 \leftarrow$$

This illustrates that the forces f_i and f_j are actually internal forces on the nodes produced by the spring element as the nodes displace. Or, in other words, these forces are simply the amount of force that the spring in question is exerting on both nodes. (Pulling on both nodes toward the center of the spring element)

In order to illustrate how to analyze models that contain more than one spring element, we will now examine the two spring element model shown in Figure 2.1. The stiffness matrix for element number 1 can be written as:

$$\begin{bmatrix} k_1 & -k_1 \\ -k_1 & k_1 \end{bmatrix}$$

eq. 2.4

and the stiffness matrix for element number 2 can be written:

$$\begin{bmatrix} k_2 & -k_2 \\ -k_2 & k_2 \end{bmatrix}$$

eq. 2.5

The next step in the solution process is to assemble the stiffness matrix of the total structure so that the combined effect of both springs is correctly defined.

2.3 Assembling the Total Structure's Stiffness Matrix

In order to maintain equilibrium, the sum of the internal forces must equal the external forces at each node. We will indicate external forces as F_i, where **i** indicates the nodal point number where the force **F** is applied. Using this notation, the equilibrium equations for our sample three nodal point structure, shown in Figure 2.1, can be written:

$$k_1 u_1 - k_1 u_2 \qquad\qquad = F_1$$
$$-k_1 u_1 + k_1 u_2 + k_2 u_2 - k_2 u_3 = F_2 \qquad\qquad \text{eq. 2.6}$$
$$-k_2 u_2 + k_2 u_3 = F_3$$

that can be written in matrix form as:

$$\begin{bmatrix} k_1 & -k_1 & 0 \\ -k_1 & k_1+k_2 & -k_2 \\ 0 & -k_2 & k_2 \end{bmatrix} \begin{Bmatrix} u_1 \\ u_2 \\ u_3 \end{Bmatrix} = \begin{Bmatrix} F_1 \\ F_2 \\ F_3 \end{Bmatrix} \qquad\qquad \text{eq. 2.7}$$

or more compactly as:

$$[K]\{u\} = \{F\} \qquad\qquad \text{eq. 2.8}$$

where the uppercase [**K**], represents the entire structure's stiffness matrix (also, sometimes referred to as the global stiffness matrix).

This total structure's stiffness matrix [**K**] will always contain as many rows as there are degrees of freedom in the structure. Since each of the nodal points in our spring models have only one degree of freedom, there will be as many equations as there are nodes. Equation number 1 will correspond to nodal point number 1, while equation 2 will correspond to node number 2, etc. The order in which the nodal points are numbered will determine how the k values of the individual spring element's stiffness matrices are combined to form the total structure's stiffness matrix [**K**].

The values shown in equation 2.7, were placed in their respective positions based on the way the nodal points were numbered, left to right. Consider now the spring structure shown below in Figure 2.3, in which the nodal points are no longer consecutively numbered.

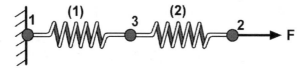

Figure 2.3 Spring structure with non-consecutive node numbering

In this structure, spring element 1 produces internal forces at nodes 1 and 3 (f_1 and f_3). Therefore, when the total structure's stiffness matrix is written, spring element number 1's stiffness matrix k_1 will affect rows 1 and 3, while spring element number 2's stiffness matrix k_2 will effect rows 3 and 2, since those nodal points are used in the definition of spring element 2. The following notation will be added to help understand the process of adding the individual spring elements' stiffness matrices to the total structure's stiffness matrix as shown below.

$$\begin{matrix} (1) & (3) \\ \begin{bmatrix} k_1 & -k_1 \\ -k_1 & k_1 \end{bmatrix} & \begin{matrix} (1) \\ (3) \end{matrix} \end{matrix} \quad and \quad \begin{matrix} (3) & (2) \\ \begin{bmatrix} k_2 & -k_2 \\ -k_2 & k_2 \end{bmatrix} & \begin{matrix} (3) \\ (2) \end{matrix} \end{matrix}$$

The numbers enclosed in parentheses indicate the degree of freedom as well as the column and row of the total structure's stiffness matrix where the individual values will be added. The structure's stiffness matrix [K] is then constructed by directly adding the individual values as follows:

$$[K] = \begin{bmatrix} k_1 & 0 & -k_1 \\ 0 & k_2 & -k_2 \\ -k_1 & -k_2 & k_1 + k_2 \end{bmatrix}$$

The resulting stiffness matrix shown above differs from the total structure's stiffness matrix [K] shown in equation 2.7 due to the numbering sequence of the nodal points.

The previous example also illustrates the concept of *bandwidth* of the total structure's stiffness matrix. By arranging the numbering of nodal points so that a minimum difference exists in each spring element, the stiffness terms, (*k's*) are concentrated closer to the diagonal of the resulting structure's stiffness matrix [K]. The term *bandwidth* refers to the number of terms we must move away from the main diagonal before we encounter all zeros. The figure shown below illustrates how a banded symmetric matrix is stored.

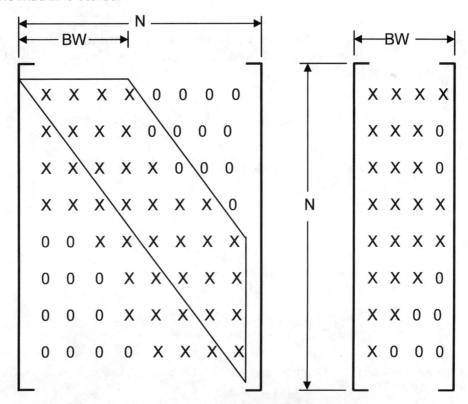

Figure 2.4 Example of how the concept of bandwidth affects the number of terms that must be stored in symmetric stiffness matrices.

2.4 Boundary Conditions

In most static structural FEA problems, the applied forces {*F*} are known, and the nodal point displacements are the unknowns. One technique for solving the resulting set of simultaneous equations is to premultiply both sides of equation 2.7 by the inverse of [*K*] (see Appendices A and B for more details on this process). However, if we try this with the model in question, we find that the inverse is singular, which means that we cannot get a unique solution. Physically this means that the structure is not in equilibrium, or simply, the structure is not restrained. This is because we have not taken into account the fact that nodal point 1 is attached to an immovable wall.

Nodal points that are restrained from movement are defined as boundary conditions (supports) for structural models. Without boundary conditions, structures would move as a rigid body. Boundary conditions are usually classified as one of two general types: homogeneous boundary conditions—the most common type—occurs at locations that are completely fixed; nonhomogeneous boundary conditions occur when a specified displacement at a nodal is given.

In order to solve problems that have homogeneous boundary conditions (structures that have a node or set of nodes fixed to ground) the equation(s) which corresponds to the degree(s) of freedom which are "fixed to ground" are eliminated from the set of equations (the structure's stiffness matrix). This produces a non-singular [*K*] matrix. An example of the entire procedure of assembling and solving for displacements and forces is illustrated below.

EXAMPLE 2.2

For the spring assemblage shown below, determine the contents of the global stiffness matrix, the displacements of nodal points 3 and 4 after the application of the 50 lb. force, and the reaction forces at the walls.

We begin by defining the contents of each spring element's stiffness matrices:

$$k_1 = \begin{matrix} (1) & (3) \\ \begin{bmatrix} 10 & -10 \\ -10 & 10 \end{bmatrix} & \begin{matrix}(1)\\(3)\end{matrix} \end{matrix} \quad and \quad k_2 = \begin{matrix} (3) & (4) \\ \begin{bmatrix} 10 & -10 \\ -10 & 10 \end{bmatrix} & \begin{matrix}(3)\\(4)\end{matrix} \end{matrix} \quad and \quad k_3 = \begin{matrix} (4) & (2) \\ \begin{bmatrix} 30 & -30 \\ -30 & 30 \end{bmatrix} & \begin{matrix}(4)\\(2)\end{matrix} \end{matrix}$$

Superimposing each of these three element's stiffness matrices into the global stiffness matrix yields:

$$K = \begin{bmatrix} 10 & 0 & -10 & 0 \\ 0 & 30 & 0 & -30 \\ -10 & 0 & 10+10 & -10 \\ 0 & -30 & -10 & 10+30 \end{bmatrix}$$

Now, since nodal points 1 and 2 are prevented from moving we will eliminate rows 1 and 2 and columns 1 and 2 of the stiffness matrix as well as the corresponding values in the force and displacement vectors. This produces the matrix equation that follows:

$$\begin{bmatrix} 20 & -10 \\ -10 & 40 \end{bmatrix} \begin{Bmatrix} u_3 \\ u_4 \end{Bmatrix} = \begin{Bmatrix} 50 \\ 0 \end{Bmatrix}$$

The unknown displacements at nodes 3 and 4 can be solved for by inverting the 2 x 2 stiffness matrix and premultiplying both sides of the equation as shown below:

$$\begin{bmatrix} 20 & -10 \\ -10 & 40 \end{bmatrix}^{-1} \begin{bmatrix} 20 & -10 \\ -10 & 40 \end{bmatrix} \begin{Bmatrix} u_3 \\ u_4 \end{Bmatrix} = \begin{bmatrix} 20 & -10 \\ -10 & 40 \end{bmatrix}^{-1} \begin{Bmatrix} 50 \\ 0 \end{Bmatrix}$$

This produces the displacement results at nodes 3 and 4 of:

$$\begin{Bmatrix} u_3 \\ u_4 \end{Bmatrix} = \begin{bmatrix} 0.057143 & 0.014286 \\ 0.014286 & 0.028571 \end{bmatrix} \begin{Bmatrix} 50 \\ 0 \end{Bmatrix} = \begin{Bmatrix} 2.857 \\ 0.7143 \end{Bmatrix}$$

To obtain the external forces at the nodal points (which will give us the reactions at both walls), we'll now back substitute the displacements we just solved for along with the zero displacements at nodes 1 and 2 back into the displacement vector, of equation 2.8, as shown below:

$$\begin{bmatrix} 10 & 0 & -10 & 0 \\ 0 & 30 & 0 & -30 \\ -10 & 0 & 20 & -10 \\ 0 & -30 & -10 & 40 \end{bmatrix} \begin{Bmatrix} 0.0 \\ 0.0 \\ 2.857 \\ 0.7143 \end{Bmatrix} = \begin{Bmatrix} F_1 \\ F_2 \\ F_3 \\ F_4 \end{Bmatrix}$$

and then perform the matrix multiplication, which yields the following results:

$F_1 = -28.57...\text{lb}$ $F_2 = -21.43...\text{lb}$ $F_3 = 50 \text{ lb}$ $F_4 = 0 \text{ lb}$

Notice that if we sum all the values of $\{F\}$, shown above, we end up with $\Sigma F = 0$. This confirms the rule from statics that states: *the sum of all external forces on a structure in equilibrium must equal zero.*

2.5 Summary

The steps that are used to solve the spring element problems can be summarized in the flowchart below:

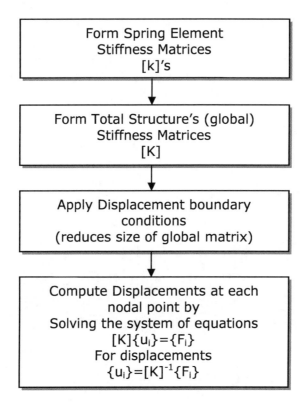

Exercises

1. For the spring assemblage shown below, develop the global stiffness matrix **[K]**, and also find the displacement and force at each nodal point. (*ans.* $u_2 = 0.25''$)

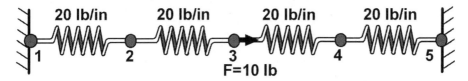

2. Repeat the process, using the figure shown above for exercise 1, with the modification of interchanging nodal point numbers 2 and 5.

3. Develop the global stiffness matrix, and then determine the displacement of nodal point 3, if the applied force F = 100 lb. (*ans.* $u_2 = 0.2''$)

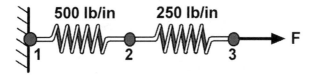

4. For the spring assemblage shown below, nodal point 3 moves 0.25 inches to the right. Determine the value of **F** that causes this to occur.

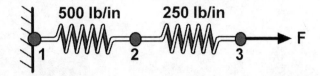

5. For the spring assemblage shown below, develop the global stiffness matrix [**K**], and also find the displacement and force at each nodal point.

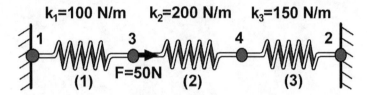

6. A 350 mm long solid steel step-down shaft is secured to supports at both of its ends. The shaft can be modeled as a two spring system, where the spring rate is defined by the equation: k=(AE/L). Determine the amount of deflection that will occur at the point where the 1500 kN load is applied. Use $E = 210 \times 10^9$ N/m^2.

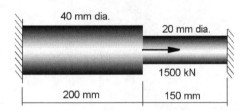

7. Explain each of the following terms:
   a) homogeneous versus non-homogeneous boundary conditions.
   b) restrained degrees of freedom.
   c) bandwidth

NOTES:

3

Introduction to Workbench

In chapter 1 we presented an overview on the Workbench environment. In this chapter we will introduce some of the Workbench functionality that is common to all the applications that run under Workbench.

In the remainder of the book we use the following shorthand convention:

Shorthand Notation	Meaning
Click	Press and release the mouse button. Normally refers to the Left Mouse button unless otherwise specified.
Drag	Click and hold the left mouse button while moving the cursor on the screen.
LMB	Left Mouse Button
RMB	Right Mouse Button
WB	Workbench
DM	DesignModeler
BOLD Text	Bold text is used to indicate the text that you see on the screen.
Bold Italic	Text or numbers you enter

3.1 Starting Workbench

Start Workbench from the Windows **Start** menu as you would other Windows programs from the **Start All Programs** menu. By default Workbench version 11.00 is installed in the **ANSYS 11.0** folder.

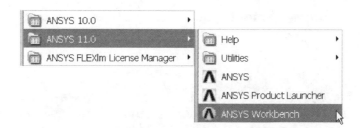

3.1.1 The Start Window

After Workbench starts, you will see the Start window as shown below.

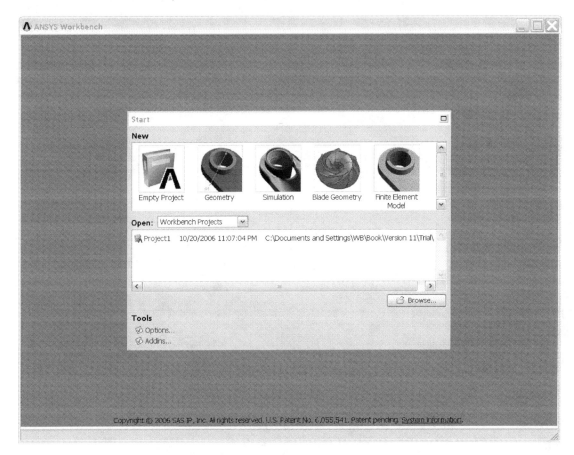

The Start window has three distinct sections which are described below.

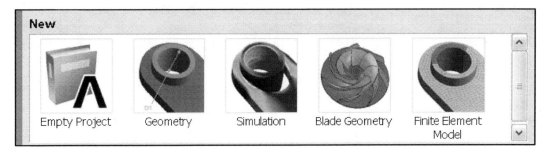

- **Empty Project**
  Click on the **Empty Project** icon to start a project that does not have any databases associated with it. You can add the appropriate databases after this step.

- **Geometry**
  Click on this icon to start a project and associate a **Geometry** database (DesignModeler) with it. Workbench will then start DesignModeler so you can start building the geometry.

- **Simulation**
  Click on this icon to start a project and associate a Simulation database with it. Workbench will then start the Simulation application. You use this option if you already have a solid model (geometry) that is ready to be used in your Simulation.

- **Other icons in this section**
  Several other icons may appear after the Simulation icon. The icons represent other applications that run under Workbench and for which your installation has the necessary license.

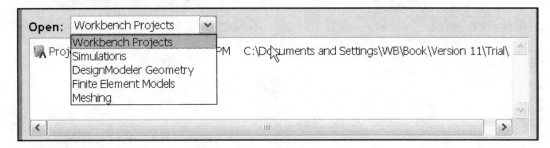

- **Open**
  In this section of the start window you can open an existing database that you have recently used by clicking on the name of the file. You can also change the type of file displayed by using the pull down menu.

  Some of the database files you may see in this window are:

  - Workbench database file (.wbdb extension)
  - Simulation database file (.dsdb extension)
  - DesignModeler geometry file (.agdb extension)
  - Finite Element Model file (.fedb extension)

- **Browse...**
  Click on the **Browse** button to search for a file that is not shown in the list. The **Browse** button will search for the file type selected in the pull down menu in the previous section.
- **Options...**
  Clicking on **Options...** opens the Options dialog box shown below which allows you to change the settings for all the Workbench applications.
- **Addins...**
  Addins is used to execute custom scripts. This topic is beyond the scope of this book.

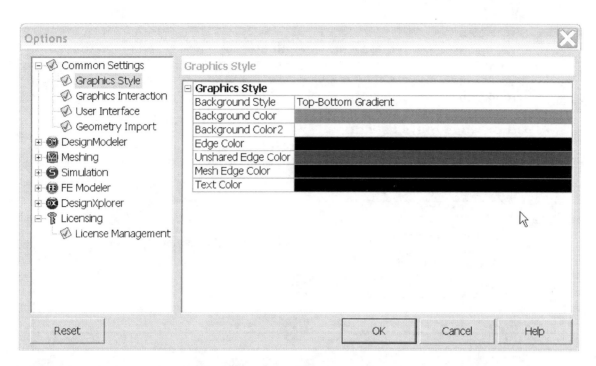

Expand the categories by clicking on the "+" next to a major category to expand that category then select a specific item. Selections for that item appear in the right pane where you can change them as appropriate. In the Figure above, **Graphics Style** under the **Common Settings** category has been selected.

3.2 The Project Page

Workbench organizes all the information related your Finite Element Analysis in a project. The project includes information on the geometry, material properties, loading conditions, etc. From the **Start Window**, you have the option of starting an empty project and add the relevant information yourself or begin the type of analysis you want to perform and Workbench will create the project automatically.

Regardless of how a project has begun, the Workbench window will have a project tab which gives you easy access to the project information.

The figure below shows an empty project page. Three areas of the window have been outlined and numbered and are explained below.

The first area marked as 1, shows the project tab. Other tabs will appear next to this one as you add to your project. For example geometry tab or simulations tabs may appear here. You can then access each of those applications by simply clicking on the appropriate tab.

The second area shows details about the project file. In this case the project has not been saved yet and the default name "Unsaved Project" is shown. Once the project is saved, the name as well as the size and the date it was last modified will appear in this area.

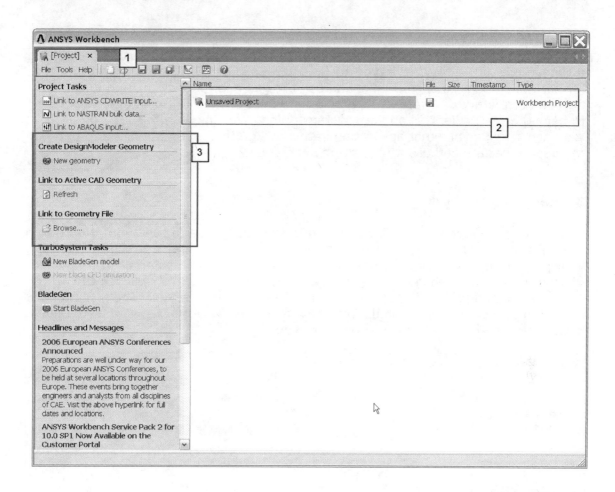

The third area is where you associate geometry with your project.   Let's take a closer look at this section.

Create DesignModeler Geometry

If you click on "New Geometry" here, Workbench will start DesignModeler, add a DesignModeler tab to your next to the project tab, start DesignModeler and you will see the DesignModeler new geometry opening dialog box. After you are done creating the geometry, you will click on the Project tab again and create a Simulation model for the geometry you just created.

Link to Active CAD Geometry

This section allows you to take advantage of a very powerful feature of Workbench which is to work with an *active* CAD model.   An active CAD model is one that is open in the CAD application at the same time Workbench is running. This means that any changes you make to the CAD model will be reflected in the simulation model. You can even drive the changes from applications such as Simulation or DesignXplorer by using parametric models. We will explore this more later. Keep in mind that in order for the CAD model name to appear in this section two important conditions must be met:

1. The CAD model must be open and active in the CAD tool
2. You must have a license for the "Plug-in" for that CAD tool

Link to Geometry File

This section allows you to open a geometry file on your system and use it to perform a simulation. If the file is of a type such as ParaSolid or IGES, the translator for that format will be used to open the file and use the geometry in a simulation task. If the file is a proprietary CAD format such as Unigraphics or ProE or SolidEdge, you have to have that particular tool on your system. When you link with this type of file, Workbench will invoke that application in the background, open the file, and bring in the geometry data and use it to perform simulation.

3.3 Saving Your Work

You can use the standard Windows functionality of File|Save to save your Workbench files. However, you should be aware that several file types may be associated with your project and each one may need to be saved. This point is demonstrated when you try to exit Workbench before you have saved your work. You will see the project page and asked to save the files that have not been saved. The files that need to be saved are highlighted. You will not be able to close this window until you have taken one of the actions presented to you.

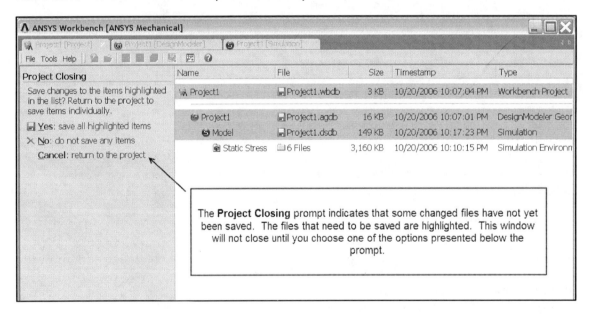

In this example the project contains a DesignModeler database (Project1.agdb) and a Simulation database (Project1.dsdb). The results of the analysis (labeled as **Static Stress** in this case) are saved automatically.

3.4 Common Interface Features

Several features of Workbench are common to DesignModeler and Simulation applications and are described in this section. The functions described below are accessible from the toolbars and from the pop-up or context menus. The pop-up menus are accessed by clicking the RMB when the cursor is in the **Geometry** pane (In DesignModeler this pane is called **Model Preview**).

3.4.1 Selecting Model Entities

You can use the icons shown below to select portions of your model. The selected entities can then be operated on. For example the selected entities can be deleted or used to construct new entities in DesignModeler or and in Simulation you can impose loads and boundary conditions on them.

Icon	Function
	Selection Mode. Allows you to select single entities or drag a box around the items you want to select.
	Point or Vertex. Select points and vertices only.
	Line or Edge. Selects lines and edges only.
	Surface or Face. Select surfaces and faces only.
	Body. Select solid bodies only.
	Adjacent. Select the adjacent faces. Pull down allows selection of immediate neighbors only if they meet an angular tolerance or extended selection in which case the selection process continues until the angular tolerance is no longer met.

3.4.2 Manipulating Model Entities

The icons shown below are used to manipulate the model displayed on the screen.

Icon	Function
	Rotate. Rotate the image on the screen by dragging the mouse pointer.
	Pan. Move (translate) the object on the screen by dragging the mouse pointer.
	Zoom in/out. Enlarge the image by dragging the mouse from the bottom of the window towards the top. Reduce the image size by dragging from top of the window towards the bottom.
	Box Zoom. Drag a box on the screen to indicate the opposite corners of the area to be zoomed.
	Fit To Window. Fit the image on the screen to the **Geometry** (**Model Preview**) pane.
	Magnifier. Open a magnifier window which can be moved around on the displayed part.
	Previous View. Display the previous view.
	Next View. Display the next view.
	Isometric View. Display the isometric view.
	Look At. Orient the view such that the line of sight is perpendicular to the face, plane or sketch that is selected.

3.4.3 Window Manager Features

The Workbench Simulation window contains a number of smaller window panes which appear depending on the selection in the outline pane. For example the figure below shows the Workbench window when a force load is selected.

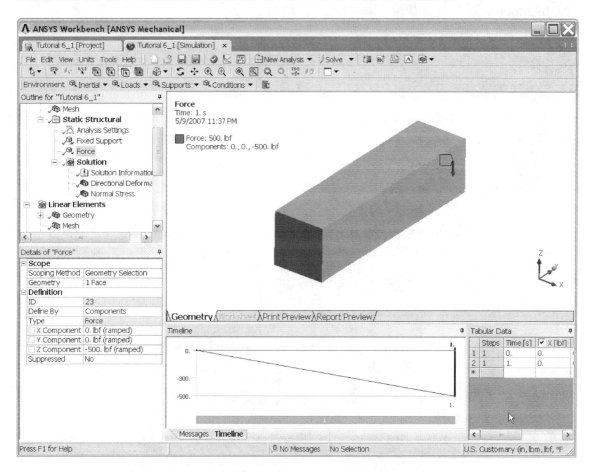

These window panes can be pinned (displayed) or unpinned (collapsed). A pinned window occupies space in the Workbench window while the unpinned or collapsed window is represented as a tab on the right hand side of the Workbench window. The terms pinned and unpinned refer to the state of the pushpin icon that appears on the top right hand corner of the window panes that have this feature. You can unpin a window pane to reclaim the space they occupy and restore them when they are needed.

- To unpin a window pane, click on the pushpin icon in the top right hand side corner of the pane.
- To restore a collapsed (unpinned) window, move the mouse cursor to the tab representing the window pane, hold the cursor there for moment and then click on the pushpin icon when the pane opens.

The figure below shows the Simulation window after the Timeline and Tabular Data panes have been unpinned and are represented by the tabs shown on the right hand side of the Simulation window.

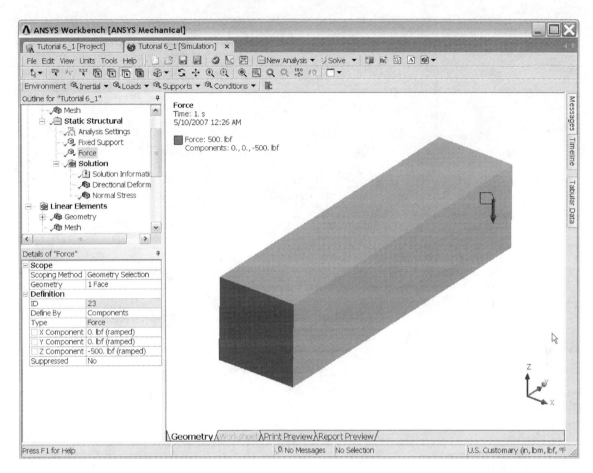

The window manager also allows you to move the window panes and doc them to different sides of the Simulation window. Refer to the online help for Simulation for more information on moving and docking the window panes. You can find this information by searching for the word Pane and then selecting **Window Manager Features**.

Note that the some panes have their own tabs which appear at the bottom of the pane. For example the **Timeline** pane has two tabs; **Messages** and **Timeline** which can be made active by clicking the tab.

3.5 Material Properties

In Workbench material property data is maintained by an application called **Engineering Data**. This application allows the user to create or import material properties, convection coefficients and load histories. Convection coefficients are used in heat transfer analyses and load histories are used in applications where the load varies with time.

Engineering Data is accessed by clicking on the **Engineering Data** icon from the project or the simulation tabs as shown below. Once the application is activated, the application tab is added to the top of the window next to the project and simulation tabs and **Engineering Data** window opens as shown below. To work with material properties, first select the Materials folder. You can then define new materials, import new materials into the project or modify existing ones.

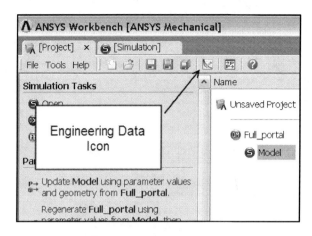

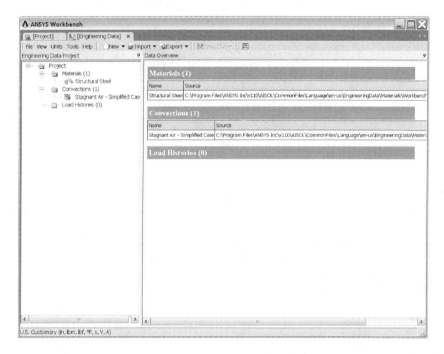

To add a new material type to the project, select **Material** from the **New** drop down menu shown below. Enter a name for the new name for the material and then enter the material properties required for your analysis.

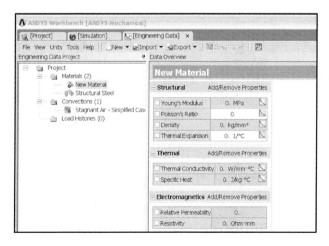

3.6 Customizing the Workbench Interface

Since Workbench supports a large number of analysis types, it has many features and capabilities that are not used in an introductory book such as the present text. However, the Workbench User Interface (UI) can be customized in a number of ways to fit the task for which it is used. The following sections describe how this customization can be performed in order to make the UI consistent with the tutorials presented in this book.

3.6.1 Orientation of the Sketching Plane in DesignModeler

By default, DesignModeler coordinates are oriented so that when you draw on the XZ plane, the Z axis is horizontal. In this book we use the more common convention of using the Z axis as the vertical axis and X as the horizontal axis. This section shows you how to orient the sketching coordinate system such that it is consistent with the tutorials in this book.

In order to set the orientation of the Z axis, perform the following steps:

Step 1 – Start Workbench by clicking on the ANSYS Workbench icon.
                                    - or -
        Start – All Programs – ANSYS 11.0 – ANSYS Workbench

Step 2 – Click on **Options**… on the Start dialog box.

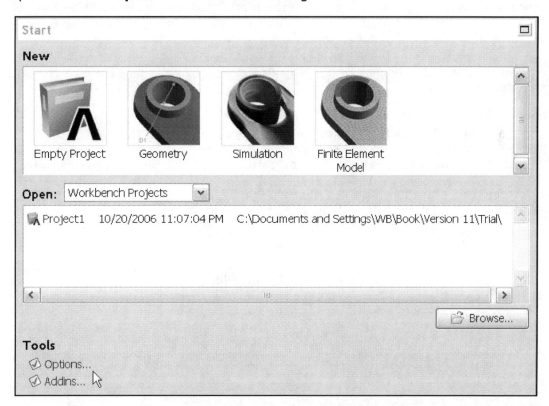

Step 3 – Expand the **DesignModeler** settings and click on **Miscellaneous**.

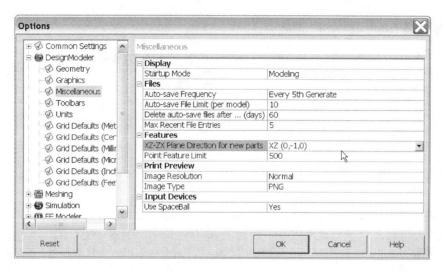

Step 4 – Under **Features**, change the setting for **XZ-ZX Plane Direction for new parts** to read **XZ (0,-1, 0)** as shown above.

3.6.2 Disabling the Map of Analysis Types in Simulation

Version 11 of Workbench introduces a new feature called the **Map of Analysis Types**. The map relates various analysis types based on their physics and inserts the appropriate environment objects into the outline tree for the project. The tutorials in this book generally don't use the map; therefore we will disable the automatic display of the map. The map can always be displayed from the **New Analysis** pull-down menu if it is needed.

In order to disable the display of the **Map of Analysis Types** by default, perform the following steps:

Step 1 – Start Workbench
Step 2 – Display the **Options** dialog box as in the previous section
Step 3 – Expand Simulation and click on Miscellaneous
Step 4 – Under **Map of Analysis Types Panel** change **Visible at Startup** to **No**.

Performing this procedure disables the map when the Simulation application is started up. The Option dialog box is shown in the figure below.

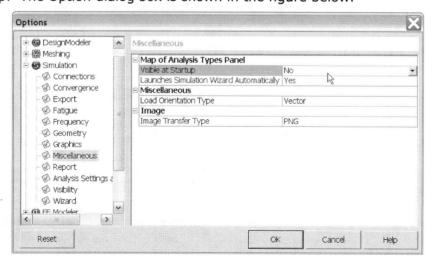

Exercises

1. Using the Engineering Data application, create a new material and name it Aluminum-2. Enter the following properties for Aluminum-2: Young's Modulus=70GPa, Poisson's Ratio=0.33, Density=2.77e-6 Kg/mm^3, Thermal Conductivity=0.15 W/mm°C, Specific Heat = 875 J/Kg°C.

2. Using the Engineering Data application, duplicate Structural Steel and name it Stainless Steel 1. Then modify the following properties to the indicated values: Young's Modulus=2.8e7 PSI, Poisson's Ratio=0.31, Density=0.28 lbm/in^3.

NOTES:

4

Using DesignModeler to create geometry

DesignModeler (DM) is the Workbench application used to create the geometry that is used in the finite element analysis. Every new Workbench analysis begins by creating or importing the geometry which will then be used to generate a finite element mesh. Older FEA tools required the user to manually create the mesh by defining the nodes and the elements that are the building blocks of an FEA mesh. Since the mid 1990s however, most FEA tools have been able to use CAD models as a starting point to generate the mesh. This process can be completely automatic or may need some user intervention depending on the robustness of the meshing algorithms and the complexity of the CAD model.

Users of Workbench can start a new analysis by either importing geometry that was generated using a third party CAD tool such as AutoCAD, Catia, SolidEdge, etc., or they can create the geometry entirely in DesignModeler. DesignModeler also allows a model that was generated in another program to be imported and modified to some extent to make it ready for use by Workbench.

Although DesignModeler is not intended to replace or compete with other commercially available CAD packages, it has the features required to create surface and line models as well as solid model assemblies most commonly used in a finite element analysis.

4.1 Introduction to 3D modeling

DesignModeler allows solid models to be created using several different methods. One of these techniques makes use of a set of pre-defined primitive solids (spheres, cylinders, rectangular blocks, etc.) being combined by Boolean operations (union, intersections, etc.). While this method works well for simply models, it becomes quite cumbersome when more complex geometric descriptions are required.

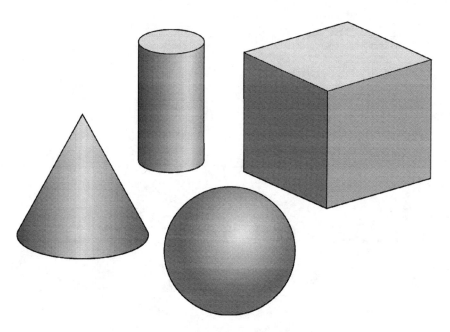

Figure 4.1 Example of several different solid modeling primitives

The more commonly used technique, which will be used in this book, is referred to as the Boundary Representation (B-rep) technique. It involves defining solid models as a collection of edges and bounding surfaces. From the user's perspective, this is usually done by drawing two-dimensional sketches that are then extruded, revolved or swept through space to create a three dimension feature. Additional features, such as cuts, holes, rounds on edges or fillets can then used to complete the model.

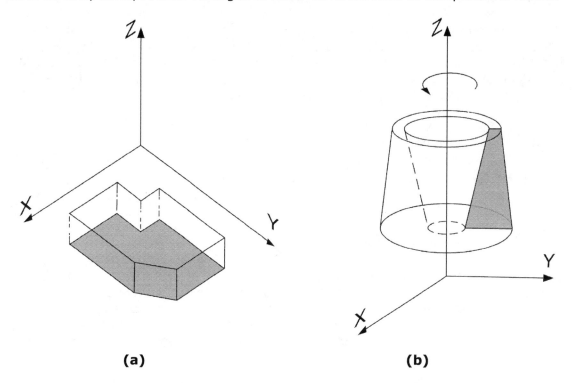

(a)   **(b)**

Figure 4.2 Examples of an extrude (a) and revolved (b) sweep

4.2 Introduction to DesignModeler

DesignModeler is the Workbench tool that you use to create new geometry or to modify geometry that was created using a CAD tool such as AutoCAD, Unigraphics, Catia, etc. It is important to point out that this book will not attempt to help you master DesignModeler but will only cover what you need to know in order to create the models necessary to perform Finite Element Analysis.

In some cases, the models will be provided as ParaSolid files which you will simply bring into your Workbench project.

The remainder of this section introduces the basic functionality and the user interface of DesignModeler. In the following sections, several tutorials are presented to help you learn how to used DesignModeler to create different kinds of geometry.

DesignModeler operates in two basic modes:

- Two-dimensional sketching mode
- Modeling mode

In sketching mode, you draw on a two-dimensional plane using geometric entities such as lines, arcs, circles, etc. to create a sketch.

In modeling mode, you use the 2-D sketch to create 3-dimensional solid shapes by extruding, rotating or sweeping the sketch.

After you have created a solid model, you can then modify it by adding or subtracting primitives such as spheres, boxes, pyramids or other shapes as necessary to create the final solid model that will be used in the FEA.

DesignModeler is feature based. In CAD jargon a feature is usually a user defined geometric shape that is added or subtracted from the model. The tree outline on the left side of the DesignModeler window shows the features in your model and the operations used to create them.

We will now take at the look at the DesignModeler window and introduce its major features. The portions of the DesignModeler window which are highlighted in Figure 4.3 will be described as they appear from the top of the window to the bottom.

Project and Application Tabs: This area shows the application tabs. When you start an empty project, only the project tab will appear. If you use the DesignModeler to create geometry, a DesignModeler tab is added and if you use Simulation in your project, a Simulation tab will appear, etc.

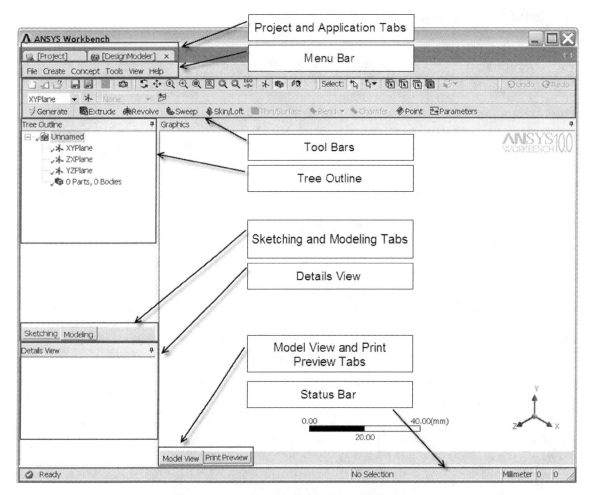

Figure 4.3 DesignModeler Window

The Menu Bar: The menu bar is where the DesignModeler menus appear.

Tool Bars: Various toolbars such as the graphical manipulation toolbar and the selection toolbars appear in this area. The toolbars are dockable and can be moved around.

Tree Outline: The Tree Outline is perhaps the most important part of the window. It shows critical information such as where the two-dimensional sketches of your model were created or how many bodies are in your model as well as their dependencies. The Tree Outline also shows the operations used to create a feature.

Sketching and Modeling tabs: Use these tabs to switch between sketching mode and 3-D modeling mode.

Detail View area: This area shows details related to the item selected in the Tree Outline.

Model View & Print View tabs: Switch to the Print View to see a picture of the active model that you can print.

Status Bar: Status bar displays a variety of information including prompts, the number of selected items and their properties and the active system of units.

4.2.1 Sketching Plane Orientation

Before proceeding further, we will need to make a modification to the default DesignModeler coordinate system orientation. This step is necessary in order to align the coordinate system in WB with that used in the book. If you use the default settings, DM coordinates orient such that when you draw on the XZ plane, the Z axis is horizontal. In this book we use the more common convention of using the Z axis as the UP or vertical axis and X as the horizontal axis.

In order to set the orientation of the Z axis, perform the following steps:

Step 1 – Start Workbench by clicking on the ANSYS Workbench icon.
- or-
Start – All Programs – ANSYS 11.0 – ANSYS Workbench

Step 2 – Click on **Options**... on the Start dialog box.

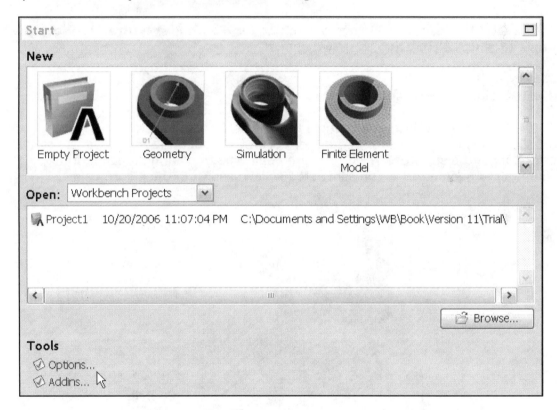

Step 3 – Expand the **DesignModeler** settings and click on **Miscellaneous**.

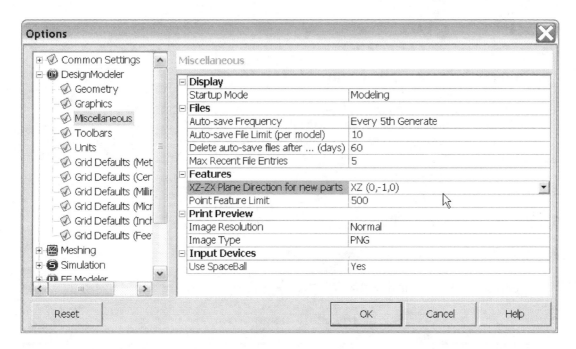

Step 4 – Under **Features**, change the setting for **XZ-ZX Plane Direction for new parts** to read **XZ (0,-1, 0)** as shown above.

4.3 Tutorial 4_1 – Rectangular extrusion

In this tutorial you will create a simple rectangular solid by sketching a rectangle on the YZ plane and extruding it in the X direction. Although the final solid is a simple brick shape, the steps described here are applicable to creating much more complicated geometries. The completed solid is shown in the Figure below.

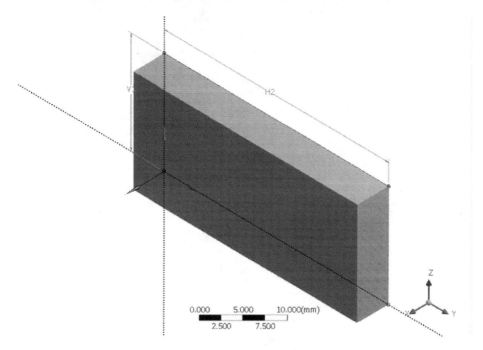

Step 1 – Start a new DesignModeler database by clicking on the Geometry icon as shown.

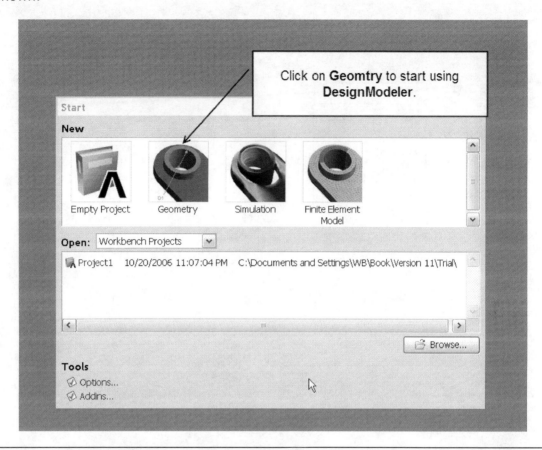

Step 2 – On the unit selection dialog box, make sure Millimeter is selected and then click OK.

Step 3 – Choose the Sketching plane and orient it parallel to the screen.

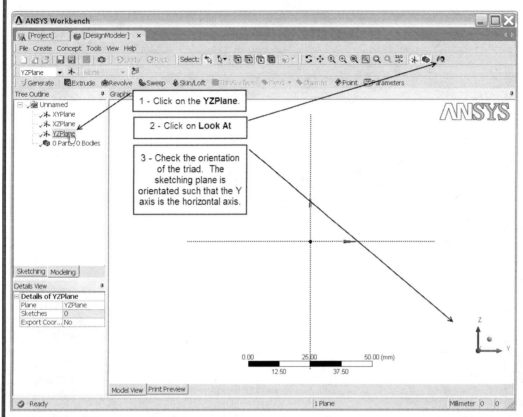

Step 4 – Begin sketching.

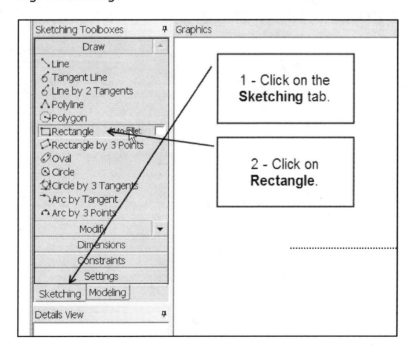

Step 5 – Draw a rectangle.

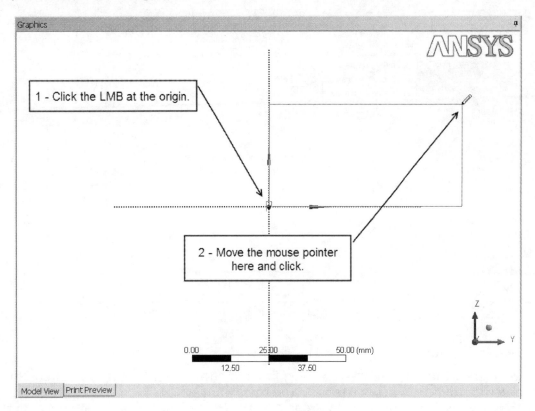

The exact location where the mouse is clicked and released is not important at this stage as long as the general shape of the drawing is correct. Also notice the outlined area on the bottom left corner of the window. Prompts appear here guiding you through the process.

Step 6 – Specify the vertical dimension for one of the edges. First you must open the Dimensioning toolbox by clicking on **Dimensions** as shown below.

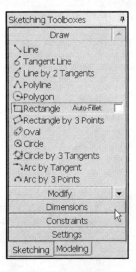

Step 6 (continued) – Finish dimensioning the vertical edge as shown.

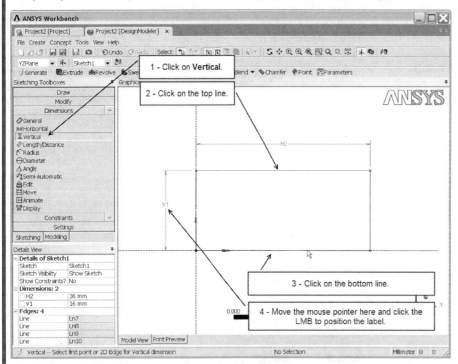

By completing these four sub-steps, you have told the program that you intend to set a vertical dimension (sub-step 1), and then you select two lines whose vertical distance you want to specify (sub-steps 2 & 3). In the last sub-step you position the location where the dimension will be displayed.

Step 7 – Set the horizontal dimension for the top edges.

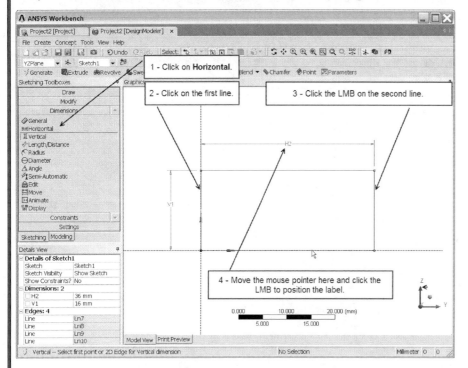

Both dimensions, V1 and H2 are now shown in the **Details View** pane.

Step 8 – Change the dimension. First select the value shown next to H2 and type *36*. Next select the value next to V1 and type *16*.

Details View	📌
Details of Sketch1	
Sketch	Sketch1
Sketch Visibility	Show ...
Show Constraints?	No
Dimensions: 2	
☐ H2	36 mm
☐ V1	16 mm
Edges: 4	
Line	Ln7
Line	Ln8
Line	Ln9
Line	Ln10

Step 9 – Extrude the sketch in the Z direction to form a solid. First change the view to isometric as shown below.

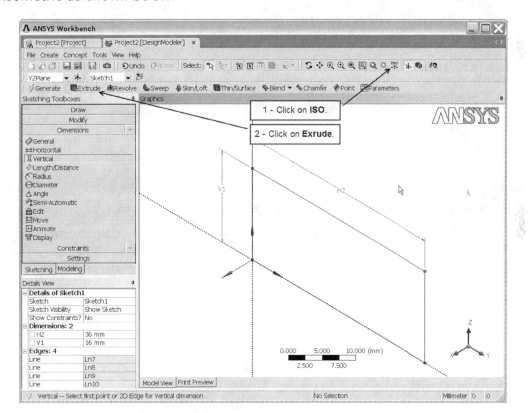

Step 10 – Set the depth dimension and generate the solid.

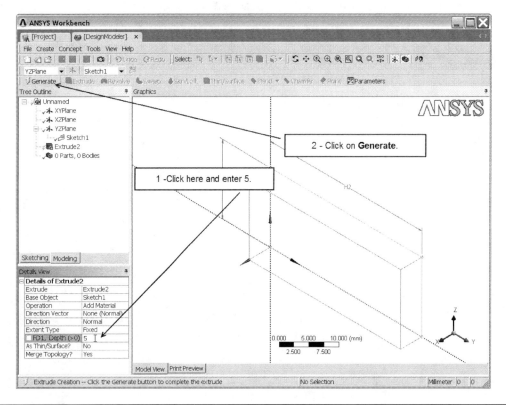

Step 10 (continued) – Your solid should now look like the figure below.

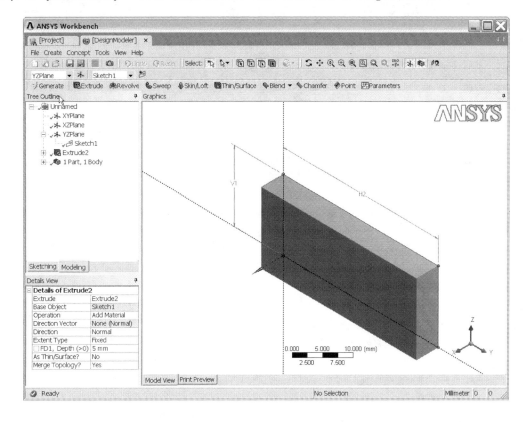

Step 11 – Save your model. Note that both the project file and the model have to be saved. If you try to exit Workbench at this point without saving, you will be prompted for file names twice, once for the project (file with wbdb extension) and once for the geometry file (file with agdb extension).

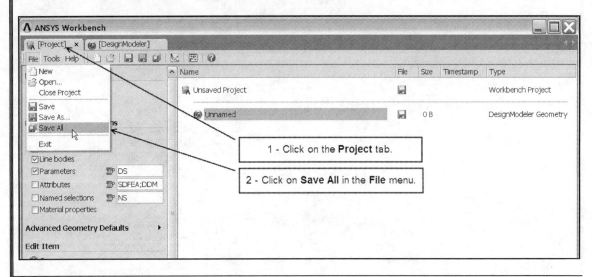

Step 11 (continued) – In the dialog box that appears, select a location and a file name for the geometry file and click on Save. Notice the file name extension which is "agdb".

Step 11 (continued) – A second dialog box will appear. Select a location and file name for the project file and click Save. Notice the file name extension is "wbdb".

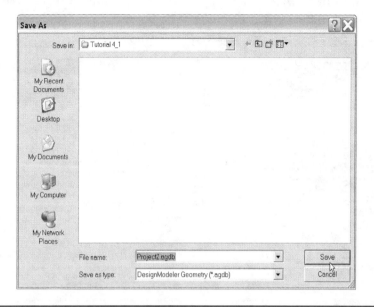

4.4 Tutorial 4_2 – Revolved extrusion

In this tutorial you will construct your sketch on the XY plane and revolve it around the Y axis to build the three dimensional part shown below.

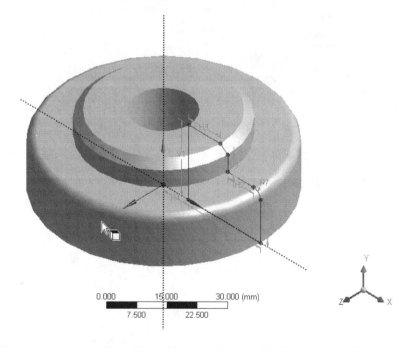

We will use the Rectangle tool in the Sketching toolbox of DM to build the initial sketch, however you can also build the sketch using individual lines. If you use lines to build your sketch, DM will aid you in drawing horizontal and vertical lines by placing a letter **H** or a letter **V** near the line you are sketching as shown below.

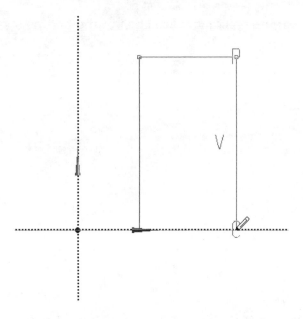

Step 1 – Start a new DM project (see step 1 of tutorial 4_1).

Step 2 – Select Millimeter as the working length unit (see step 2 of tutorial 4_1).

Step 3 – Click on the **XYPlane** in the Tree Outline and orient the view to it by clicking on **Look At Face/Plane Sketch**. See Step 3 of tutorial 4_1 but make sure you select the **XYPlane**.

Step 4 – Enter **Sketching** and select the **Rectangle** tool. Move the cursor to the drawing area. The Cursor becomes a pencil. See Step 4 of tutorial 4_1.

Step 5 - Draw a rectangle as shown. Click on the horizontal axis to mark the bottom left corner of the rectangle, them move the cursor to the approximate location shown and click the LMB. Make sure you leave a gap between the left edge of the rectangle and the Y axis. This gap will become the hole at the center of the part.

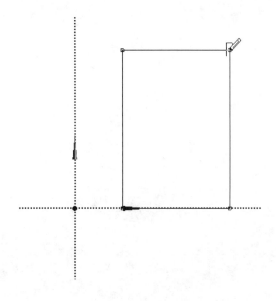

Step 6 – Draw a second, shorter rectangle attached to the first as shown.

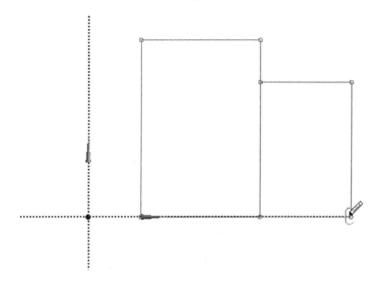

Note: At any time during the session you can click on the **Zoom to Fit** icon (🔍) to center and enlarge the image.

Step 7 – Trim the vertical inside line.

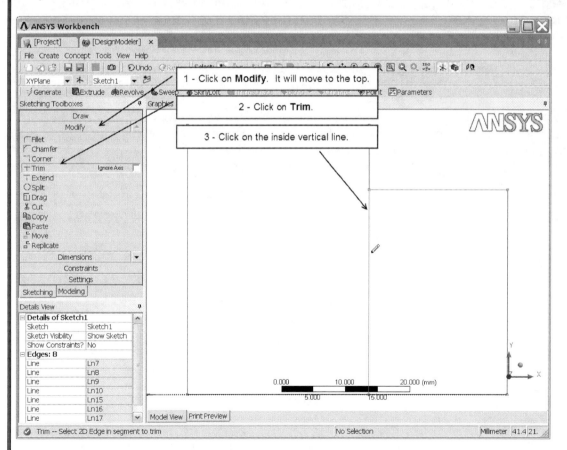

Step 8 – Adjust the display by using the **Zoom** tool (🔍) to move the sketch above the scale. Then Click on **Zoom** again to cancel the zoom mode.

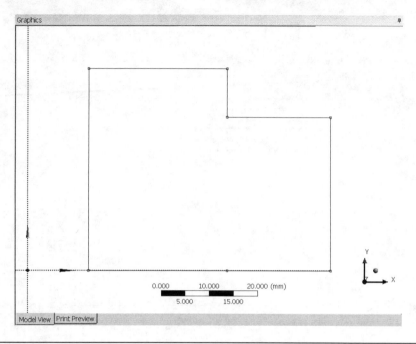

Step 8 (continued) – Delete the horizontal line segment at the bottom right portion of the sketch.

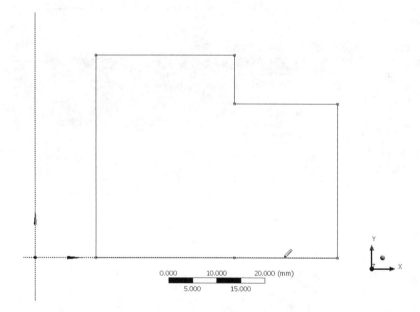

In step 9, we will extend the remaining horizontal segment to close the sketch.

Step 9 – Extend the remaining horizontal line to close the sketch.

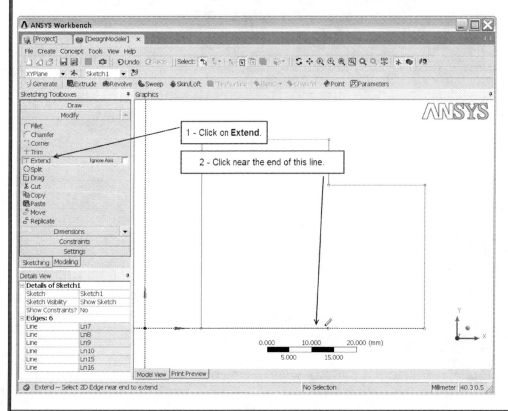

Step 10 – Create a Chamfer.

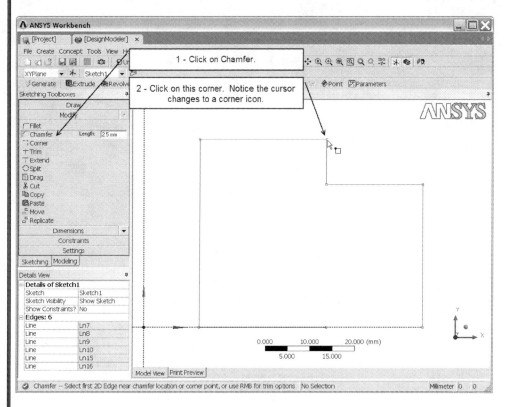

Step 11 – Create a Fillet.

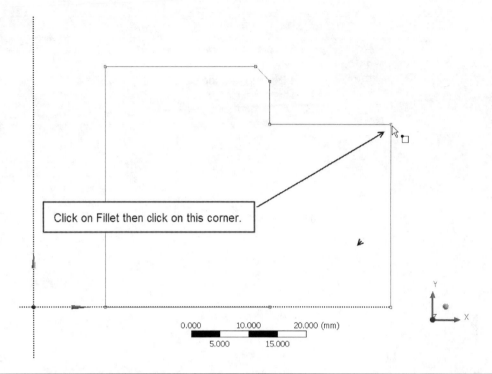

Click on Fillet then click on this corner.

Step 11 (continued) – Your sketch should now look like the sketch shown below. Note that at this point, we have not dimensioned the sketch; therefore, your sketch may look slightly different.

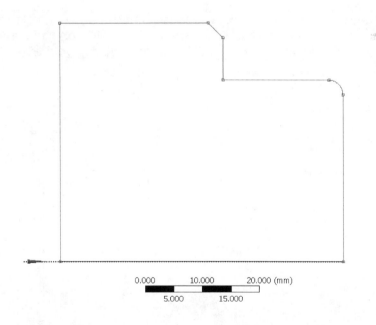

Step 12 – Dimension the sketch.

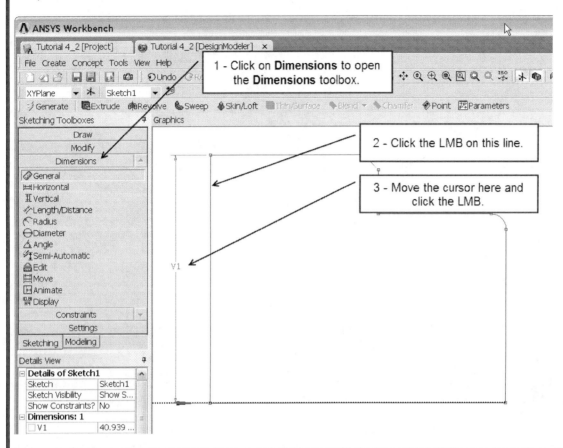

Step 12 (continued) – Using the **General** dimensioning tool, Dimension the remaining lines. Then dimension the Fillet radius by clicking on the **Radius** tool and selecting the Fillet. The length of the chamfer is left free to avoid over-constraining the sketch.

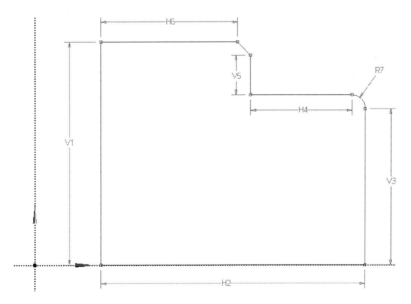

Step 12 (continued) – In the detail pane of the sketching toolbox enter the values shown below. Note that the dimension labels in your case maybe different. In that case, match the values in the table below to the appropriate line.

Details View	🔩
⊞ **Details of Sketch1**	
⊟ **Dimensions: 7**	
☐ H2	25 mm
☐ H4	9 mm
☐ H6	11 mm
☐ R7	2.5 mm
☐ V1	22 mm
☐ V3	12.5 mm
☐ V5	5 mm
⊞ **Edges: 8**	

Step 13 – Set the hole size. The solid will be generated by rotating the sketch about the Y axis, therefore, the hole radius is the horizontal distance between the left edge of the sketch and the Y axis. In the **Details View** pane set the value of this distance to be 9mm.

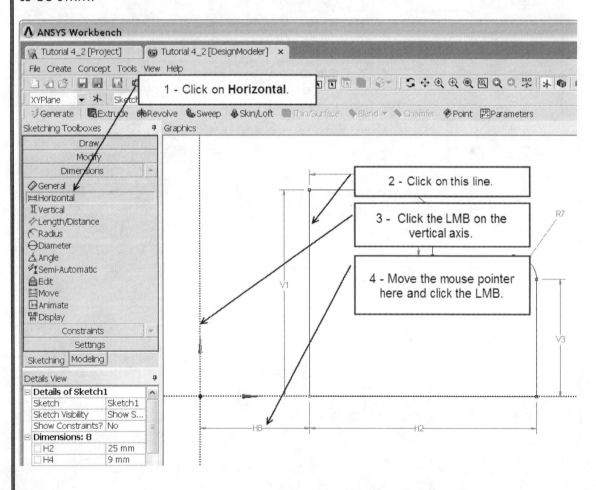

Step 13 (continued) – The completed and dimensioned sketch is shown below.

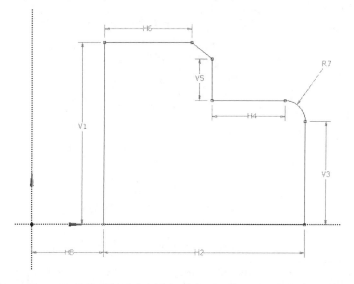

Step 14 – Create a revolved extrusion.

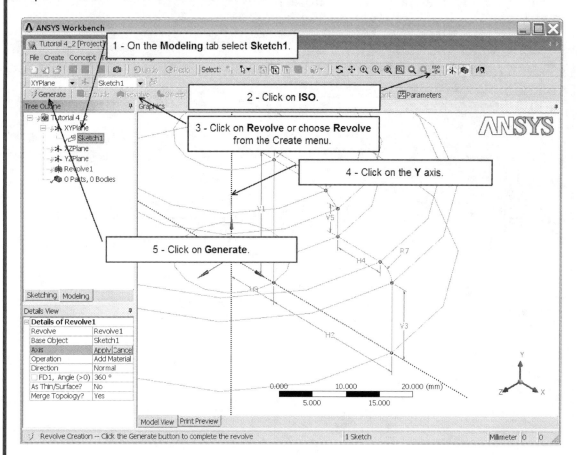

Step 14 (continued) – Completed solid is shown below.

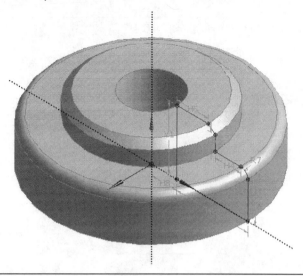

Step 15 – Save your model.
  A. Click on the **Project** tab.
  B. Click on the **Save all** icon or choose **File | Save All**.
  C. Save the Workbench project file (wbdb extension).
  D. Save the DesignModeler file (agdb extension).

4.5 Tutorial 4_3 – 3D Bracket with Two Holes

In this tutorial we will use the DesignModeler to build the bracket shown below. We will use three sketch planes; the first sketch is the profile of the bracket which when extruded creates the base solid. The second and third sketches are used to create cylinders which when subtracted from the bracket create the two holes. The first sketch is constructed on the XZ plane and extruded in the Y direction. The second is constructed on the XY plane and extruded in the Z direction. The third sketch is constructed on the face of the bracket which is not parallel to the principal axes.

Note: This tutorial assumes that you have oriented the sketching coordinate system as described in section 4.2.1.

Step 1 – Start a new DM project (see step 1 of tutorial 4_1).

Step 2 – Select Inch as the working length unit.

Step 3 – Choose the sketching plane and orient the view.

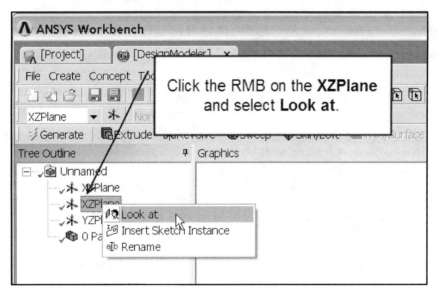

Step 4 – Begin building the sketch.
  A. Click on the **Sketching** tab.
  B. Click on the **Line** icon. The cursor becomes a pencil. Draw two lines on the screen by clicking the left mouse button at the endpoints of each line. The numbers in the figure below correspond to the mouse clicks. Points 2 and 3 are at the same location and designate the end of the first line and the beginning of the second line.

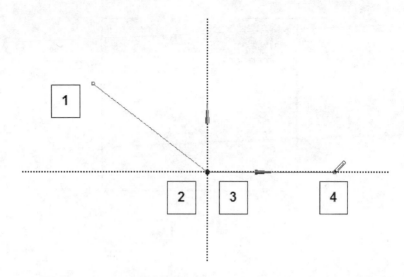

Step 5 – Add a Fillet between the two lines.
  A. Click on **Modify** to open the modify toolbox.
  B. Click on **Fillet**.
  C. Select the first line (note the prompts at the bottom left part of the window). Select the second line. The default fillet radius may make the radius difficult to see but you should notice the two end points of the radius after it is created.

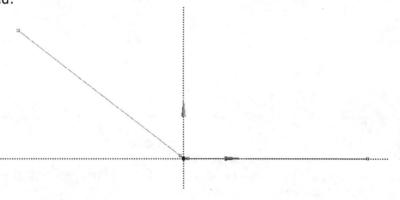

Step 6 – Dimension the drawing.
  A. Click on **Dimensions**.
  B. Use the **General** tool to dimension the two lines as you did in step 12 of the previous tutorial.
  C. Use the **Angle** tool to set the angle between line 1 and the horizontal axis.
    a. Click on Angle.
    b. Click the first line close to point 1.
    c. Click the LMB on the horizontal axis.
    d. Move the cursor to the desired location for the label and click the LMB.
  D. Use the **Radius** tool to dimension the fillet.
  E. In the **Details View** type the values shown in the figure below.

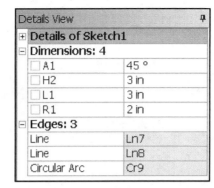

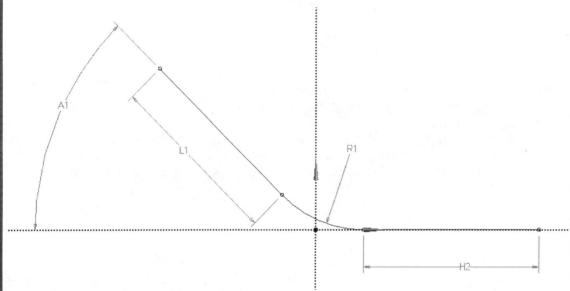

Step 7 – Save your work.
 A. Click on the Project tab to open the project page.
 B. From the File menu choose **Save All**.
 C. When prompted, type *Tutorial 4_3* for both the project and the DesignModeler database file names.
 D. Click on the DesignModeler tab to return to DesignModeler.

Step 8 – Create an offset copy of the sketch.
 A. In the **Modify** toolbox click on **Offset**.
 B. Select the first line, the fillet and the second line in that order. As you select these entities, they are highlighted. After the last selection, check the status bar to make sure 3 items are selected.
 C. Click the right mouse button and from the context (pop-up) menu select **End Selection/Place offset**.
 D. Move the pencil cursor in the positive Z direction and click the left mouse button.
 E. Press the escape key to end the process. Your drawing should look like the figure below.

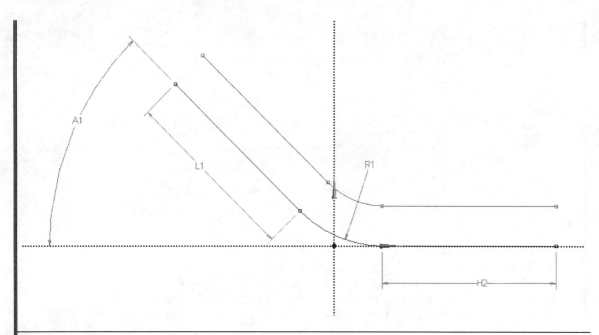

Step 9 – Close the ends of the sketch profile. Use the Line tool in the Draw toolbox and draw a line at each end of the sketch to close the profile.

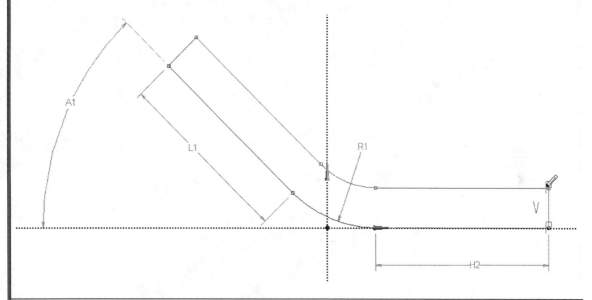

Step 10 – Set the thickness of the profile. Use the **General** tool from the **Dimensioning** toolbox to set the thickness. Enter a value of **0.375** inches for the thickness in the **Details View**.

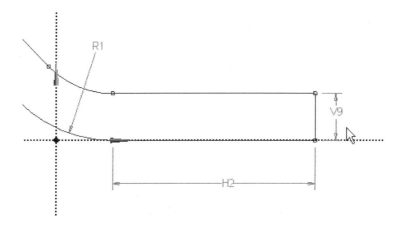

Step 11 – Extrude the sketch in the Y direction to create a solid.
    A. Click on the **Extrude** icon in the toolbar.
    B. Click on the **ISO view** icon in the toolbar.
    C. In the **Details View** pane change the value of **FD1, Depth** to 2.
    D. Click on **Generate** in the toolbar to complete the process.

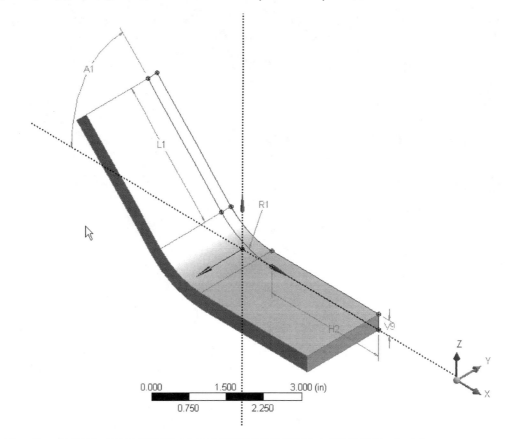

Step 12 – Create a new sketch plane for the first hole.
    A. In the **Tree Outline**, select the project icon (If you saved your work as instructed in step 7, this will be named **Tutorial 4_3**).
    B. From the **Create** menu select **New Plane**.
    C. Change the type to *From Face* in the **Details View** pane.
    D. The item **Base Face** will show Unselected and will be highlighted. Click on the highlighted area to select a face.

E. Select the top face of the horizontal portion of the bracket which is parallel to the XY plane then click **Apply**.
F. Change the **Reverse Normal/Z axis** to Yes (so that +Z points into the part).
G. Click on **Generate** in the toolbar.

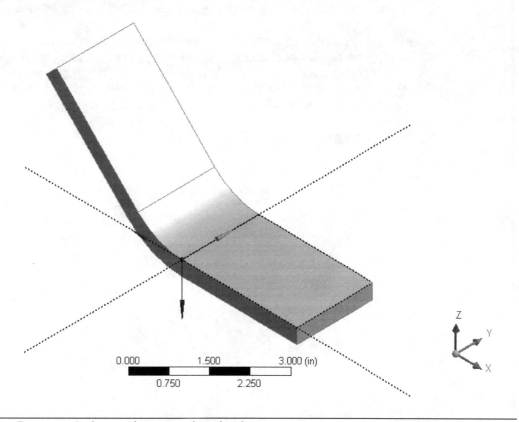

Step 13 – Draw a circle on the new sketch plane.
A. From the **Draw** toolbox select **Circle**.
B. Draw the circle on the sketch plane by clicking once to set the center and moving the cursor until the circle is of the desired size and then click the left mouse button.

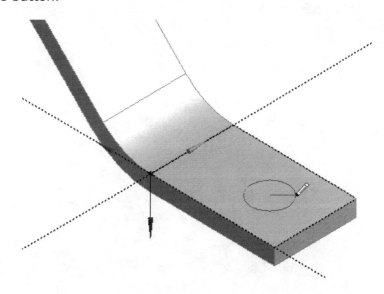

Step 14 – Dimension and position the circle.
  A. Using the **Diameter** tool from the **Dimensions** toolbox dimension the circle
  B. Position the circle.
      1. Select **Length/Distance** from the toolbox.
      2. Select the center of the circle, and then click the LMB on the nearest edge of the solid.
      3. Move the pointer to position the dimension and click the LMB.
      4. Select the center of the circle again then click the LMB on the second edge (perpendicular to the first).
      5. Move the pointer to position the dimension and click the LMB.
      6. Modify the diameter (D1 in the figure) to 0.5 in the **Details View** pane.
      7. Modify the first and second distance to 1 (L2 and L3 in the figure).

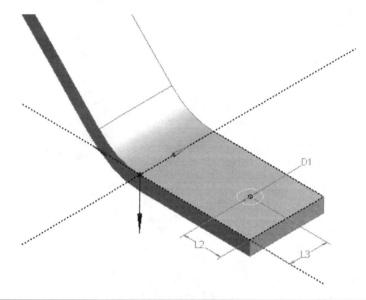

Step 15 – Create a hole in the bracket by extruding the circle into a cylinder and subtracting it from the bracket.
  A. Click on the **Extrude** button in the toolbar.
  B. In the **Details View** change the **Operation setting** to "Cut Material".
  C. In the **Details View** change the **Direction** to **Normal**.
  D. Click **Generate**.

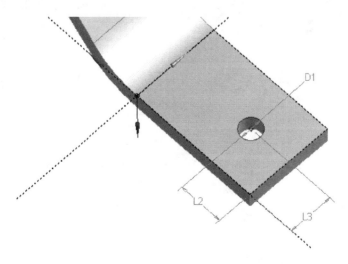

Step 16 – Create a new sketch plane for the second hole.
  - A. In the **Tree Outline**, select the project icon (If you saved your work as instructed in step 7, this will be named **Tutorial 4_3**).
  - B. From the **Create** menu select **New Plane**.
  - C. Change the type to *From Face* in the **Details View** pane.
  - D. The item "Base Face" will show Unselected and will be highlighted. Click on the highlighted area to select a face.
  - E. Select the top face of the angled portion of the bracket then click **Apply**.
  - F. Change the **Reverse Normal/Z axis** to Yes.
  - G. Click on **Generate** in the toolbar.

Step 17 – Draw a circle in the new sketch plane. This step is identical to step 13.

Step 18 – Dimension and position the circle. This step is identical to step 14 except for the values you enter for the diameter of the circle. In the **Details View** change the value of D1 to *1.0*.

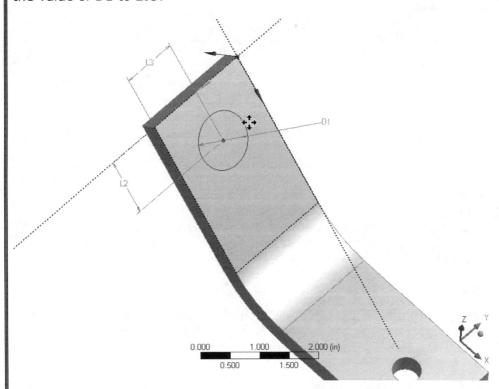

Step 19 – Create a hole in the bracket by extruding the circle into a cylinder and subtracting it from the bracket. This step is identical to step 15.

Step 20 – Final solid. The final solid should appear as the figure below.

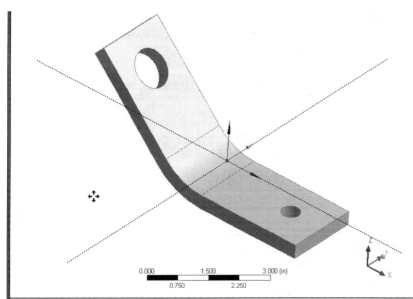

```
        0.000          1.500          3.000 (in)
              0.750          2.250
```

Step 21 – Save the project and the DesignModeler database.

4.6 Additional Topics

- **Multiple Sketches on a plane**

  When constructing solid models, it occasionally becomes necessary to place a second or third sketch on a plane that already contains a sketch. In order to accomplish this, the plane on which the sketch is to be placed should first be selected in the outline window, followed by clicking on the new sketch icon that is located in the toolbar. The name of the new sketch should then be selected followed by constructing the sketch. An example of this process is illustrated in tutorial 5_2.

- **Displaying Mass Properties**

  In order to display the physical properties such as volume, and surface area, the line under "1 Part, 1 Body" that is labeled "Solid" in the Tree Outline window should be selected. This will cause the numerical values to appear in the Details View window pane.

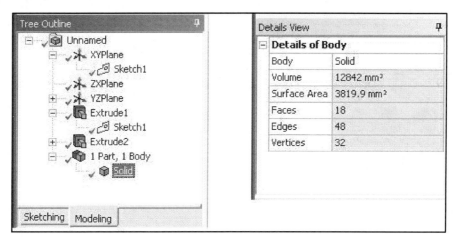

Exercises

Use DesignModeler to create each of the 3-D parts shown below. After completing the part, use DesignModeler to determine its volume.

1. The dimensions of the part shown below are in millimeters.

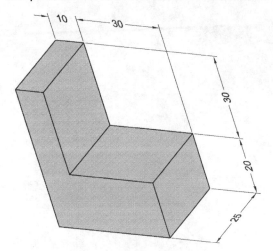

2. The dimensions of the part shown below are inches.

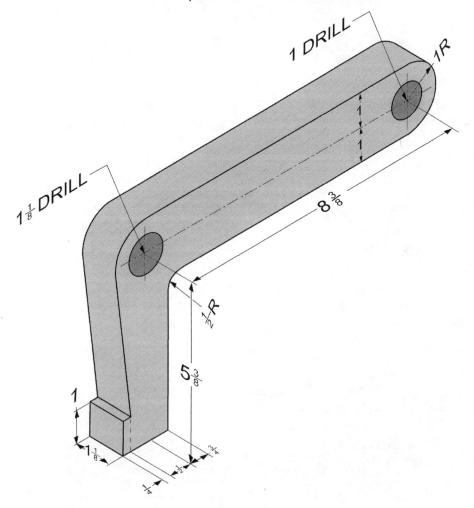

3. The dimensions of the part shown below are inches.

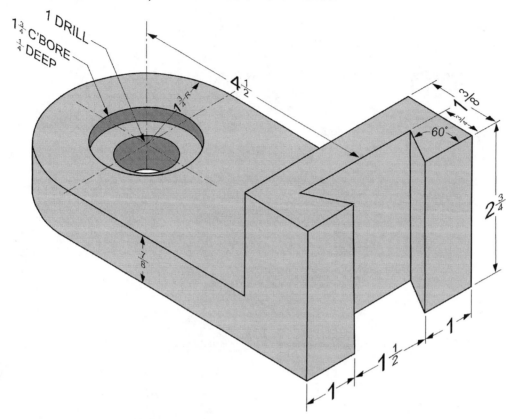

4. The dimensions of the part shown below are inches.

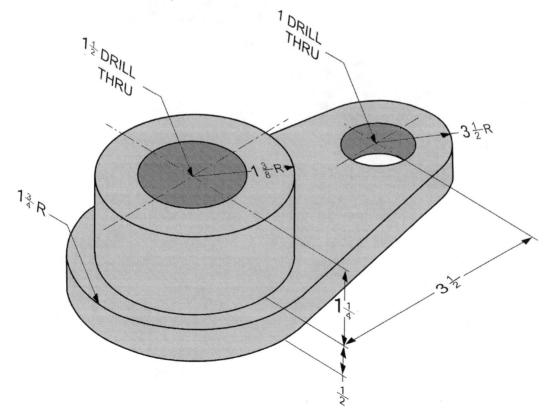

Use DesignModeler to create a 270 degree revolve of each of the 3-D parts shown in exercise 5,6 and 7, and then determine the volume.

5. The dimensions of the part shown below are inches. The radius of the round is both ½ inch and the fillet is ¾ inch.

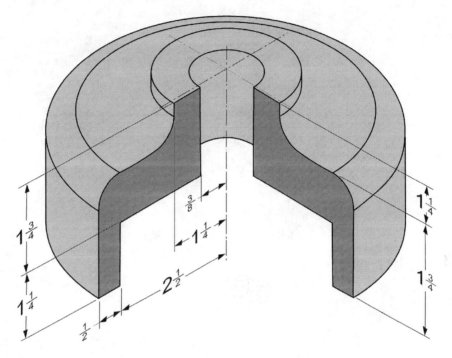

6. The dimensions of the part shown below are millimeters. The radius of the fillet is 25 millimeters.

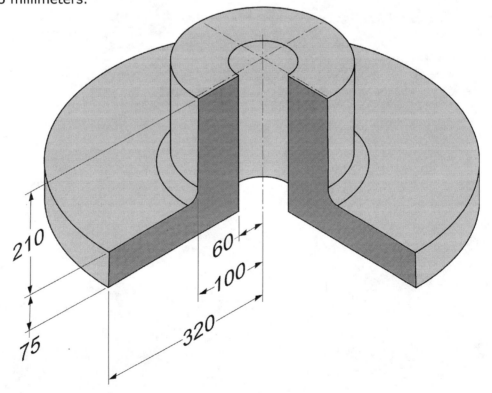

7. The dimensions of the part shown below are millimeters.

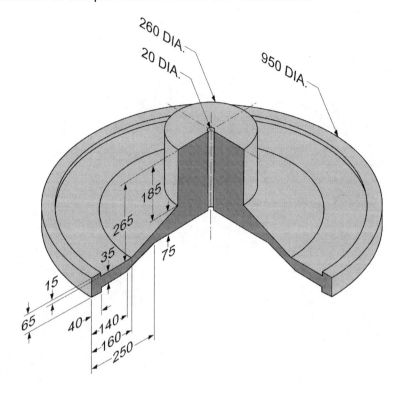

5

Using DesignModeler to Create Surface and Line Geometry

5.1 Surface and Line Bodies defined

In DesignModeler as well as other CAD tools, physical objects can be represented by Solid Bodies, Surface Bodies or Line Bodies as needed. Solid, Surface and Line bodies are used to generate solid, plate/shell and beam elements respectively. In most cases, solid models are used but in some cases the use of surface or line bodies results in more efficient modeling of the systems under consideration.

Chapter 4 illustrated how to create solid models in DesignModeler. In this chapter, we will demonstrate how to create surface and line bodies.

Surface Bodies are CAD models (parts or assemblies) that when used in Simulation, result in shell or plate elements being generated to represent them instead of solid elements. Surface Bodies have no volume associated with them. They are a conceptual representation of a thin solid body, for example a part that is made of sheet metal. However, in order to be able to use such a conceptual representation in an FEA tool, we must first assign the thickness of the physical object to the surface body.

The reasons for using plate and shell elements rather than solid elements are described in more detail in Chapter 11 **Plate and Shell Element Modeling**. In this chapter, we are only concerned with using DesignModeler to generate various types of geometry.

Similarly, line bodies result in the generation of beam elements when they are used in Simulation. In order to completely define the properties of the beam elements, we must specify the beam cross-section geometry and orientation in DesignModeler.

Tutorial 5_1 demonstrates the generation of a surface body that lies entirely on the sketch plane. In this case, we simply draw the profile on a sketch plane and use the function **Surfaces From Sketches** in the **Concept** menu to generate a surface body of the desired thickness.

Tutorial 5_2 demonstrates how to create an imprinted face that can be individually selected to apply loads or boundary conditions.

Tutorial 5_3 demonstrates generating a three dimensional surface body by extruding the profile of the body constructed from lines.

Finally, Tutorial 5_4 shows how to create line bodies.

Note: In the following tutorials the exact dimensions of the geometric entities are not critical to the goal of the tutorials which is to demonstrate creation of surface bodies. We will therefore not dimension the sketches as we would under normal circumstances.

5.2 Tutorial 5_1 – 2D Surface Model (Surface From Sketch)

Step 1 – Start a new DesignModeler project and choose Millimeter as the desired length units.

Step 2 – Create a sketch.
On the **XYPlane**, draw a rectangle and a circle as shown

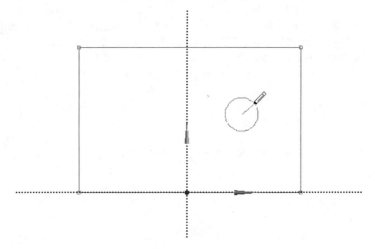

Step 2 (continued) – Create a surface body.
   A. From the **Concept** menu choose **Surfaces From Sketches**.
   B. Click the **Modeling tab** of the tree outline window, select **Sketch1**.
   C. Click the **Apply** button next to **Base Objects**.
   D. In the **Details View** enter a value of **2** for thickness.
   E. Click **Generate**.

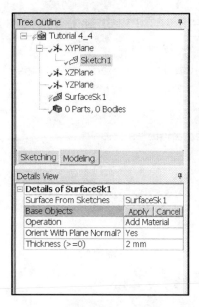

Step 2 (continued) – You have now created a surface body from the sketch. If you do not specify a thickness value as we did in the previous, you will have to enter the value in Simulation before this model can be used to perform an FEA.

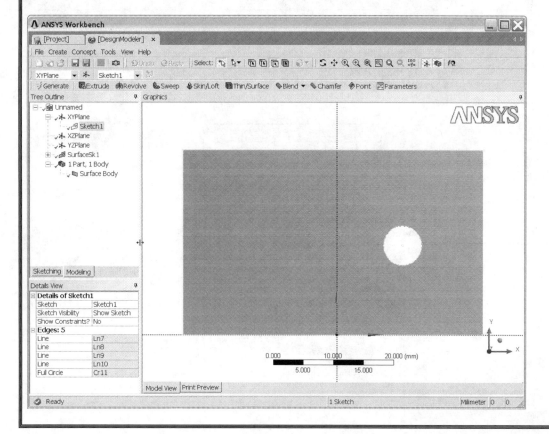

5.3 Tutorial 5_2 – Creating an "imprinted" surface patch for loads and boundary conditions

Step 1 – Start a new DesignModeler project and choose Millimeter as the desired length units.

Step 2 – Create a sketch.
On the **XYPlane**, draw a rectangle as shown.

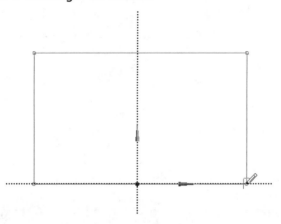

Step 3 – Create a surface body.
  A. From the **Concept** menu choose **Surfaces From Sketches**.
  B. In the Modeling toolbox, select **Sketch1**.
  C. Click the **Apply** button in front of **Base Objects**.
  D. In the **Details View** enter a value of **2** for thickness.
  E. Click **Generate**.

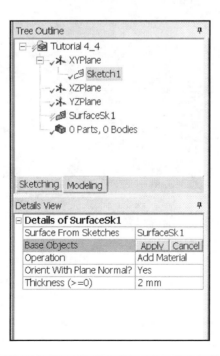

Step 3 (Continued) – You have now created a surface body from the sketch. If you do not specify a thickness value as we did in the previous, you will have to enter the value in Simulation before this model can be used to perform an FEA.

Step 4 – Create the surface patch. We will first create a second sketch on the **XYPlane** and draw the surface patch (a circle) on it.

    A. Select the **XYPlane** and click the New Sketch icon 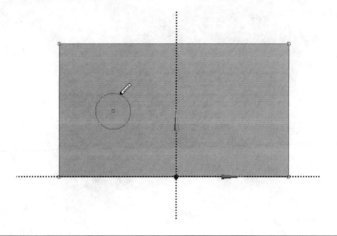 in the toolbar.
    B. Select the new sketch named **Sketch2**.
    C. Click on the Sketching tab.
    D. Select the Circle icon.
    E. Draw a circle as shown below.

Step 5 – Extrude the new sketch.

    A. Switch to Isometric view by clicking on the **ISO** icon in the toolbar.
    B. Click on **Extrude**.
    C. In the Details View change the Operation to **Imprint Faces**.

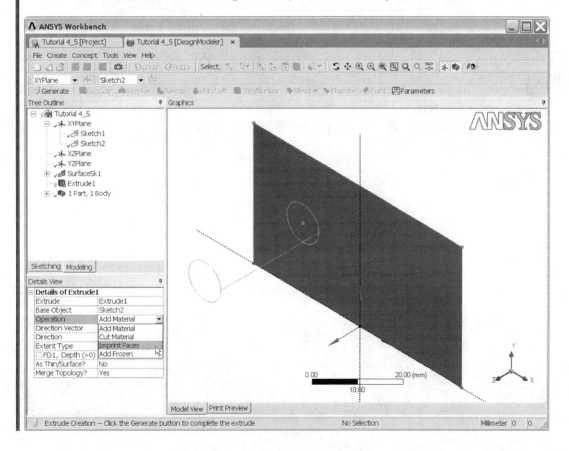

Step 5 (Continued) – Click **Generate**.
You now have two distinct areas. When this model is used in Simulation, the second area can be selected separately so that loads or boundary conditions can be imposed on it.

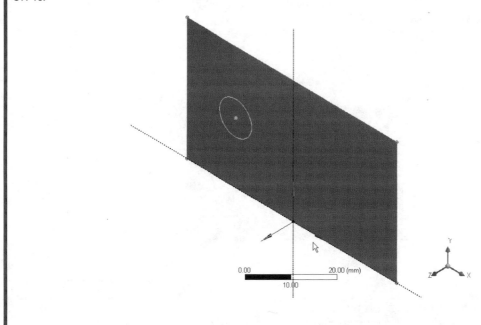

5.4 Tutorial 5_3 – Creating a surface model by extruding lines

Step 1 – Start a new DesignModeler project and choose Millimeter as the desired length units.

Step 2 – Create a Sketch.
On the **XYPlane** create the profile shown below using the **Line** tool.

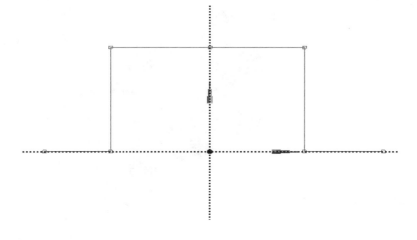

Step 3 – Add Fillets to the sketch.

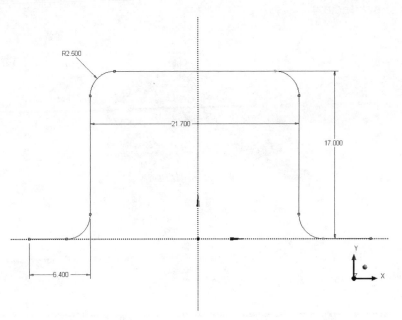

Step 4 – Extrude the Profile.
Click on **Extrude** and then **ISO**.

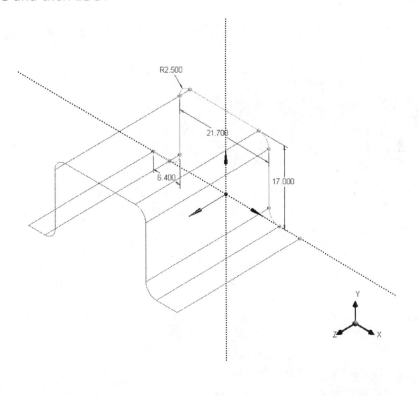

Step 4 (Continued) – Click on **Generate** to complete the extrusion. The completed extrusion is shown below.

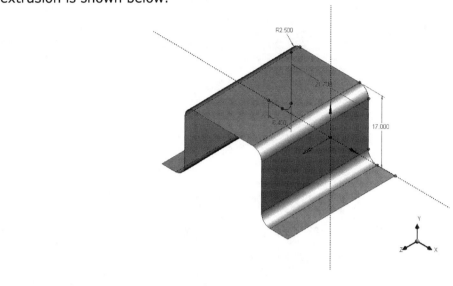

5.5 Tutorial 5_4 – 3-D Line Body

Step 1 – Start a new DesignModeler project and choose Millimeter as the desired length units.

Step 2 – Create a Sketch.
Draw a line in space parallel to the X axis.

Step 3 – Dimension the line. Set the line length to 100mm.

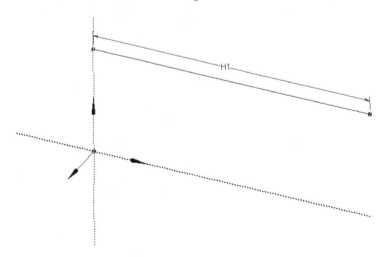

Step 4 – Generate the line body.
From the **Concept** menu select **Lines From Sketches**. Select the line and click **Apply** in the Details View. Click **Generate** to complete the operation.

Step 5 – Select a cross section for the beam. From the **Concept** menu select Cross **Section** > **I Section.**

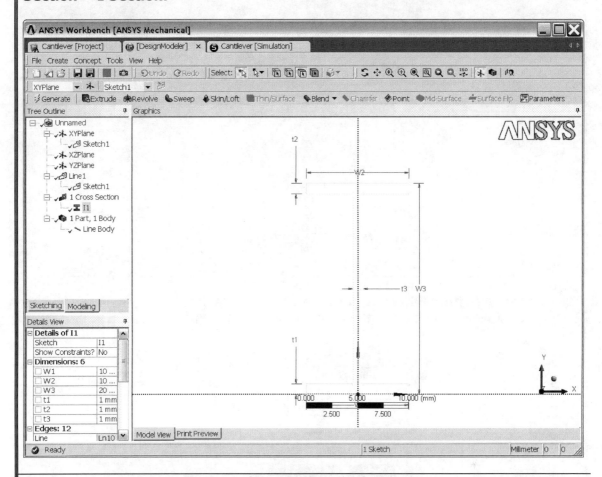

Step 6 – Assign the cross section (I section) to the line body.
In the Tree Outline expand **1 Part, 1 Body** and select **Line Body**. In the Details View select **I1** from the **Cross Section** pull-down menu.

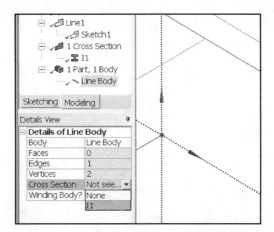

Step 7 – Change the view to show the beam cross section.   From the **View** menu select Cross **Section Solids.**

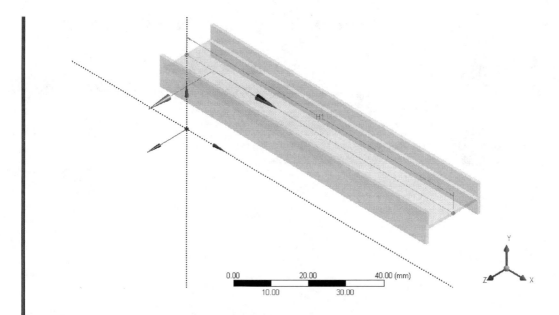

Step 8 – Rotate the beam to change its orientation
Click on the **Selection Filter: Edges** then select the line.
In the Detail View pane change the Rotate angle to 90 degrees.

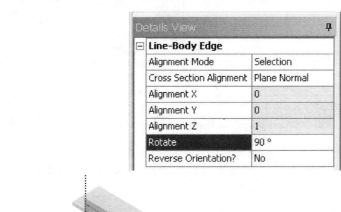

Details View	
Line-Body Edge	
Alignment Mode	Selection
Cross Section Alignment	Plane Normal
Alignment X	0
Alignment Y	0
Alignment Z	1
Rotate	90 °
Reverse Orientation?	No

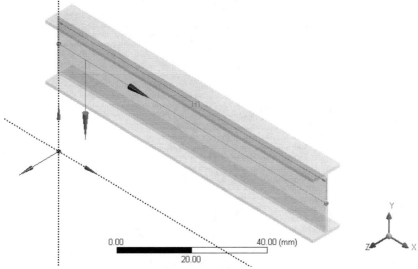

Exercises

1. Create a surface model of the 10mm thick plate shown below. All dimensions are in mm.

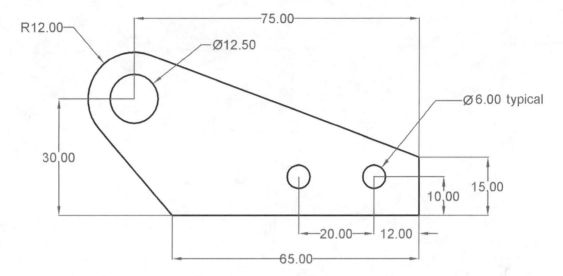

2. Create a surface model of the 0.25 inch thick plate shown below, then imprint the 1 inch diameter circular surface on the plate. All dimensions are in inches.

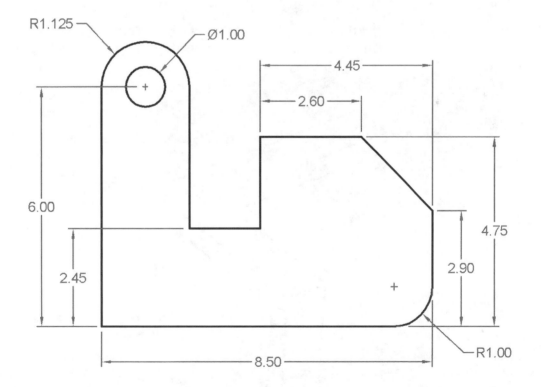

3. Create a surface model of the part shown below. Make sure to place the sketch of your lines, arcs, etc. along the mid-line of the part. All dimensions are in inches.

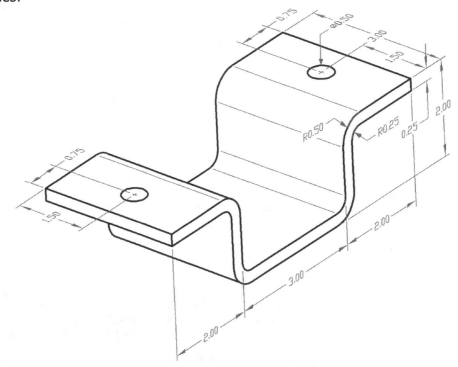

4. Create a line body of the three dimensional beam below. The 80 mm by 40 mm cross section is common to each segment of the beam. All dimensions are in mm.

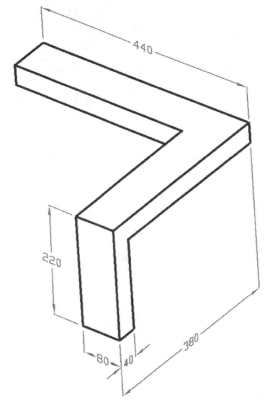

6

Introduction to Finite Element Simulation

Historically, finite element modeling tools were only capable of solving the simplest engineering problems which tended to reduce the problem to a manageable size and scope. These early FEA tools could generally solve steady-state, linear problems in two dimensions. The factors that forced these simplifications were lack of efficient computational techniques and the computing power to model more complex real-life problems.

As numerical computation techniques have advanced and computing power has increased, analysis tools have also advanced to solve more complex problems. A real-life engineering problem may involve different physics such as fluid flow, heat transfer, electromagnetism and other factors. The finite element method has been used to solve engineering problems in all of these areas successfully and the goal of most software developers is to include as much of the real-world in the simulation they perform as possible.

However, in many situations, use of simplifying assumptions such as symmetry, axisymmetry, plane stress, plane strain, etc., is still preferable to using a complete three dimensional model because of the efficiency they provide. These assumptions should be used if the problem being solved requires it. In other words, there is no need or justification to perform a full three dimensional analysis if symmetry is present in the problem being solved.

The ANSYS philosophy can be summarized as one that aims to simulate the complete real-life engineering problem. The simulation usually begins by using a three dimensional CAD model to construct a finite element mesh followed by imposing loads and boundary conditions and then computing the solution to the finite element problem.

6.1 Steps required to solve a problem

In general you follow the same steps to perform a finite element analysis. However, it is important to note that it is possible to use Workbench to perform a large number of different analysis types. These analysis types may include various material non-linearities, transient loads, rigid body dynamics, etc. which may require additional steps to be performed. The steps described below are aimed at solving a static, linear stress, heat transfer or free vibration analysis. Also remember that the following steps are performed in the **Simulation** application of Workbench.

1. **Attach to geometry**
2. **Define/Assign material properties**
3. **Define the analysis type**
4. **Set loading and boundary conditions**
5. **Request results**
6. **Solve**
7. **Review the results**
8. **Generate a report**

Below is a brief explanation of each step.

1. **Attach to geometry**. In this step you identify the geometry (CAD) model that will be used in your simulation. The model may have been created in DesignModeler or in some other CAD tool.
2. **Define/Assign material properties**. In this step you specify the type of material each part of your model is made of. You can assign material types from a small database supplied with Workbench or if the material is not in the database you must define it using the **Engineering Materials** application.
3. **Define the analysis type**. In this step you set the type of analysis you will be performing such as Static Structural, Modal or Steady-state heat transfer.
4. **Set loading and boundary conditions**. In this step you specify how your model is constrained and what loads are acting on it.
5. **Request results**. In this step you specify the results quantities that you want to see once the problem has been solved.
6. **Solve**. In this step you request that Simulation solve the problem you have defined and compute the results you requested.
7. **Review the results**. In this step you review the analysis results that you requested in step 5.
8. **Generate a report**. This step is optional but is recommended. In this step you generate an HTML report which includes the inputs to your simulation, the results and any comments you want to add. You can publish the report or e-mail it in various formats.

6.2 Tutorial 6_1 – 4"x1"x1" 3-D cantilevered beam

In this tutorial you will create a cantilevered beam, and perform a stress analysis after constraining it and loading it with a 500lb load. The beam is 4 inches long and has a 1 inch square cross-section.

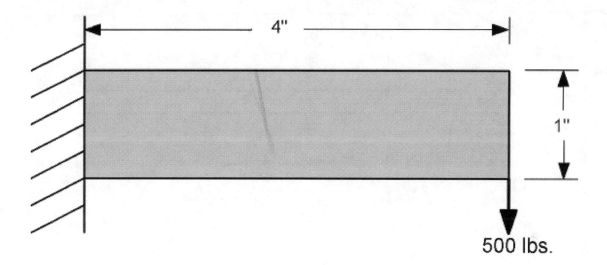

Manual calculation of the deflection at the end of the cantilevered beam can be done using the following formula introduced in strength of materials courses: $\delta = (PL^3)/(3EI)$, along with an additional term that takes into account the deflection due to shear $(6PL)/(5AG)$. Although the deflection due to shear for the cantilevered beam is small, we will include it here for sake of completeness[1]. Since the beam is made of structural steel, we will be using a modulus of elasticity $E = 29,007,557$psi, and determining the shear modulus, from the formula $G= E/(2 (1 + \mu)) = 11,156,753$psi (based on the values stored in the ANSYS database for structural steel). Substituting these values into the deflection equation yields an expected deflection of:

$$\delta = \frac{PL^3}{3EI} + \frac{6PL}{5AG} = \frac{(500lb)(4in)^3}{3(29.01e6\,psi)(\frac{(1in)(1in)^3}{12})} + \frac{6(500lb)(4in)}{5(1in)^2(11.16e6\,psi)} = 0.004627in$$

The maximum bending stress in the beam is expected to occur at the top and bottom of the beam where it contacts the wall. Again, from strength of materials, we would expect a maximum bending stress value of:

$$\sigma = \frac{Mc}{I} = \frac{(500lb)(4in)(0.5in)}{\frac{(1in)(1in)^3}{12}} = 12,000\,psi$$

We will use these two values to compare with our finite element results.

Step 1 – Start a new DesignModeler database and select **Inch** in the unit selection dialog box.

Step 2 – On the **XZPlane** construct a 1"x1" square section.

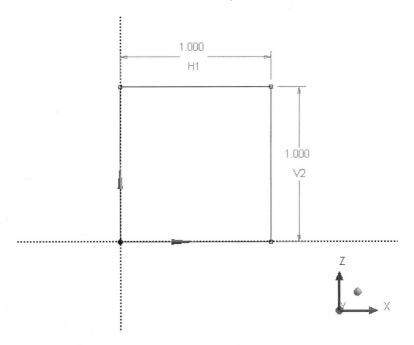

Step 3 – Create a beam by extruding the section 4 inches in the Y direction.
   A. Switch to Isometric view by clicking on the **ISO** icon in the toolbar.
   B. In the **Details View** switch the **Direction** to **Reversed**.
   C. Enter **4** for **FD1, Depth(>0)**.
   D. Click **Generate**.

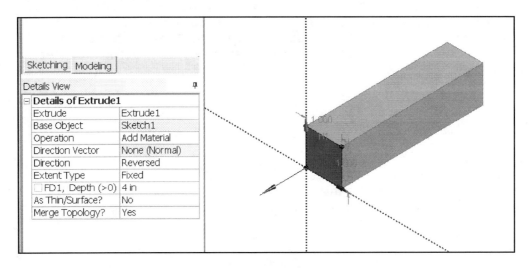

Step 4 – Save the solid model. Click on the **Save** (Floppy disk) icon, browse to a desired location and save the file as *Tutorial 6_1*.

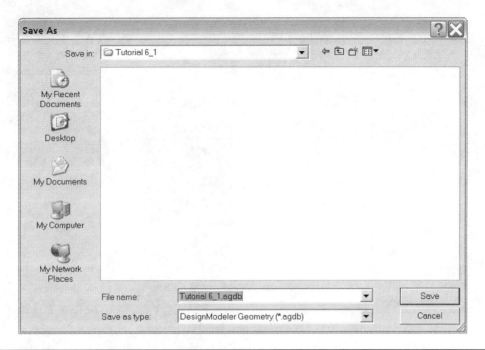

Step 5 – Begin a simulation using the solid model of the beam.
   A. Go to the project page by clicking on the project tab.
   B. Select the solid model (Tutorial 6_1.agdb) and click on **New Simulation**.

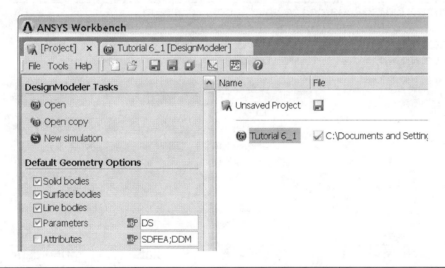

Step 5 (continued) – The simulation window will open and the part file will be brought in and displayed as shown.

Note: If you see the **Map of Analysis Types** window pane on the right hand side, click on the **X** at the top of the window pane to close it. See section 3.6.2 for steps to prevent the map from being displayed when the Simulation application starts.

Check the bottom right portion of the Simulation window to make sure the units are set correctly. In this tutorial the working units are "**US Customary (in,lbm,lbf,F,s)**". If a different system is displayed, use the **Units** pull down menu to change working units.

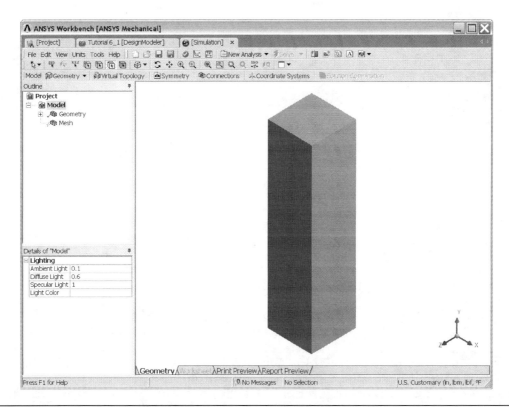

Step 5 (continued) – Rename the solid model to **Beam**.
  C. In the **Outline** pane expand the **Geometry** object.
  D. Click the RMB on **Solid** and select Rename.
  E. Type **Beam**.

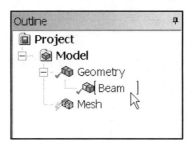

Step 6 – Set the material type. By default, the Simulation application sets all materials in the model to be Structural Steel. In this step we simply check that the material type has been set.

Select **Beam** in the **Outline** pane look at the **Material** setting in the **Details** pane below.

See section 3.5 in chapter 3 for instructions on adding new material types to your project.

Step 7 – Define the analysis type. Click on the **New Analysis** pull-down menu and select **Static Structural**.

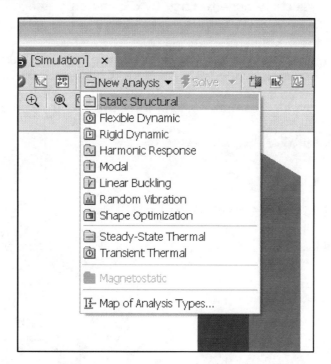

Step 7 (continued) – The **Static Structural** folder and the **Solution** folder are added to the **Model** in the **Outline** pane.

Note the question mark icons next to the Static Structural folder and the Solution folder. The reason for the question marks is that we have not yet defined any loading, boundary conditions or desired results for this analysis. Once these quantities are specified, the questions marks will be replaced by green check marks or other appropriate icons.

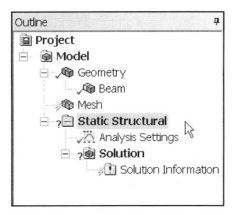

Step 7 (continued) – Set the load. The loading for this analysis consists of a 500lbf force in the −Z direction.

   A. Select the **Static Structural** folder in the Outline view. The Environment toolbar is displayed.
   B. Orient the beam by rotating it so that the Z axis is in the vertical direction and one end of the beam is visible as shown. The Y-axis should point towards you.
   C. Change the selection mode to **Face** by clicking on the face icon in the graphics toolbar (called the **Selection** toolbar in DesignModeler) and then select the visible end face.
   D. Click on **Loads** in the toolbar and select **Force** from the menu.
   E. In the **Details** pane, change **Define By** to **Components** if it is not already set.
   F. Enter **-500** for the Z component and **0** for the X and Y components.

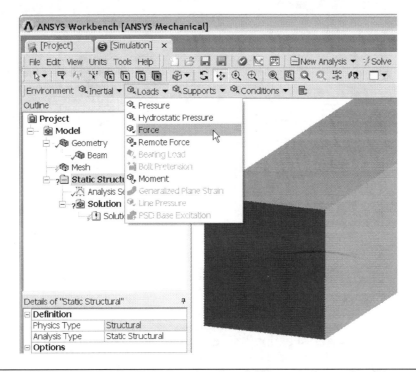

Step 8 – Set The boundary conditions. The boundary condition for this analysis consists of a fixed support at one end of the beam.

A. Orient the beam by rotating it so that the Z axis is in the vertical direction and the opposite end of the beam (opposite end on which you imposed the force in step 7) is visible. The Y axis will point away from you.
B. Select the visible end face of the beam.
C. Select the **Static Structural** folder.
D. Click on **Supports** in the toolbar and select **Fixed Support**.
E. Click on **Apply** in the **Details** window pane.

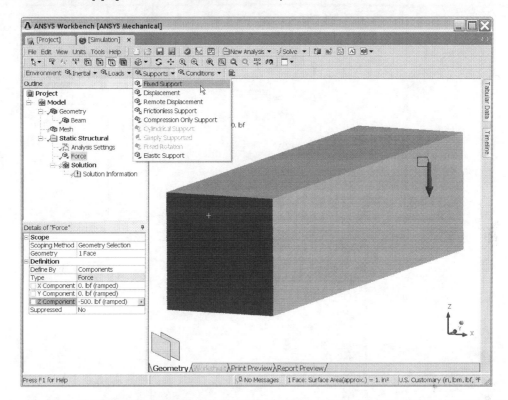

Step 9 – Request results. First request deformation.
A. Select the **Solution** folder.
B. In the Solution toolbar click on **Deformation** and select **Deformation-Directional**.
C. In the **Details** pane change the **Orientation** to **Z Axis**.

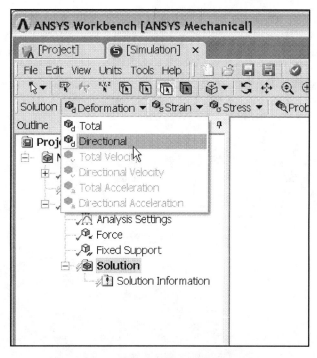

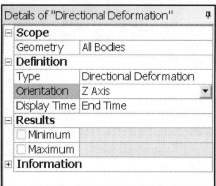

Step 9 (continued) – Request normal stress
   D. Click on **Stress** in the toolbar and select **Stress-Normal**.
   E. In the **Details** pane change the Orientation to **Y Axis**.

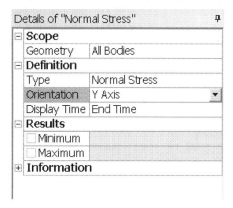

The Project Outline pane now appears as shown below. The question mark next to **Static Structural** folder has been replaced by a green check mark indicating that loads and boundary conditions sufficient to solve this simulation haven been specified. The question mark next to the Solution folder is replaced by a yellow lightning bolt. This icon indicates that the solution has not been calculated yet.

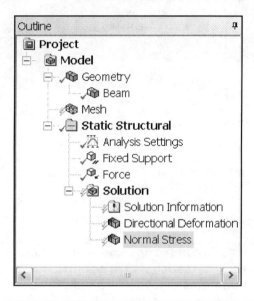

Step 10 – Solve.
Click on the Solve icon in the toolbar.

The solution status window will appear and display the various stages of the solution process. The solution is complete when this window disappears.

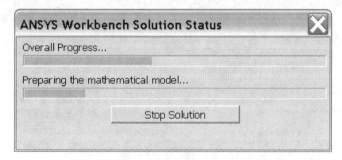

Step 10 (Continued) – Once the solution is successfully completed, green check marks will be placed next to the solution quantities you had requested.

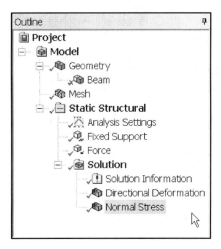

Step 11 – Save the analysis. Click on the floppy disk icon in the toolbar and click the **Save** button in the dialog box that appears next. The file name will be automatically entered as **Tutorial 6_1.dsdb** and the directory will be the same one you selected when you saved the DesignModeler file.

Step 12 – Review the results. When the solution is complete, click on one of the solution quantities you requested such as **Directional Deformation** or **Normal Stress** to display those quantities as contour plots. For example, the figure below shows the contour plot of the normal stress in the Y direction superimposed on the deformed shape of the beam. Note that since in most cases deflections and deformations are too small to be perceptible, these quantities are automatically scaled (exaggerated) to make them easily visible. In this way you can quickly determine if you have set the loads and boundary conditions correctly. The scale factor can be modified from the **Result** toolbar and set to various values including 1.0 (True Scale).

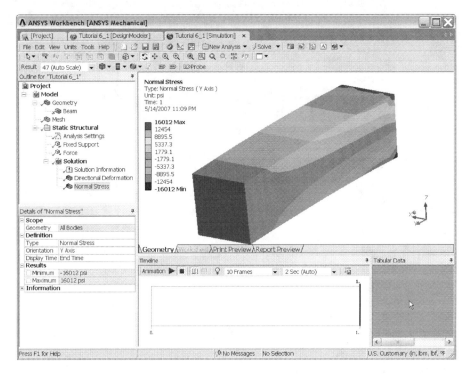

Step 12 (continued) – Enlarge the displayed results area.

By default, when displaying graphical results, a considerable portion of the Workbench window is occupied by window panes such as the **Timeline** and **Tabular Data** window panes. These window panes can be unpinned (collapsed) in order to enlarge the graphical results display as described in section 3.4.3, Window Manager Features. To unpin the **Timeline** and **Tabular Data** Window panes, click on the push-pins located at the top right hand corner of each pane. The resulting display is shown below.

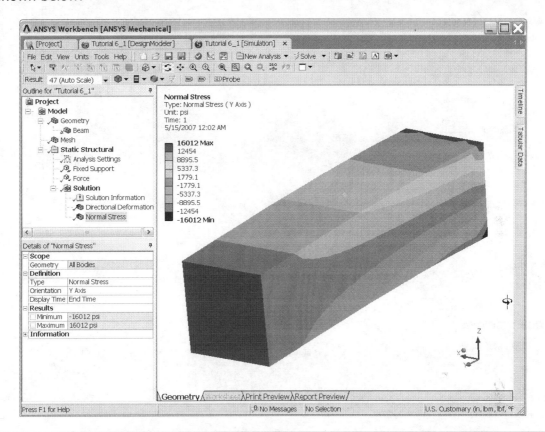

Step 12 (continued) – The displayed contour plots can be modified in several ways in order to better represent the results of the analysis. The modifications are performed from three pull-down menus as shown below.

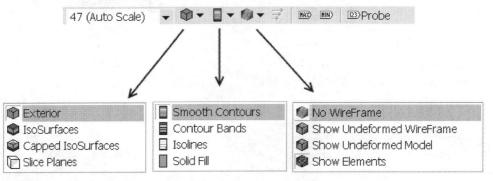

The previous display is set to display **Exterior**, **Contour bands** and **No WireFrame**.

Step 12 (continued) – Select **Contours Bands** and **Show Elements** from the pull-down menus. The resulting display is shown below.

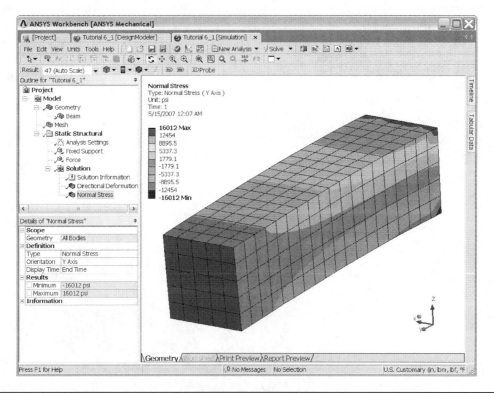

Step 12 (continued) – Click on **Directional Deformation**. The resulting display is shown below.

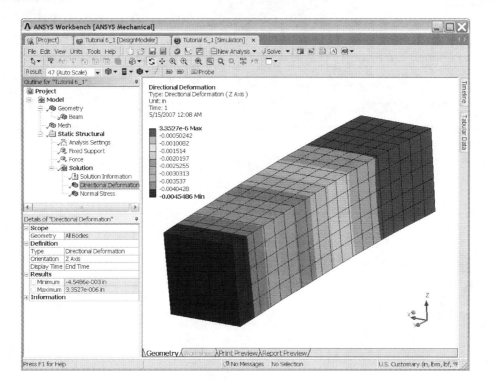

Step 12 (continued) – Note that the maximum and minimum values displayed are the range values for the contours. For example, on the **Normal Stress** plot, the red contours represent stress values ranging from 12,454. PSI to 16,012. PSI. In order to get a more precise value, use the Probe tool:

A. Rotate the beam and position it as shown below.
B. Click on **Probe** in the toolbar.
C. Move the cursor over the contoured part and observe the contour values at the position of the cursor.
D. Click the LMB to place a tag indicating the value at that location.

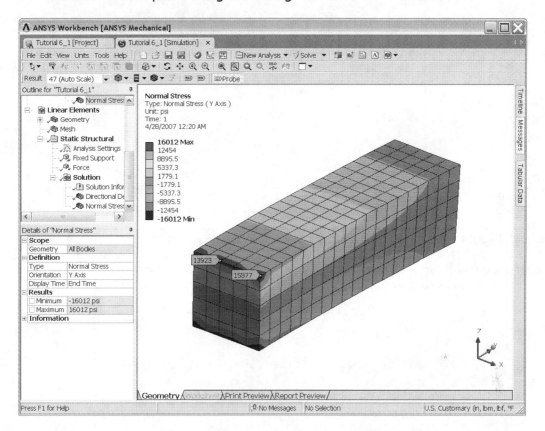

To remove a tag, click on the **Label** icon in the toolbar 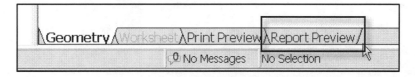, select the tag to be deleted and press the Delete key on the keyboard.

Step 13 – Generate a report. A simple HTML report can be automatically generated by simply clicking on the **Report Preview** tab.

The report generated in this way includes basic information about the analysis such as the type of analysis, material properties of the materials used, boundary conditions, etc.

Step 13 (continued) – The table of contents of the default report is shown below. The entries in the table of contents are hyperlinked to the location of the information in the report.

Contents

- Model
    - Geometry
        - Beam
    - Mesh
    - **Static Structural**
        - Analysis Settings
        - Loads
        - Solution
            - Solution Information
            - Results
- Material Data
    - Structural Steel

Step 13 (continued) – The default report includes the calculated results in tabular form but deformed shapes and contour plots are not automatically included in the report. Below is an example of tabular results.

TABLE 10
Model > Static Structural > Solution > Results

Object Name	Directional Deformation	Normal Stress
State	Solved	
Scope		
Geometry	All Bodies	
Definition		
Type	Directional Deformation	Normal Stress
Orientation	Z Axis	Y Axis
Display Time	End Time	
Results		
Minimum	-0.11553 mm	-110.4 MPa
Maximum	8.5159e-005 mm	110.4 MPa
Information		
Time	1. s	
Load Step	1	
Substep	1	
Iteration Number	1	

Step 14 – Include contour plot of normal stress in the report.
   A. In the Project tree click on **Normal Stress**.
   B. Click on the **Geometry** tab at the bottom of the window.
   C. Adjust the figure as desired by zooming, rotating, etc.
   D. From the Figures pull down menu in the toolbar select **Figure**.

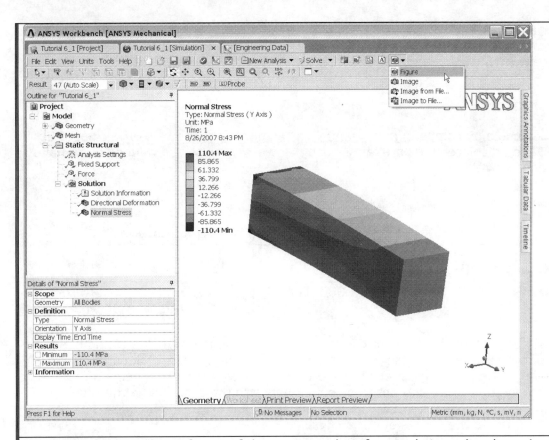

Step 14 (continued) – A figure of the contour plot of normal stress has been inserted in the project tree under **Normal Stress**. The figure can be renamed using the **RMB** and you can also add text that appears as caption with the figure.

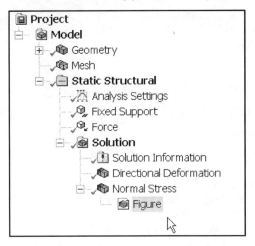

Step 15 – Regenerate the report. Click on the **Report Preview** tab as before to regenerate an updated report which includes the contour plot figure.

Note: Figures inserted in the project tree are updated with the latest results every time a new report is generated. Therefore, they always reflect the latest conditions of the analysis. In order to include a static picture, select **Image** in Step 14, sub step D.

Step 16 – Save the project as *Tutorial 6_1*.

Summary

As we can see by comparing our manual calculations with the values calculated by ANSYS, the displacements are fairly close. However, the stress values do not have very good correlation.

	Manual Calculation	**ANSYS Results**	**% difference**
Max. Deflection	0.004627 in.	0.0045486 in	1.694%
Max. Bending Stress	12,000psi	13,923psi 15,877psi	16.03% 32.31%

The primary reason for the poor correlation of stress values was due to the boundary condition occurring at the same location as our maximum stress values. However, our goal during this chapter was to become familiar with the steps needed to get a very simply job to run, and not to be concerned with the accuracy of the results. During the next chapters we will investigate several different techniques that can be used to improve the results of our analysis.

Reference

[1] Popov, E. P., Mechanics of Materials, 2nd Edition, Prentice-Hall, Englewood Cliffs NJ, 1976

Exercises:

1. Use ANSYS Workbench to build a finite element model of the beam shown below, that has a 20mm x 20mm cross section and is made from structural steel. Determine the maximum deflection and bending stress in the beam. Then compare these values with those that you manually calculate using strength of material formulas from your textbooks (you do not have to take into account the deflection due to shear, as was done in the example problem in this chapter).

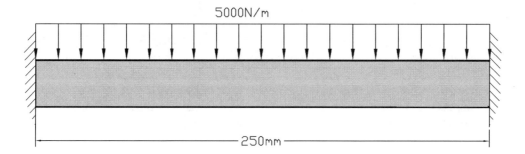

5000N/m

250mm

2. Use ANSYS Workbench to model and analyze the 36 inch long beam shown below. Imprint lines on your model of the beam, to use as edges on which to apply the 1500 lbs. loads. The beam is made from 1/2" thick, structural steel. Determine the deflection and normal (bending) stress at the center of the beam. Then compare these values with those that you manually calculate using strength of material formulas from your textbooks (you do not have to take into account the deflection due to shear, as was done in the example problem in this chapter).

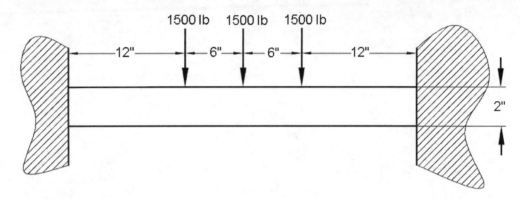

3. Use ANSYS Workbench to build a finite element model of the cantilevered beam shown below, that is made from structural steel. Determine the maximum deflection and bending stress in the beam. Then compare these values with those that you manually calculate using strength of material formulas from your textbooks (you do not have to take into account the deflection due to shear, as was done in the example problem in this chapter).

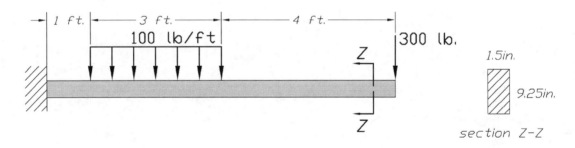

NOTES:

7

Using the Wizards

7.1 Introduction to Simulation Wizards

Most if not all computer users are familiar with wizards. In their most general form, wizards prompt the user to respond to a limited number of questions and based on the responses the wizard produces a certain outcome. The user's response at each step determines the next question and in this way the user is able to accomplish the task with a minimum of effort.

Workbench wizards are somewhat different in that they are also instructional. Based on the initial selection of the analysis type, the user is instructed to take certain actions. The wizard does not actually accomplish a task such as imposing a boundary condition, but indicates how the Workbench user interface should be used to impose boundary conditions.

The Workbench wizards, however, do control the process flow of the analysis by dividing the tasks into the required and optional ones. They also disable some tasks until a prerequisite task has been completed.

The behavior of the Workbench wizards can be summarized as follows:

- The tasks required to perform a certain type of analysis are listed in the wizard window pane which appears on the right hand side of the Workbench window.
- Clicking on each task displays and flashes a callout which points to a location in the Workbench user interface where the task can be accomplished.
- The callout tells the user what needs to be done to complete the step.
- The state of each step is indicated visually. These can be Informational, Incomplete, or disabled. A step that is not selectable (grayed out) requires a previous step to be completed first.
- The callouts can be dismissed by clicking on them.

7.2 Map of Analysis Types

As explained in section 3.6.2, version 11 of Workbench introduces a new feature called the **Map of Analysis Types**. Section 3.6.2 gives a brief description of the map and instructions for disabling it which prevents it from appearing when the simulation application is started. Since we will not be using the map, you should follow the procedure for disabling it. The map can also be disabled by clicking on the **X** icon located on the top right corner of the map and if needed, it can be restored from the **New Analysis** menu.

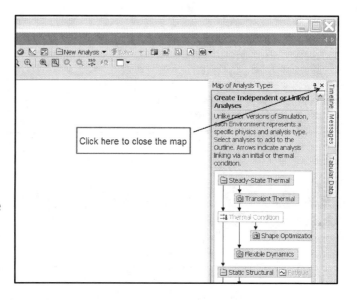

7.3 Wizards supplied with Workbench

The Workbench installation includes a number of wizards including stress analysis, thermal analysis, and modal Analysis wizards. The **Simulation Wizard** window pane which gives access to these wizards can be activated either by clicking on the Simulation Wizard button 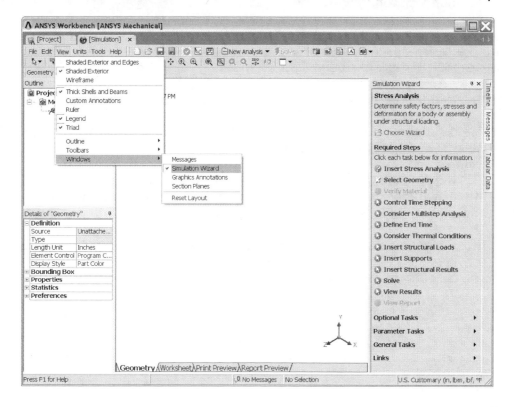 in the toolbar or from the **View** menu by selecting **Windows-Simulation Wizard** to activate the **Simulation Wizards** window pane.

Note that until a specific analysis type is chosen, the Wizard presents a number of options under **Required Steps** that will be eliminated once a choice is made. Selection of the analysis type is accomplished by clicking on the **Choose Wizard** link as shown below. The three wizards that relate to the analysis types discussed in this book, namely Stress analysis, Modal analysis and Thermal analysis are outlined in the figure below. The **Choose Wizard** pop-up can be closed by clicking on **Close this callout** which is the last item in the pop-up.

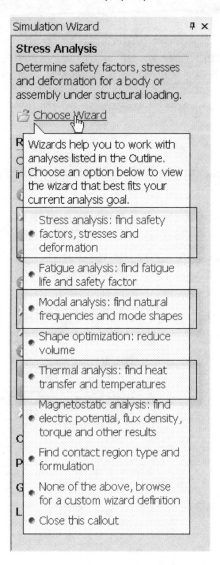

Clicking on one of the Wizards activates it and shows the steps required in performing the selected analysis type as well as optional actions which can be taken to improve or enhance the analysis.

The use of wizards will be illustrated in the next section in which one will be used to perform a Stress analysis.

7.4 Tutorial 7_1 – Stress analysis using the Stress Wizard

In this tutorial we will repeat the analysis performed in chapter 6 (Tutorial 6_1) using the Stress wizard. Although the wizards are intended to guide the user through the analysis and make further explanation unnecessary, the Workbench wizards are very general and only indicate to the user the steps necessary to perform an analysis. Therefore, the following tutorial highlights their use so that they can be used more effectively.

Once a wizard is activated, the most effective way to complete the analysis is to proceed to complete the steps presented by the wizard in the order they are presented. For example, in the following tutorial, after Stress Analysis has been selected, we will proceed to select the geometry, set the material, insert the structural loads, insert the supports and structural results before solving the FEA problem.

Step 1– Start a new simulation database by clicking on **Simulation** in the **Start** dialog box.

Step 2 – Start the Simulation Wizard and Select the Stress Analysis wizard
  A. From the **View** menu select **Windows-Simulation Wizard** or click on the Simulation Wizard button 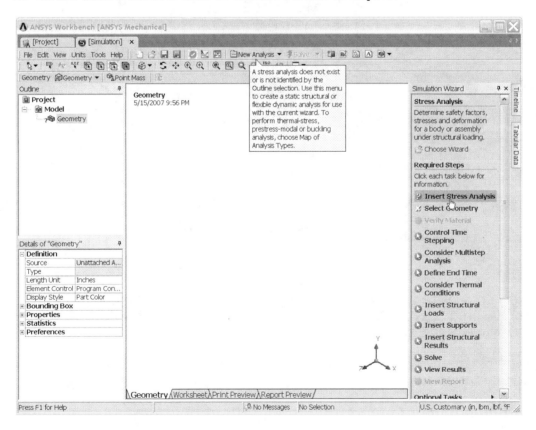 in the toolbar.
  B. In the wizard window click on **Insert Stress Analysis**.

A Callout will appear and point to the New Analysis pull-down menu. The callout instructs you to use this menu to create a static structural or other type of stress analysis.

Step 3 – Select Static Structural analysis. From the **New Analysis** menu select **Static Structural**.

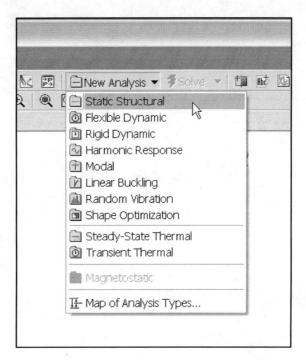

Step 3 (continued) – The Structural Analysis folder is inserted into the Outline and the wizard window pane is modified to reflect the selection of the wizard. In the Simulation Wizard window pane the **Required Steps** section is now changed to reflect the steps necessary to perform a static structural analysis and the text describing each step is preceded by an icon which indicates the state of that step as explained below.

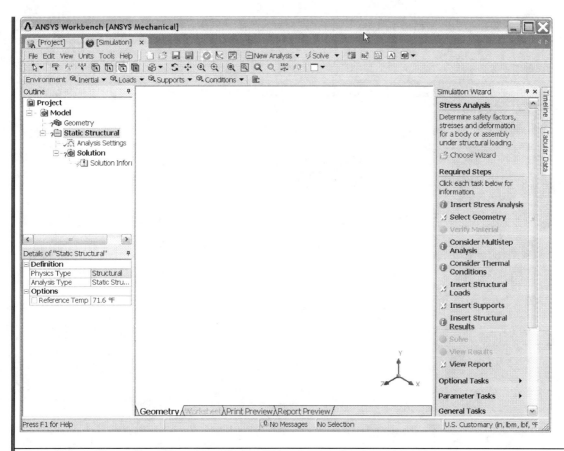

Step 3 (continued) – The meanings of the icons displayed in the wizard pane are given below.

Information: Clicking on this icon displays a callout which provides additional information about the step.

Incomplete Task: This step is yet to be performed. Therefore, all the steps that depend on it will be grayed out and inactive.

Inactive (grayed out) Task: A preceding step has to be completed first.

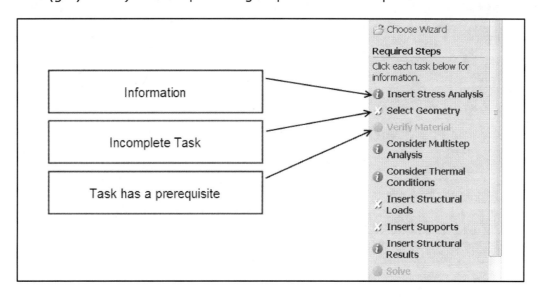

Step 4 – Link to geometry.
   A. Click on **Select Geometry** in the wizard window pane. The Callout that appears points to the toolbar **Geometry** icon and indicates that the analysis can be linked to CAD geometry from this location.
   B. Click on **Geometry** in the toolbar and select **From File**.
   C. Browse to the **Student Files\Models** directory and select the Parasolids file **Cantilever-4x1x1.x_t** which was created in a CAD program.

The geometry file is read and the model is displayed in the Geometry window pane. Notice that the Select Geometry task has a green check mark next to it, indicating that the task is complete.

The three steps that follow: **Verify Material**, **Consider Multistep Analysis** and **Consider Thermal Conditions,** are optional as indicated by the letter *i* in the icon next to each step and will be skipped in this tutorial.

Step 4 (continued) – Insert Loads. Click on **Insert Structural Loads**. The wizard selects the **Static Structural** folder and the **Environment** toolbar is displayed
   D. Orient the beam by rotating it so that the Z axis is in the vertical direction and one end of the beam is visible. Refer to the triad for orientation.
   E. Change the selection mode to **Face** by clicking on the face icon in the graphics toolbar (called the **Selection** toolbar in DesignModeler) and then select the visible end face.
   F. Click on **Loads** in the toolbar and select **Force** from the menu.
   G. In the **Details** pane, change **Define By** to **Components** if it is not already set.
   H. Enter *-500* for the Z component and *0* for the X and Y components.
   I. Click on **Apply**.

Note: Sub-steps D-H are the same as sub-steps B through F of step 7 in Tutorial 6_1 in Chapter 6. See step 7 of that tutorial for further clarification.

Step 5 – Impose the boundary conditions. Click on **Insert Supports**. The callout points to **Supports** in the **Environment** toolbar. Orient the beam and impose a Fixed Support boundary condition as described instep 8 of Tutorial 6_1. See step 8 of Tutorial 6_1 for further clarification.

Step 6 – Request results. Click on Insert **Structural Results**. The Solution folder is selected and the callout points to **Tools** in the toolbar. The callout suggests the use of the **Solution** toolbar to add Tools, Results or Probe. We will use the Results option which refers to the **Deformation**, **Strain** and **Stress** items in the toolbar which are outlined below. The **Tools** menu inserts the **Stress Tool** into Outline which includes a safety factor calculation and **Probe** enables us to probe the solution to retrieve solution values at specific locations.

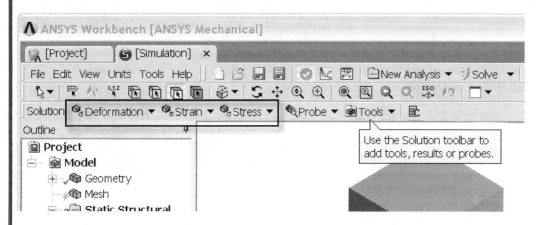

A. In the Solution toolbar click on Deformation and select Deformation-Directional.
B. In the Details pane change the Orientation to Z Axis.

Step 6 (continued) – Request Normal Stress.
C. Click on **Stress** in the toolbar and select **Stress-Normal**.
D. In the Details pane change the Orientation to **Y Axis**.

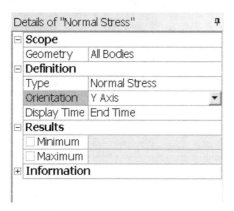

The Project Outline pane now appears as shown below. The question mark next to the **Static Structural** folder has been replaced by a green check mark indicating that loads and boundary conditions sufficient to solve this simulation have been specified. The question mark next to the Solution folder is replaced by a yellow lightning bolt. This icon indicates that the solution has not been calculated yet.

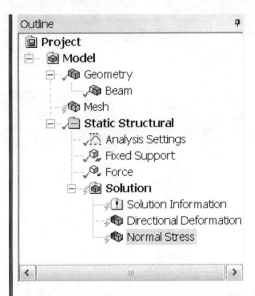

Step 7 – Click on Solve in the wizard pane. The callout directs you to use the Solve menu to generate results for this analysis.
Click on **Solve** to solve the FEA problem.

The solution status window will appear and display the various stages of the solution process. The solution is complete when this window disappears.

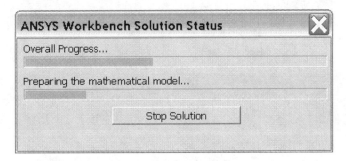

Step 8 – Review the results. The remaining steps are the same as those described in Chapter 6, Tutorial 6_1, step 12.

Step 9 – Generate a report. Click on **View Report** in the wizard pane.

NOTES:

8

Modeling Techniques

The importance of using proper modeling techniques to insure that a finite element analysis produces the correct results cannot be overemphasized. Competent users must understand how to specify: suitable types, sizes, and shapes of elements in order to correctly represent the physical part. Since finite element analysis is a numerical approximation of the actual physical part, it is important for the user to have a good understanding of both the part being analyzed as well as the limitations of the finite element method. Within this chapter we will begin to examine several modeling techniques that should be used when creating finite element models. Additional modeling techniques that are particular to specific element types will be discussed in the following chapters. As these additional techniques are discussed, it will be beneficial to return to this chapter and review the material presented here.

8.1 Meshing

Generally, the finer the mesh the closer the results will be to those in the corresponding physical part. Comparisons of FEA models containing different numbers of elements show that finite element model results approach the *exact* solution as the number of elements increase. Figure 8.1 shows the results of the deflection of the cantilever beam that was presented in chapter 6, but this time, using several different finite element models. Notice that the exact solution is approached as the number of elements is increased.

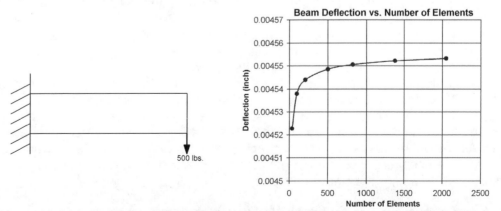

Figure 8.1 The deflection at the end of a cantilevered beam converges to the exact solution as the number of elements increases

Since finer meshes produce more accurate results, the obvious question then becomes: "why not make the mesh as fine as possible?" This question must be answered with regard to both the available computing power and time to do the analysis. If an unlimited amount of time is available to prepare the model and the computing power is quite large, then the mesh should be made as fine as possible. However, this is usually never the case. So we must make "trade-offs". One of these "trade-offs" involves, using a fine mesh of elements in regions where the stress is rapidly changing (high gradients) and a relatively coarse mesh in regions of small stress gradients. A classical example of this is shown in Figure 8.2. The stress gradient is very large in the region next to the hole due to the stress concentration, so the corresponding finite element mesh consists of smaller elements in this region and larger elements elsewhere.

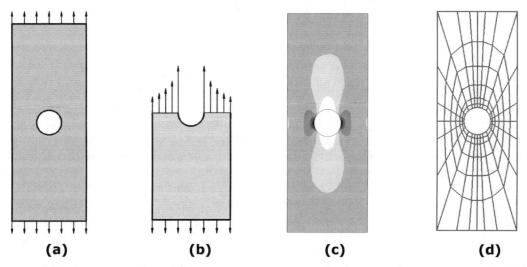

(a)   **(b)**   **(c)**   **(d)**

Figure 8.2 Axially loaded plate with center hole (a), and the resulting stress gradient (b) and (c), and the corresponding finite element model - using a finer mesh in regions of high stress gradients

Figure 8.2(d) shows a finite element model that correctly models the axially loaded plate with a centrally located hole. The plate's stress concentration factor is well documented in many books [1, 2]. The results of the finite element analysis for this model can, therefore, be compared to these book's stress concentration values in order to determine if the mesh is fine enough to correctly predict accurate results. However, the reason for performing most finite element analyses is that there is no handbook formula that *fits* the design being analyzed. For these cases, the question becomes: "When do you know that the mesh is fine enough". If several analyses are carried out using progressively finer meshes as was illustrated in Figure 8.1, each subsequent analysis will have less numerical error than the previous model, provided good element shapes are employed. Therefore, one technique that can be used is to perform multiple analyses, where each subsequent analysis has a finer mesh than the preceding model. Then when two subsequent analyses produce results that are similar, the point has been reached where further refinement will not provide any benefit. As we will discuss later in this chapter, Workbench provides an automated procedure called convergence that re-meshes the FEA model until two subsequent results are within a user specified tolerance.

Creation of the finite element mesh in Workbench is highly automated and requires very little or no intervention from the user. This is particularly advantageous in the case of a beginner who will be performing linear static analysis. Given reasonably *clean* CAD geometry, the Workbench mesher will generally produce a mesh that accurately represents the solid model and maximizes the quality of the elements in the mesh.

The finite element mesh representing a physical object is very important since the finite element method relies on the quality of the mesh as a first step in producing accurate results. Without an accurate representation of the solid, important details of the geometry can be missed and distorted and misshapen elements can produce highly inaccurate results.

8.2 Aspect Ratio and Badly Shaped Elements

Aspect ratio is defined as the ratio of the length of an element's longest side to its shortest side. Under optimum situations, all elements should have an aspect ratio of 1, and all interior angles of quadrilateral elements should be 90 degrees. However, in order to model irregularly shaped parts, it is not possible to maintain this optimum situation. They should, however, serve as the standard to strive toward. The figure below shows examples of good aspect ratio (a) and bad (b).

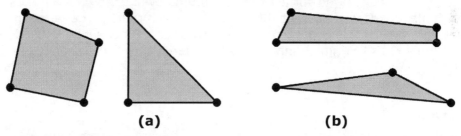

(a)   **(b)**

Figure 8.3 Examples of (a) "good" and (b) "bad" aspect ratios

In regions of a part where the stress gradient is small, aspect ratios can be higher that in areas where stresses vary rapidly. However, in any region where stress results are of interest, the aspect ratio should be kept as close to unity as possible.

Skewing of an element occurs when the interior angles vary from 90 degrees for quadrilateral elements and 60 degrees for triangle elements. Of course, just as it is nearly impossible to maintain an aspect ratio of 1, it is also impossible to maintain an ideal interior angle. The figure below shows examples of skewing.

Figure 8.4 Examples of "bad" elements caused by excessive skewing

Of course, since finite element models are usually created for parts that have irregular shapes, at least some area of the mesh will have elements that are less that the ideal aspect ratio and contain some skewing. Regions in the model that contain these less than ideal elements should be located several element layers away from any area of interest.

8.3 Mesh Refinement in Workbench

As was stated in section 8.1, mesh generation in Workbench is highly automated but because Workbench accommodates many advanced applications that may require manual adjustment to the mesh, the user can still control the mesh generation process if he or she chooses to do so. The mesh adjustment tools include a broad range of controls which act globally as well as those that allow local control of the mesh generation process. Since this book is intended for new users of the Finite Element analysis method and Workbench, our main focus will be on the mesh refinement controls that act globally rather than locally.

In the following sections of this chapter, it is helpful to keep in mind that to manually generate a mesh, the user has to explicitly specify how a model (solid or surface body) is subdivided into discrete elements. This involves specifying the coordinates of all the nodal points and how they are connected to each other to form the elements. Automatic mesh generation tools such as those used in Workbench free the user from having to do this. From the geometry, Workbench extracts information such as the overall size of the model, the size of the smallest feature such as an edge, proximity of features to each other, etc., and uses this information along with the default settings, such as the type of element to be used and how closely the curved edges and surfaces should be followed, to produce a mesh. Workbench also takes into account the type of analysis that will be performed with the generated mesh. This is particularly important if the mesh will be used for a CFD (Computational Fluid Dynamic) analysis rather than a Stress or other type of analysis.

8.4 Relevance

The first mesh refinement method we will introduce is called Relevance. It is the simplest way to improve the mesh generated by the program. Relevance simply allows the user to modify the default settings that would normally be used to generate the mesh for a body. Using this method, the relevance or importance of a part is specified relative to the default settings. The user simply sets the relevance level on a scale from -100 to +100; where, 0 is the default. On this scale, a -100 setting means the least relevance or the coarsest mesh, 0 is the default and +100 means the most relevance or the finest automatically generated mesh.

Relevance can only be applied to an entire solid body or surface body. It is not applicable to portions of a body such as surfaces and edges.

The following steps should be followed to apply relevance to a part:

1. Select the **Mesh** icon in the **Outline** window pane
2. From the **Mesh** pull down menu select **Part Relevance**
3. Select the part and click Apply in the **Details** window pane
4. Click the area next to **Part Relevance** in the **Details** window pane
    o Type a value from -100 to +100, OR
    o Use the mouse cursor to drag the slider to the set the value

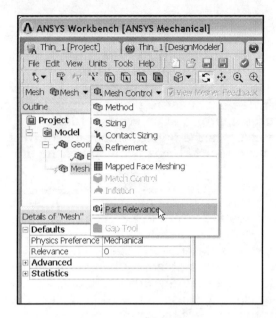

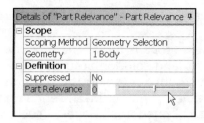

The following figure shows the results obtained by varying the relevance setting of a rectangular cross-section beam.

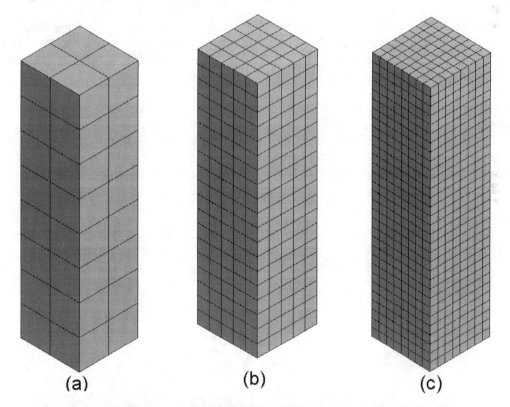

Figure 8.5 Relevance settings of –100 setting results in the mesh shown in (a), the default setting or a 0 setting results in the mesh shown in (b) and the maximum setting of +100 results in the finest mesh which is shown in (c)

8.5 Convergence

Convergence is by far the most powerful feature of Workbench in improving mesh quality and solution accuracy because it is driven by the results. The term convergence refers to the solution converging to a final and most accurate solution possible by way of mesh refinement. Finite element analysis is an approximation of physical phenomena and as such, it introduces approximation errors into the analysis. The first source of approximation errors is the finite element mesh which represents the physical structure. Traditionally the mesh has been one of the most important sources of error in a finite element analysis. This is due to the presence of one or more of following problems: the elements are too large to capture the variation of the quantity (such as stress) of interest, the elements are distorted or have large aspect ratios, or critical geometric features were not modeled correctly.

The solution to the problem of meshing errors was described in section 8.1 and consists of refining the mesh and the solving the FEA problem multiple times where each solution uses a finer and more accurate mesh than the preceding one. Once the results of an analysis are the same as or close to those obtained in the previous analysis, the process can stop. In the past, this process had to be performed manually. However, because this was a very time consuming process, often times it was not done.

Workbench simulation can perform this process automatically and in a way that is far superior to the manual process. While a manual mesh refinement process requires the analyst to decide how and where to refine the mesh, the Convergence feature in Simulation automates this task.

The mesh refinement is based on the computed results so that finer elements are generated in the areas of the structure where the solution shows the most rapid change is occurring. This technique is called Adaptive Mesh Refinement and has the advantage of refining the mesh only in the areas where it needs to be refined. The flowchart shown below describes the procedure used in the convergence process.

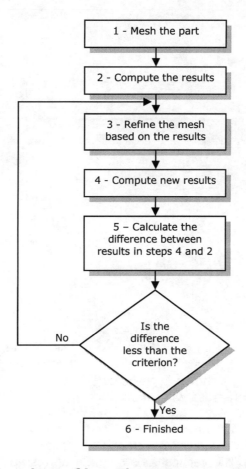

Figure 8.6 Flowchart of how the convergence feature works.

The following are some important characteristics of the convergence feature:

- Convergence can be applied to any solution quantity such as displacement or stress
- Convergence can be applied to either the maximum or the minimum value of the solution quantity
- Convergence uses adaptive mesh refinement which is solution driven
- In most cases, the **Max Refinement Loops** setting of the **Solution** object in the **Outline** view has to be increased to obtain a converged solution (see step 11 of the following tutorial)

8.6 Tutorial 8_1 – Using Convergence to improve the results

In this tutorial we will use the convergence feature of Workbench to illustrate how the calculation of the normal stress in the fillet region of a T-section can be improved. The section is loaded as cantilevered beam. It is fixed on the left side (the side whose longest edge is 3") and top and bottom and loaded with a vertical force of 100 lb. that is distributed on the vertical face at the free end as shown in the figure below.

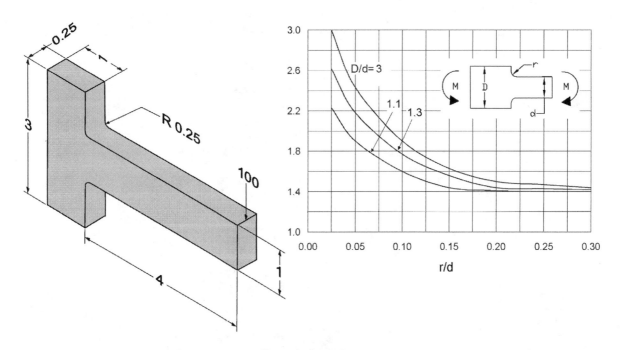

The maximum stress in the fillet area will occur at the location where the fillet meets the 1 inch wide portion of the part. The stress concentration factor can be approximated from the case shown in the chart, so we will use the moment at the point where the maximum stress will occur.

The curve which we will use from the chart: **D/d = 3/1 = 3**
The value on the horizontal axis: **r/d = 0.25/1 = 0.25**
Therefore, the value from the vertical axis of the graph is approximately: **K=1.49**
The maximum stress can then be calculated to be approximately:

$$\sigma_{max} = K\,\frac{Mc}{I} = 1.49\,\frac{(100\ lb \times 3.75in)\ \ 0.5in}{\dfrac{0.25in\ \times 1in^{\,3}}{12}} = 13,410\ \ PSI$$

Step 1 – Start a new Simulation project by clicking on the Simulation icon in the start up dialog box. The simulation window opens and **Geometry** is selected in the **Outline** window pane.

Step 2 – Link this simulation to a geometry file.
   A. From the **Geometry** pull down menu select **From File...**
   B. Browse to the "Student Files\Models" directory and select "T-Section.agdb".
   C. Verify that the working units are set to U.S. Customary (in,lbm,lbf....) as shown in the **Units** pull down menu and in the status bar at the bottom of the Simulation window (U.S. Customary (in, lbm, lbf, °F, s, V, A)).

Step 3 – Check the material type. In the **Outline** view expand **Geometry**, select **Part 1** and in the Details window check that the material is set to **Structural Steel**.

Step 4 – Set the analysis type. From the **New Analysis** pull down menu select **Static Structural**.

Step 5 – Apply a fixed support to the top, back and bottom faces of the vertical portion (the longest face of this portion is parallel with the Y axis). First orient the image. Rotate the image so that the back face is visible.

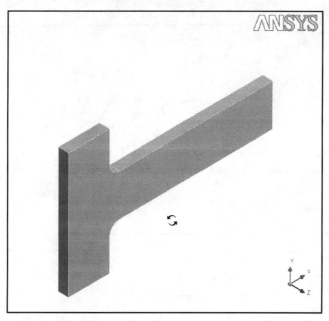

Step 5 (continued) – Apply a fixed support...
   A. While the **Static Structural** folder is selected, select **Fixed Support** from the **Supports** pull down menu.
   B. Set the selection filter to **Face** 🔲 if necessary.
   C. Select the back, top and bottom faces of the vertical portion.
         a) Select the top face.
         b) Press and hold the Control key and then click the back face.
         c) Rotate the part to expose the bottom face.
         d) Set the selection filter to **Face** 🔲 then press and hold the Control key and click the bottom face.
         e) Click **Apply** in the **Details** pane.
   D. Verify that the fixed support was applied to 3 faces by insuring that **3 Faces** is shown in the **Details** pane in front of **Geometry**.

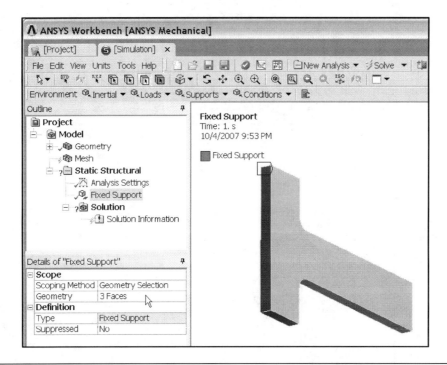

Step 6 – Apply the load.
   A. From the **Loads** menu select **Force**.
   B. Rotate the model and select the opposite face from the one used in the previous step.
   C. Click **Apply** in the **Details** pane.
   D. In the **Details** pane change **Define By** to **Component** if necessary.
   E. Enter **-100** for the **Y Component**.
   F. Click on the **Static Structural** folder icon. The model should appear as shown below.

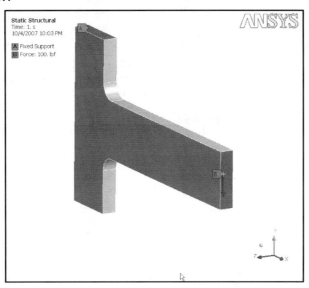

Step 7 – Request Results.
   A. Select the **Solution** folder in the **Outline** view pane.
   B. From the **Deformation** pull down menu select **Directional**.
   C. In the **Details** pane change the **Orientation** to **Y Axis**.

D. From the **Stress** pull down menu select **Normal**.
E. If needed, in the **Detail** pane change the **Orientation** to **X Axis**.

Step 8 – Solve the problem. Click on **Solve** in the toolbar.

Step 9 – Review the results. Select **Normal Stress** under **Solution** in the **Outline** pane to view the stress contours. The following figure shows the resulting display. The maximum normal stress is 10733 PSI and the contours correctly show that the top surface of the beam is in tension (positive stress) and the bottom surface is in compression (negative stress).

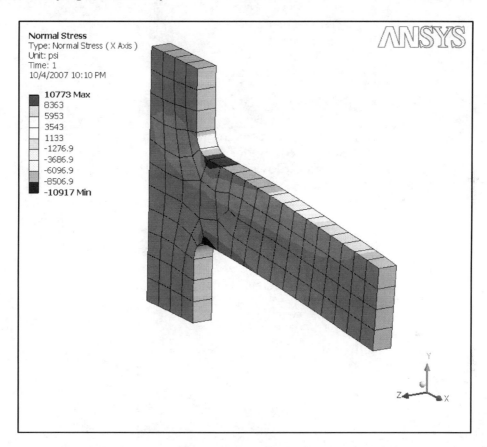

Step 10 – Duplicate the model. The purpose of this step is to preserve the model in its current default state in order to provide a clear comparison with the results after the Convergence feature is used.
A. Select the **Model** icon in the **Outline** window pane, then click the **RMB** and choose **Duplicate**. An exact duplicate of the model is created and named **Model 2**.
B. Select **Model 2**, click the **RMB** and select **Rename**.
C. Enter **_Convergence Model_** to distinguish this model from the original. The Outline window pane now appears as shown below.

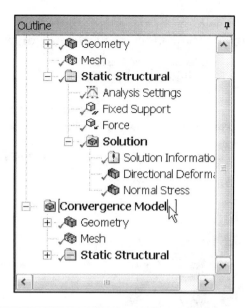

Step 11 – Request solution convergence for the Normal Stress results.
  A. Select the **Normal Stress** icon under the **Solution** folder. First expand the
      Static Structural and the **Solution** folders by clicking in the **+** icon.
  B. Click the **RMB** and select **Insert Convergence**.
  C. Click on **20%** to the right of **Allowable Change** in the **Details** window pane
      and enter **5** (You can also use the slider).

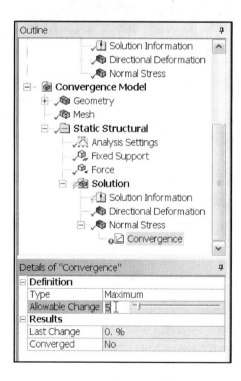

  D. Click on the **Solution** Folder icon and then in the **Details** window pane
      change the **Max Refinement Loops** to **3**.

Step 12 – Solve the convergence problem. Click on **Solve** in the toolbar. Once the solution is complete, if a converged solution is achieved, a green checkmark will appear next to **Convergence** below **Normal Stress** under **Solution** (If the solution had not converged, a red exclamation mark would appear instead).

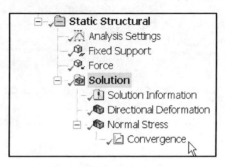

Step 13 – Review the results.
  A. Click on **Convergence** in the **Outline** window pane under **Normal Stress**. A chart and a table of the results, in this case **Normal Stress** are shown in the **Worksheet** tab.
  B. If the **Timeline** and **Tabular Data** window panes are shown, unpin them to maximize the results area (See section **3.4.3 Window Manager Features** in chapter 3 for instructions on unpinning window panes).

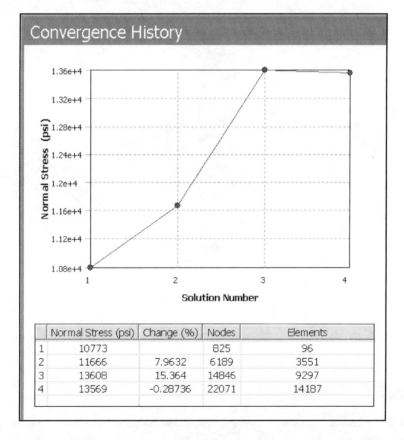

	Normal Stress (psi)	Change (%)	Nodes	Elements
1	10773		825	96
2	11666	7.9632	6189	3551
3	13608	15.364	14846	9297
4	13569	-0.28736	22071	14187

The table shows that the Maximum Normal Stress found in step 9 of the tutorial has increased to 13569 psi. The chart shows that the final solution changed only slightly from the previous run (-0.28736%; far less the specified 5% allowable change) which indicates that a converged solution has been achieved.

Step 13 (continued) – Review the results; understanding the convergence history worksheet:

- Below the chart the results of each run are presented in tabular form. The table includes the percent change between solutions and the number of nodes and elements used in each case.
- The convergence operation was performed on the **Maximum Normal Stress** as indicated in the **Details** window pane under Type. This can be changed to the minimum value if appropriate.
- The solution does not always converge. In some cases as the calculated values continue to change more than the specified **Allowable Change** after the **Max Refinement Loops** is reached in which case the process is halted and marked as **Failed**.
- To see the mesh before the convergence process, click on the Mesh icon.
- To see the mesh after the final refinement, display one of the results quantities, e.g., Normal Stress and from the **Edge Options** pull down menu select **Show Elements**.

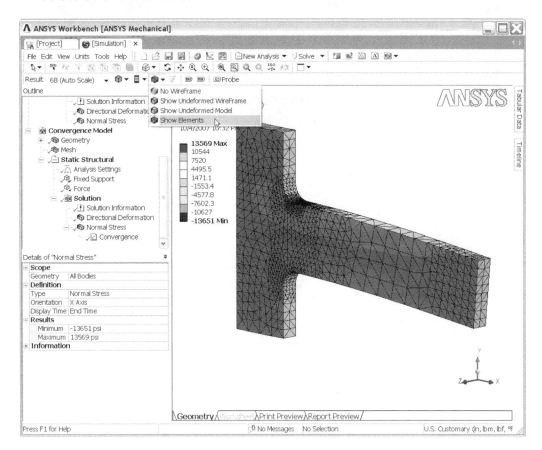

Step 14 – Save the project.

As we can see from the above tutorial, the maximum stress computed in Step 9 was much lower than the results found in Step 13, after convergence was employed.

	FEA Result	Manual Calculation	Percent Difference
Max. tensile Normal Stress in Step 9 (without using convergence)	10,773 psi	13,410 psi	-19.7%
Max. tensile Normal Stress in Step 13 (using convergence)	13,569psi	13,410 psi	+1.2%

8.7 Supports

As we discussed in chapter 2, in order to generate a solution to the set of global stiffness equations, the assemblage of spring elements had to be supported at some location. This is also true for our 3D FEA models. They must be supported (constrained) in space and have loads (external or internal) which act upon them in a manner that complies with Newton's laws. The supports prevent the model from moving in space (resulting in rigid body motion) in response to the applied loads acting on it.

Rigid body motion can take place in any one of six degrees of freedom (three translation and three rotation) if a structure is not properly restrained. Each of these degrees of freedom must be restrained by defining supports at one or more of the finite element model's surfaces, edges or vertices.

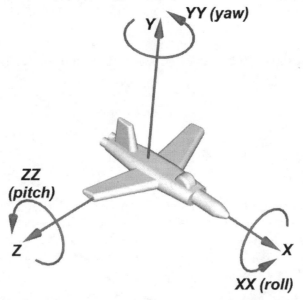

Figure 8.7 Illustration of the six possible directions (*X, Y, Z, XX, YY, ZZ*) that nodal points can move if not restrained by imposing supports

These supports (also called boundary conditions) are usually defined at locations in finite element models where a part is connected to another part, or where it is embedded in concrete or simply resting on a foundation. The number of degrees of freedom that are restrained depends on the type of connection that the part has to its surroundings.

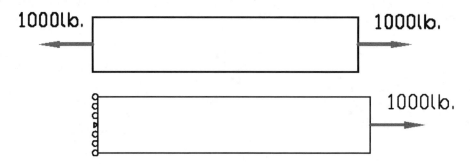

Figure 8.8 Lack of boundary conditions (supports) on the rectangular plate shown at the top will most likely produce rigid body motion. The proper boundary conditions are applied on the left end of the lower model to analyze the 1000 lb. tensile load.

In Workbench, loads and supports, are located under a folder in the **Project** tree named after the type of analysis you are performing, such as **Static Structural** or **Steady-State Thermal**. Generically, this folder is referred to as the Environment Folder and represents the external influences on the model being analyzed. The results (**Solution**) depend on the environment and are therefore located below the environment.

In a traditional finite element program, the supports can be applied directly to nodes, while in Workbench these constraints or supports are applied to solid model entities (vertices or points, edges, or surfaces) and are then transferred to the nodes once the finite element mesh has been generated.

There are a number of different types of supports available under Simulation, as summarized below.

- Fixed Supports
- Displacements
- Frictionless Supports
- Simply Supported (Surface or line bodies only)
- Fixed Rotation

Fixed Supports: This type of support can be applied to vertices, edges or faces. When this type of support is applied to a geometric entity, all the degrees of freedom for that entity, and by extension, the nodes generated for that entity are immobilized. In other words, the resulting nodes are prevented from moving or rotating. This is illustrated below.

■ Immobilized face   ■ Immobilized edge   ■ Immobilized vertex

Note: Fixed vertices and edges are not realistic in a physical sense and may lead to stress singularities (stresses that approach infinity near the fixed point or edge) and should be avoided if possible.

Displacements: Displacements can also be applied to points, edges, and faces. When a displacement constraint is imposed on an entity, the entity experiences displacement by one or more components of displacement vector in the global (world coordinate system) or a local coordinate system. In the case of faces and edges, the face or edge subjected to the displacement condition retains its original shape and is simply translated or rotated in space by the amount specified.

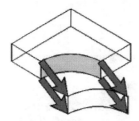 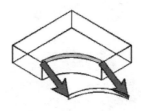 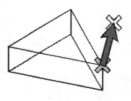

Note: When imposing displacement constraints on an entity, remember the following:

- A non-zero value imposes that value on the specified DOF
- A zero value for a DOF means that degree of freedom is fixed (can not move)
- No value specified (Free) means that degree of freedom is free to move

Consider the **Details** view shown below, of the Displacement boundary condition imposed on an edge. The edge will experience a translation of 1m in the X direction; it will be prevented from moving in the Y direction and is free to move in the Z direction.

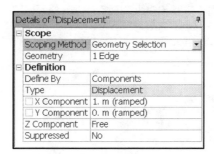

Details of "Displacement"	⊕
Scope	
Scoping Method	Geometry Selection
Geometry	1 Edge
Definition	
Define By	Components
Type	Displacement
☐ X Component	1. m (ramped)
☐ Y Component	0. m (ramped)
Z Component	Free
Suppressed	No

This concept is illustrated below where the solid arrows indicate a zero value or fixed DOF while the outline arrows indicate unspecified or free DOF.

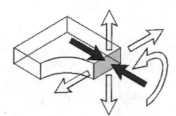 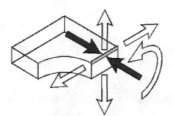 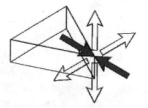

Frictionless Support: This type of support is applicable to faces. It prevents a face subjected to this support from moving or deforming in the direction normal to the face. The face is free to move or deform in the tangential direction. This boundary condition is analogous to placing an object on a table whose top surface is frictionless. In the following figure the solid arrows indicate the direction in which the face can not move while the outline arrows indicate free DOF.

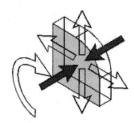

Note: For a flat face, this boundary condition is equivalent to a symmetry condition.

Simply Supported: This type of support is applicable to vertices and edges in surface and line bodies. When imposed on these entities, they can rotate freely but their translational DOF are fixed. In the case of an edge, the edge itself defines the free axis of rotation. In the following figure, the solid arrows indicated fixed (immobilized) translational degrees of freedom while the outline arrows are the free rotational DOF.

Fixed Rotation: This support is applicable to faces, edges or vertices. The entity subjected to this support is free to translate but its rotational DOF are fixed. The figure below shows a vertex that is constrained using this boundary condition.

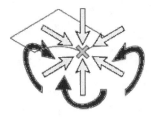

8.8 Loads

Loads are the external influences on the finite element model and since Workbench is capable of performing a large number of different types of analyses, naturally, there are a large number of load types available to the analyst. In this section we will describe some of the loading types necessary to perform static structural, steady-state thermal and modal analyses.

Note: Once an analysis type such as **Static Structural** or **Steady-State Thermal** has been inserted into the project tree, the available loads are filtered so that only the loads applicable to that type of analysis are visible in the menus and toolbars.

Loads can be divided into the following categories:

- Inertia Loads
- Structural Loads
- Thermal Loads

Inertia Loads: These loads result from accelerating the body and may be either translational or rotational. A special type of translational acceleration is the standard earth gravity which accelerates the selected bodies at a rate of 9.8066 m/s^2 in the specified direction. Acceleration loads can be applied in the global (world) coordinate system or a local coordinate system if one is defined.

Note: In order to simulate standard earth gravity, acceleration has to be applied in the opposite direction of gravity. For instance if, in your model the downward direction (pull of gravity) is in the −Z direction, to simulate standard earth gravity you have to accelerate the structure in the +Z direction.

Structural Loads: The structural loads described in this section are:

- Force
- Remote Force
- Pressure

Force: Forces can be applied to faces, edges or vertices. When applied to a single face or edge, the force is distributed on that entity; if multiple entities are selected, the force distributed over all the selected entities.

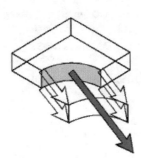 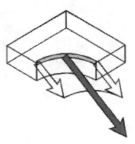 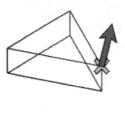

Forces and other vector quantities can be defined by a vector direction or by specifying components. When vector direction is used, the user selects an entity whose vector is parallel with the direction of the applied force. If an edge is selected to orient the vector quantity, the vector is parallel to the edge, but if a face is selected, the vector is parallel to the normal to the face. See Tutorial 9_2 for instructions.

Remote Force: A remote force is simply a force which acts at a distance. In other words, a remote force also exerts a moment on the selected entity. This loading type is useful when there is a rigid member between the point of application of the load and the portion of the structure subjected to the force. In such cases, the rigid member does not experience any deformation or stress and is simply a means of transferring the load. For example, when a force is applied to a steel member which in turn transfers the load to a softer material such as one made of plastic, rather than build the steel member as part of the model; the load can be applied as a remote force, permitting a more detailed model of the plastic part to be used.

Pressure: In 3-D simulations, this type of loading simply distributes the specified pressure (force per unit area) over all the selected faces. Pressure is applied uniformly and normal to the face at all locations, such that a positive pressure acts into the body; compressing it. If the face changes (increases or decrease in size due to interaction with a CAD package), the force per unit area remains the same, therefore, the total force may increase or decrease.

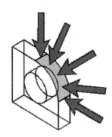

In a 2-D simulation, pressure is applied to one or more edges.

8.9 Application of Loads and Supports

Application of load and supports can be accomplished by following the four step process below.

1. Select the **Environment** (for example Static Structural or Steady-State Thermal) folder.
2. Select the geometric entity to which the load or support applies.
3. Select the desired load or support from the toolbar pull-down menu. Alternatively, click the **LMB** and from the pop-up menu select **Insert** and then the appropriate load or boundary condition.
4. In the **Details** pane enter the required values or adjust other settings as required.

A brief description of each of these steps follows:

Select the Environment folder – This step is necessary in order to activate the loads and boundary conditions toolbars and context (pop-up) menus.

Select the geometric entity – In this step you select the portion of the model where the load or boundary condition is to be applied.

Select the desired load or support – In this step you apply the actual load such as force, deflection, pressure, etc., or boundary condition such as fixed, simply supported etc.

Details View – In this step you can enter magnitudes such as a force or deformation values or set the components of vector quantities.

Note: A question mark appearing in the **Outline** to the left of a load or boundary condition indicates an ambiguity that must be resolved before you can continue. In most cases, this means that the load or boundary condition is not associated with a geometric entity. To resolve this problem, select the ambiguous condition, select the geometry where it is to be applied and then click on the **Apply** button in the **Details** pane next to **Geometry** as shown below.

8.10 Example Model that illustrates how supports and loads are applied

The diving board shown in Figure 8.9 is modeled in DesignModeler as a rectangular solid as shown in Figure 8.10 on the left. Edges (lines) are then imprinted on the top and bottom surfaces, as shown on the right, using techniques illustrated in tutorial 5_2. A simply supported boundary condition is then applied on the lower edge where the pipe roller exists, and the 1500N force is applied on the edge on the top surface.

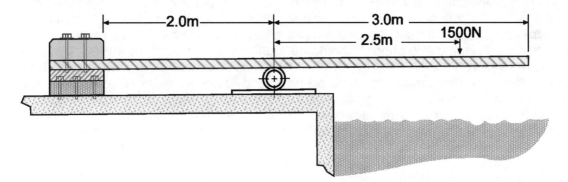

Figure 8.9 Diving board used to illustrate application of loads and supports.

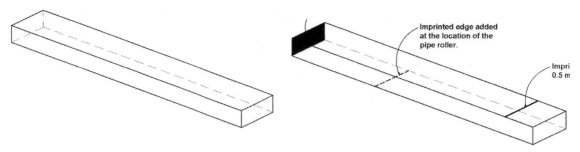

Figure 8.10 Diving board as modeled in DesignModeler

8.11 Use of Symmetry

Symmetry is a very useful concept because it allows a smaller model to be used to represent the entire part. Since the size of the model is reduced, a more accurate model (one built using a finer mesh), can often times be created. Symmetry modeling techniques can be taken advantage of when a part has symmetrical: shape, loads, material properties, and boundary conditions about a symmetrical dividing line or plane. The deformed shape of the part must also be symmetrical about the same line or plane. By correctly applying boundary conditions and loads along the line or plane of symmetry, a finite element model of only a portion of the physical part can be used to correctly represent the entire part. These smaller models can obviously be prepared much more quickly, and the computational time will be less.

In order to correctly model symmetrical parts, boundary conditions are used to restrict the displacements of the nodal points that lie along the line or plane of symmetry. These boundary conditions cause nodal points that are on the line or plane of symmetry to remain on the line or plane as the part deforms. This is done by constraining the displacements of these nodes in a perpendicular direction to the line or plane of symmetry. However, motion is allowed for these nodes in other selected directions that allow them to move along the line or in the plane of symmetry. Boundary conditions should be judicially assigned so that they reflect as realistic as possible the actual behavior of the part. Care should be exercised when specifying boundary conditions, because incorrectly applied boundary conditions will prevent the part from deforming normally and therefore, yield incorrect solutions. If in doubt about whether symmetry exists, it may be beneficial to build and analyze a coarse model of the entire structure which can be checked for symmetrical deformations.

Any loads that occur in the plane of symmetry are reduced to half their original value. This is because in the entire model, the left and right halves of the model equally support the load. Several examples of symmetrical structures are shown below in order to illustrate how boundary conditions and loads are defined.

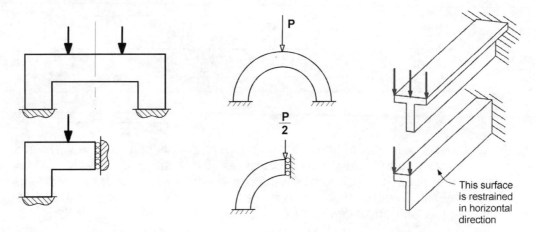

Figure 8.11 Examples of applying boundary conditions (with frictionless surfaces) and modifying loads to take advantage of symmetry conditions

Symmetry boundary conditions are often defined by specifying surfaces that lie on the plane of symmetry to be frictionless surfaces. Or alternatively, in Workbench, symmetry can be specified as follows:

- Insert a Coordinate Systems object into the Project tree under the model object if one is not present
- Insert a Symmetry object into the project tree under the model object
- Insert a Symmetry Region object
- Specify the geometry region to which the Symmetry Region applies
- Specify the type of Symmetry

The above steps are illustrated as part of example 9.1.

References

[1] Beer, F. P., Johnston, E. R. and DeWolf, J. T., Mechanics of Materials, 3rd Edition, McGraw-Hill, 2001, New York, NY

[2] Juvinall, R. C. and Marshek, K. M., Fundamentals of Machine Component Design, 3rd Edition, John Wiley & Sons, Inc., 2000, New York, NY

Exercises

1. Use the relevance mesh refinement technique in ANSYS Workbench to build several finite element models of the beam shown below, that has a 20mm x 20mm cross section and is made from structural steel. Determine the maximum deflection at the center of the beam. Vary the relevance factor from -100 to +100 in increments of 50, and then graph your results similar to the graph shown in figure 8.1. Finally, compare your results with those that you manually calculate using deflection formulas found in handbooks or textbooks.

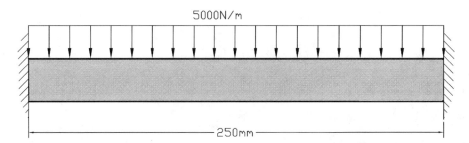

2. A finite element model of an entire "U-shaped" part is shown below. Sketch how the part could be modeled, if we wish to take advantage of symmetry. Make sure and label each nodal point where you would place boundary conditions, and the degrees of freedom that would be restrained at each of these nodes. Also show the location and magnitude of the load.

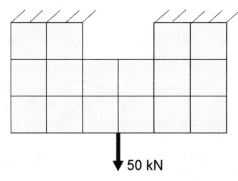

Exercises 3-7: If symmetry is used whenever possible, sketch the portion of each part that would be included in the "symmetry model" and indicate the locations that must be restrained and how they will be restrained (fixed edge or surface, frictionless surface, etc.). If the part cannot be analyzed using symmetry, indicate why it is not possible.

3. The part shown below is welded along its left end and the 500 lbs. load is evenly distributed along the right edge. The part has a uniform thickness.

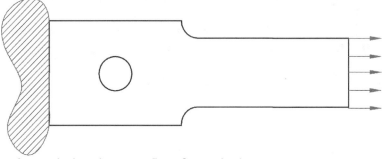

4. The beam shown below has a ½" uniform thickness.

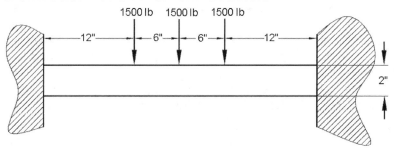

5. Each end of the part shown below has a load of 2000 lb. that is evenly distributed, and the part has a uniform thickness.

6. The left end of the part shown below is welded and the 500 lb, load is evenly distributed along the right end, and the part has a uniform thickness.

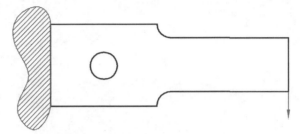

7. The plate shown below is cantilevered on its left end (the shaded end), while the holes and 500 N load lie on the centerline.

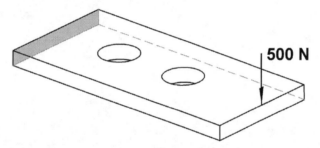

8. Use ANSYS Workbench to build a "full" finite element model of the 6" long by 3" wide plate that subjected to a tensile load of 1000 lb. The notches have a 0.5" radius and the plate has a uniform thickness of 0.25" and it is made from structural steel. Determine the maximum normal stress in the plate (which will occur in the notch areas) and compare these stress values with those that you manually calculate using stress concentration factors. Use convergence to within 2%.

   Then re-analyze the model by building a symmetry model of the plate again using convergence to 2%. Compare all three of your results.

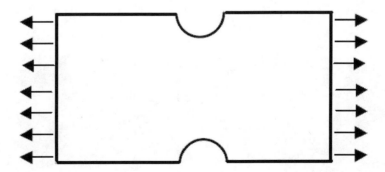

NOTES:

9

3D Solid Elements

The element type that will be discussed in this chapter can be used to model irregularly shaped 3 dimensional parts. Typical parts modeled with 3D solid elements include: forgings, cast parts and other parts that have a thickness that is comparable to the other two dimensions.

The advantage of using 3D solid elements is that the results provide information about the variation of stress through the thickness of the part as well as the other two dimensions. As we will see in later chapters, this type of in depth information is not provided by other element types.

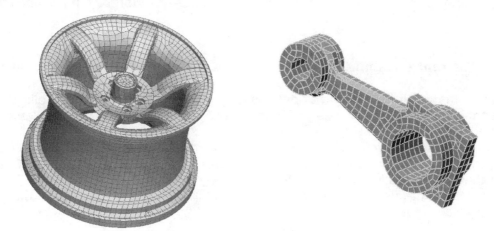

Figure 9.1 Typical 3D solid finite element models

The most basic 3D solid elements are defined as tetrahedral (4 nodes) or hexahedral (8 nodes) shapes. However, there exist many variations to these basic shapes. These include elements with mid-side nodes, and/or collapsed edges. The meshing process consists of defining enough elements to occupy the same volume of space as is occupied by the part being modeled. The nodal points that define the corners of 3D solid elements actually describe the volume of space occupied by the elements.

Tetrahedral elements are the most basic type of solid element, having a base that is a triangle and vertical edges that converge to a single point some distance above the base. It is a 4 noded element, however, by placing mid-side nodes along each edge, it becomes a 10 noded element.

The hexahedral element (8 nodes) is defined by a quadrilateral, which describes the bottom surface, and a second quadrilateral, that describes its top surface. On the sides are four additional quadrilateral shapes. Hexahedral elements are often referred to as *brick8* elements. Degenerate hexahedral elements can be defined which have collapsed edges. For example, if two adjacent edges are collapsed a wedged shaped element is defined.

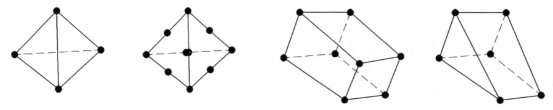

**Figure 9.2 Four node and ten node tetrahedral elements
and 8 node brick and wedge element**

Numerous automatic meshing programs are available today. Most are dependent on the part first being defined in a CAD program, as a solid model. The most commonly available *meshers* produce tetrahedral meshes. One of the reasons for this is that tetrahedral elements (like triangles) are more easily used to model intricate details and transition regions. However, since hexahedral elements are often considered more accurate, hexahedral biased meshing is often used. Workbench provides this option as will be explained later in this chapter.

9.1 3D Element Capabilities and Limitations

The mathematical formulation that defines the value of strain across 3D solid elements is basically an extension of that used to define 2-D plane stress elements. Four noded tetrahedral elements are similar to constant strain triangles and, therefore, should be avoided if possible. Ten noded tetrahedral elements define the variation of strain as quadratic and, therefore, are an improvement over the 4 noded elements. As discussed above, The 8 noded hexahedral element is often the preferred element due to its isoparametric formulation. This formulation allows the element to be warped.

Both tetrahedral and hexahedral elements are defined to have only 3 translational Degrees of Freedom (D.O.F.). Therefore, care must be used when combining 3D solid elements with other types of elements that have additional D.O.F.

9.2 Stress Results

Workbench provides output for several different types of stresses. The examples shown in chapters 6 and 8 used normal stress, because we were comparing our results with the beam bending stress formula Mc/I, which calculates stress normal to the beam's cross section.

For ductile materials, the evaluation of stresses within a part is usually based on either the maximum distortion energy criterion or the maximum shear stress criterion[1]. Workbench provides stress contour displays for both the von Mises equivalent stress (which is based on the maximum distortion energy criterion) and the Tresca (which is based on the maximum shear stress criterion). In the tutorial problem of this chapter, we will be examining the von Mises equivalent stress. The von Mises equivalent stress is given by the following formula:

$$\sigma_e = \sqrt{\frac{(\sigma_1 - \sigma_2)^2 + (\sigma_2 - \sigma_3)^2 + (\sigma_1 - \sigma_3)^2}{2}}$$

where: σ_1 and σ_2 and σ_3 are the maximum, intermediate and minimum principal stresses

Note that because of its mathematical definition, the value of the von Mises equivalent stress will always be positive, and therefore, does not give an indication of tensile or compressive stress. For this reason it is always a good idea to examine some of the other individual stress component displays.

9.3 Modeling Techniques

The modeling guidelines discussed in chapter 8 apply when creating a mesh. That includes: using a finer mesh in regions of high stress gradients, keeping the aspect ratio as close to one as possible, and not distorting the element so that interior angles deviate too far from 90 degrees. However, as mentioned above, 3D hexahedral elements do give the user a little more flexibility. The optimum shape of a brick element is a cube, but, in order to describe *real life* parts, it is usually not practical to expect that exact cube shaped elements will be able to model very many parts.

The process of preparing 3D finite element models of complicated parts usually begins with a CAD model. We will illustrate this process in the example tutorial by making use of an IGES file that was created by a CAD program.

9.4 Tutorial 9_1 – 5mm thick Stepped plate with fillets

The goal of this tutorial is to further demonstrate the concept of symmetry that was discussed in chapter 8 and to illustrate another technique that can be used for mesh refinement.

This will be done by performing a stress analysis of a 5mm thick stepped plate under tensile loading as shown below. The narrowing of the cross section of the plate causes a sharp rise in the value of the calculated stress in the area near the step. When performing manual calculations, a stress concentration factor must be used to calculate the correct stress value as shown below.

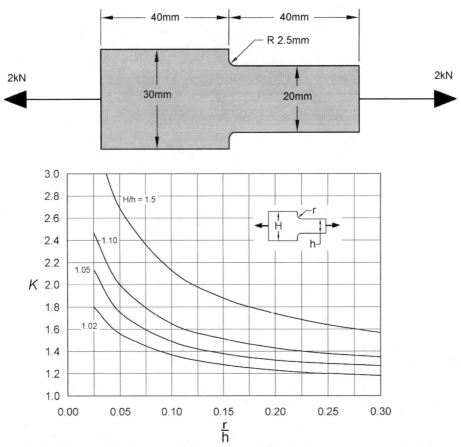

Figure 9.3 Stepped plate and the associated stress concentration chart

The curve which we will use: *H/h = 30/20 = 1.5*
The value on the horizontal axis: *r/h = 2.5/20 = 0.125*
Therefore, the value from the vertical axis of the graph is approximately: *K=1.98*
The maximum stress can then be calculated to be approximately:

$$\sigma_{max} = K\frac{P}{A} = 1.98 \frac{2kN}{(0.020m)\ (\ 0.005m)} = 39.6MPa$$

To simplify the model, we will take advantage of the part's symmetry and only model the top half. To do this correctly, we must impose the appropriate boundary condition on the model where it was split.

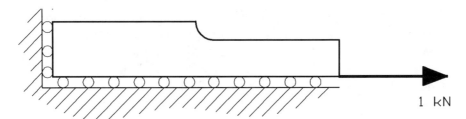

Figure 9.4 Symmetry boundary conditions applied that allow a half model of the stepped plate to be used

As shown in the figure 9.4, the lower surface of the model should be allowed to move in only the horizontal direction, while the surface along the left edge of the model be allowed to move in only vertically. The lower left edge corner of the model should be completely restrained.

Step 1 – Start an empty project by clicking on Empty Project in the Start window.

Step 2 – Link to the geometry file "Stepped Plate.igs" and start a new simulation. Under **Link to Geometry File**, click **Browse**, navigate to the "Student Files\Models" directory and select "tutorial 9_1.igs".

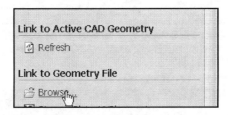

Step 2 (continued) – Click on **New Simulation** to start a new simulation.

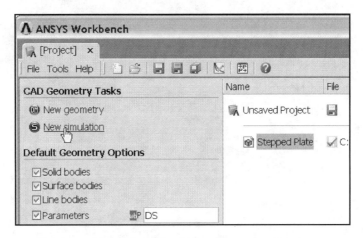

Step 3 – In the **Units** menu check that the working units are set to **Metric (mm, kg, N, °C, s, mV, mA)**. If the units are different, select **Metric (mm, kg, N, °C, s, mV, mA)**.

Step 4 – Set the material to Aluminum Alloy. We can either import Aluminum Alloy from the materials supplied with Workbench or define its properties as a new material. In this tutorial we will use the Workbench supplied data.

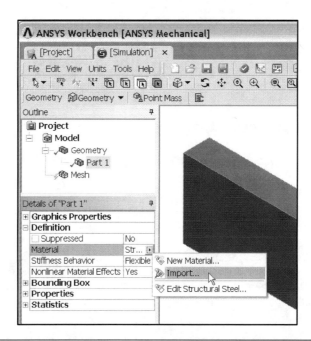

Step 4 (continued) – A dialog box appears displaying material properties supplied with Workbench, click the radio button next to **Aluminum Alloy** to select it and then click OK.

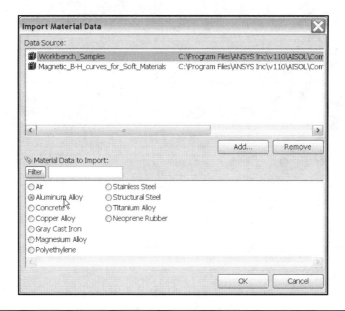

Step 5 – Insert a coordinate system into the **Outline**. First click on **Model** in the **Outline** view and then click on **Coordinate Systems** in the toolbar. This will insert the global Cartesian coordinate system into the Outline which will be referenced by the symmetry condition which will be specified in step 7.

Step 6 – Insert a Symmetry boundary condition.
   A. First click on Model in the **Outline** view and then click on the **Symmetry** icon in the toolbar.
   B. Click on **Symmetry Region** in the toolbar.
   C. Select the bottom face of the half model.
   D. Click on **No Selection** in front of **Geometry** in the **Details** window pane then click **Apply**.
   E. Change the **Symmetry Normal** in the **Details** pane to **Y Axis**.

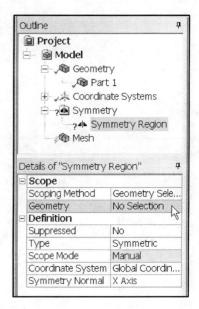

Note that the symmetry region appears as an object under **Model** in the **Outline** view and not with the rest of the boundary conditions imposed in the following steps.

Step 7 – Insert a Static Structural Analysis environment into the outline.

Step 8 – Insert a displacement boundary condition on the long, vertical face.
   A. Select the long vertical face.
   B. Click on **Supports** in the toolbar and select **Displacement**.
   C. In the detail view enter *0* for X Component. Leave the Y and Z components as Free.

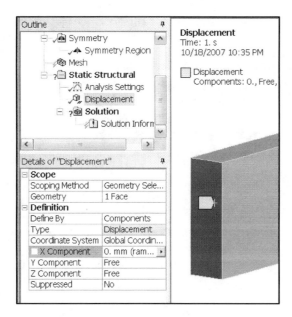

Step 9 – Fix the bottom left edge of the part.
   A. Select the edge.
   B. Click Supports in the toolbar and then select Fixed Support.

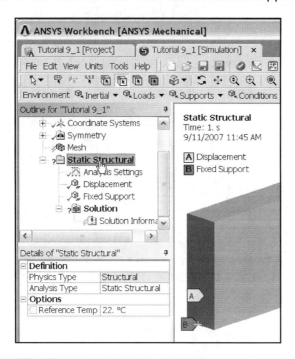

Step 10 – Impose a 1000N force on the short vertical face.
   A. Select the vertical face opposite the supported side of the part.
   B. Click on Loads in the toolbar and select Force.
   C. Change Define By from Vector to Components.
   D. Enter 1000 for the X Component.

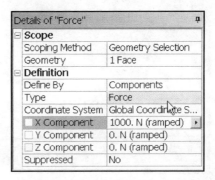

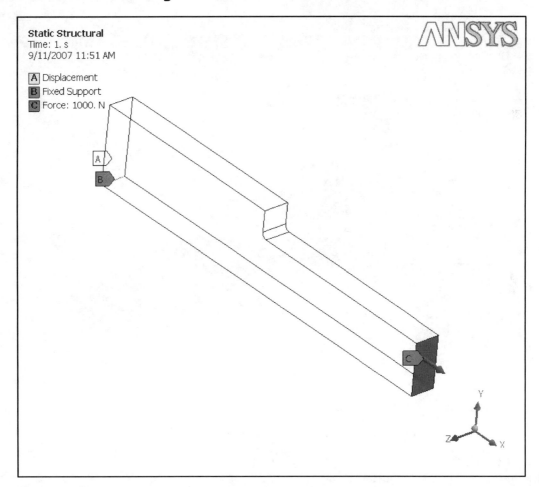

Step 10 (continued) – Click on **Static Structural** in the outline window to display the loads and boundary conditions. You can switch to wireframe display from the **View** menu to produce the figure below. To switch back to shaded view, select **Shaded Exterior and Edges** or **Shaded Exterior** from the **View** menu.

Step 11 – Request deformation and equivalent stress results.
   A. Click on **Solution**.
   B. In the Solution toolbar click on **Deformation** and select **Total**.
   C. In the Solution toolbar click on **Stress** and select **Equivalent (von-Mises)**.

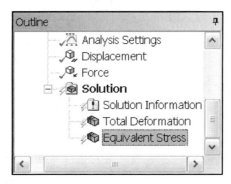

Step 12 – Solve.
   A. Click on **Solve**.
   B. After the solution is completed, click on **Equivalent Stress** and observe the
       maximum value.

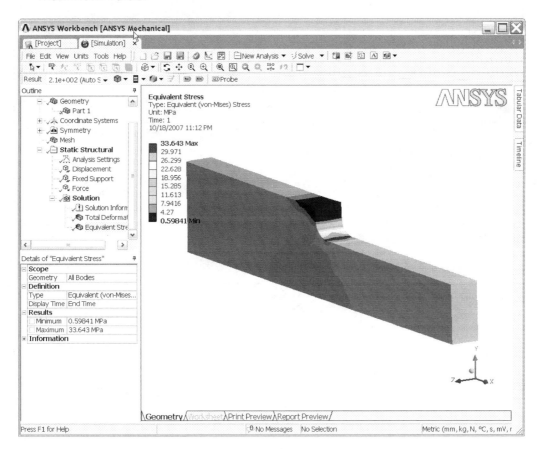

Step 13 – Compare the results with hand calculations.
Our hand calculation resulted in a stress value of 39.6MPa as compared to the
33.6MPa value computed by Workbench resulting in a 15% difference. In step 16
we will use the mesh refinement capability of Workbench to improve the solution.

Step 14 – Refine the mesh.
   A. Duplicate the model. This is step is necessary to preserve the current mesh
       and results for comparison.
   B. Under **Model 2** click the RMB on **Mesh** then **Insert** and **Refinement**.
   C. Select the short edge at the base of the fillet.

D. In the **Details** window pane change the **Refinement** value to **2**.
E. Click **Apply**.

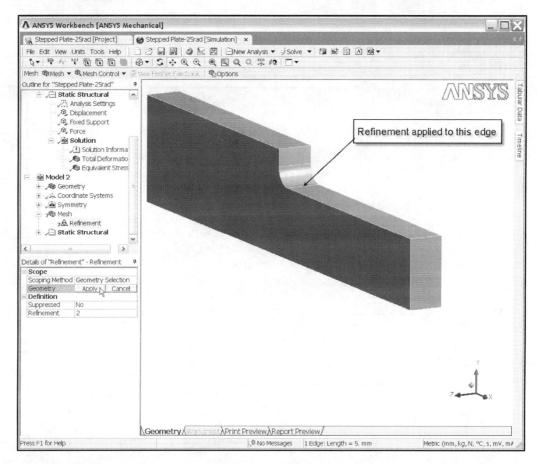

Step 14 (continued) – Generate the mesh
Click the **RMB** on Mesh and then **Generate Mesh**.

Step 15 – View the two FE meshes in a split-screen view.
  A. Click on the Viewport icon in the toolbar (⊟▾) and select **Horizontal Viewports**.
  B. Click inside the top Viewport to activate it.
  C. Click on **Mesh** under **Model** (the first model).

Note that the mesh refinement at the base of the fillet has resulted in smaller elements in that area. Note also that the mesh refinement in the fillet area has propagated to the rest of the model. This is topology dependant and in some models regions far from the refinement region may remain unaffected. The propagation of the mesh refinement is due to the fact that the mesh refinement process is attempting to produce a gradual transition from the refined area to the rest of the model while maintaining element quality.

After comparing the meshes, Click on the Viewport icon in the toolbar and select One Viewport to restore the graphics window to its previous state.

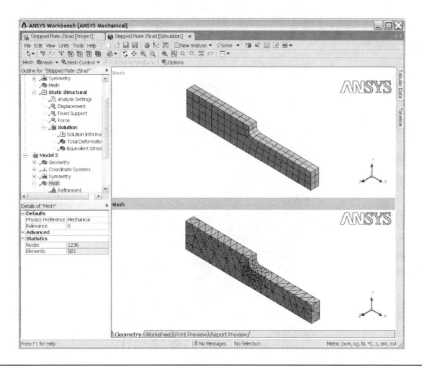

Step 16 – Solve.

Step 17 – Review the Equivalent stress results.

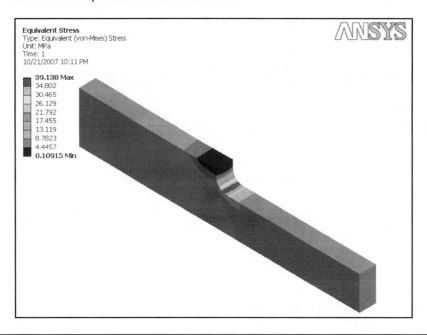

Step 18 – Compare the refined mesh solution results with hand calculations. Our final result of 39.1MPa is 1.3% lower than our hand calculation value of 39.6MPa. This is a very good result considering that our hand calculation is based on reading the stress concentration factor from a chart which can potentially lead to errors.

Step 19 – Save the project.

Tutorial problem conclusion

As we can see from the above tutorial, the maximum stress shown in Step 16 is very close to the manually calculated value of 39.6Mpa.

Manually calculated maximum stress	39.6 MPa
Maximum (FEA) Stress shown in Step 16 (using mesh refinement)	39.1 MPa

9.5 Stress Concentrations

As the stress concentration chart at the beginning of tutorial 9_1 illustrates, as the radius of the fillet decreases the stress concentration factor K increases, approaching an infinite value for a zero radius. Finite element models of the stepped plate that have a zero radius will report high stresses, but not an infinite stress. If the mesh is refined using smaller and smaller elements, the corresponding stress continues to increase, illustrating that we are not converging to a finite value. Continuing this process would be fruitless, because we are mathematically, "chasing a singularity". This illustrates the importance of using generous fillets in regions of cross sectional changes.

The results of running a model of the stepped plate with zero radius fillets shown below illustrates this process of "chasing a singularity" with the convergence option in Workbench employed.

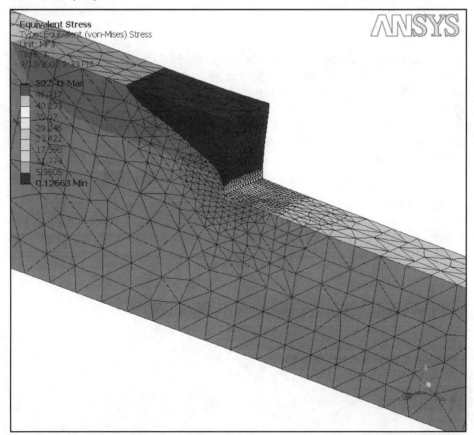

Figure 9.5 Stress Singularity in the zero radius fillet

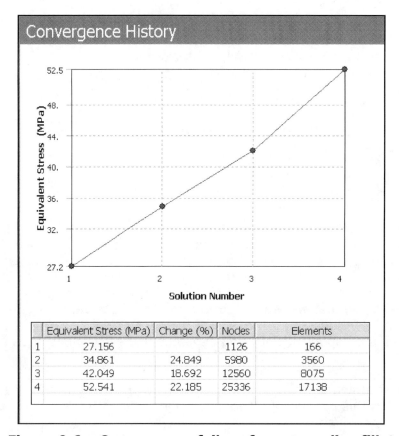

Figure 9.6 – Convergence failure for zero radius fillet

As shown in the convergence chart above, the level of stress at each step is considerably higher than the example problem and it is not leveling off. The reason that the stress values are not converging is not because our mesh is too course, but because the sharp corners in the region of the maximum stress are creating an infinite stress concentration factor. Our design recommendation for parts similar to this, therefore, would be to incorporate generous fillets in order to reduce these stress concentrations.

9.6 Hex Dominant meshing

As mentioned above, Workbench provides the user the option of controlling the mesh to be primarily tetrahedral or hexahedral. This is done by using the options:

Mesh > Insert > Method
Select the body > Apply
Then in the detail window: **Method>Hex Dominant**

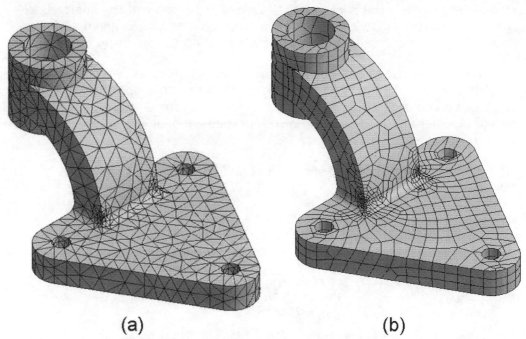

(a)   (b)

Figure 9.7 Tetrahedral (Tet) dominant and Hexahedral (Hex) dominant mesh of the same part.

Exercises

1. Build a finite element model of the 6" long step-down shaft that has a 1.5" large diameter and a 1" small diameter. It is made from steel. The 1.5" diameter portion is 3" long and the 1" diameter portion is 2.75" long. The fillet's radius is 0.25". The geometry of the shaft is contained in the IGES file: Exercise9_1.igs that is contained on the accompanying CD-Rom.

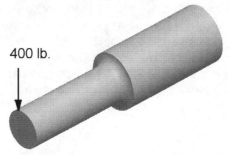

The shaft is loaded like a cantilevered beam with a load of 400 lb. applied over the circular surface at the end of the shaft. Determine the maximum principal stress at the base of the fillet area and then compare your results with the manual calculation:

$$\sigma = k\,\frac{M}{S} = 1.34 \bullet \frac{(400\ lb \bullet 2.75")}{\dfrac{\pi \bullet 1"^3}{32}} \cong 15,000\ psi$$

You should start by running an unrefined mesh, and then create several more models, each one having a smaller mesh size than the previous model in the high stress region of the fillet. Do this by using the refinement option applied to the circular edge where the fillet meets the smaller diameter of the shaft. Use refinement values of 1, 2, and 3. Then graph you results in a similar fashion to figure 8.1, in order to show that you are beginning to converge.

2. The 3 meter long 50mm x 50mm square shaft is loaded at one end with a torque of 4000 N-m. It will be made from structural steel. The opposite end of the shaft can be considered fixed like a cantilevered beam. Create the geometry in Designmodeler and load the part with four loads applied along the edges as shown.

    Determine the angle of twist of the shaft and compare your results with handbook values.

3. The support bracket shown below is made from Aluminum Alloy and is subjected to a 500 lb. vertical load that should be distributed over the top surface of the hollow cylinder as shown. The boundary conditions consist of restraining all 6 d.o.f. of the edges of the holes on the top surface, and restraining the entire bottom surface as a frictionless surface. The geometry of the part is defined in inches and is contained in the IGES file: Exercise 9_3.igs.

    Determine the maximum downward deflection of the support bracket as well as the maximum von Vises stress. You should start by running a standard unrefined mesh, and then create several more models, each one having a smaller mesh size in the high stress region of the fillet. Do this by using the refinement option applied to the three tangent edges that occur where the fillets on the base of the part meet the rectangular swept neck portion of the part. Use refinement values of 1, 2, and 3. Then graph the four maximum stress and deflection results (using number of nodes-on the horizontal axis vs. stress or deflection values-on the vertical axis), in a similar fashion to figure 8.1, in order to determine if the stress and deflection values are converging or not.

10

Plane Stress/Plane Strain and Axisymmetric Modeling

In chapter 9 we discussed 3D elements and their use in finite element analysis. In this chapter we introduce plane stress, plane strain and axisymmetric elements and their use in Workbench. The concepts of plane stress, plane strain and axisymmetry are simplifications that allow us to reduce a three-dimensional problem to a two-dimensional problem. We can only use these techniques for models and environments (geometry, loads and boundary conditions) where the influence of the third dimension is negligible. When these conditions are present in a structural problem, the simplifications do not substantially reduce the accuracy of the solution.

As the robustness of 3D meshing algorithms has improved and accurate solid models have become available, the use of these simplifications has diminished. However, they are important concepts in stress analysis and their use can result in accurate and efficient models. For these reasons, this chapter will describe how to make use of these techniques.

10.1 Plane Stress/Strain Models in Workbench

In Workbench plane stress, plane strain and axisymmetric models are all built on the XY plane. A description of each problem type follows. In the sections that follow we will describe how CAD models are used to perform each type of analysis.

- Plane Stress models are constructed on the XY plane and experience zero stress in the Z direction. In a plane stress model, the Z dimension is much smaller than the X and Y dimensions. A typical example of plane stress is a plate which is loaded on one of its narrow edges (in-plane loading).

- Plane Strain models are also constructed on the XY plane. However, they experience zero strain and non-zero stress in the Z direction. In plane strain problems, the Z dimension is much larger than the X and Y dimensions. An example of a plane strain problems is a long, constant cross section structure.

Figures 10.1 and 10.2 show typical plane stress and plane strain problems respectively.

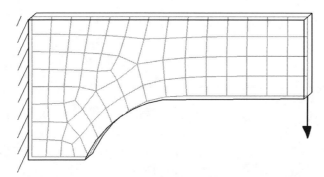

Figure 10.1 Plane Stress Problem

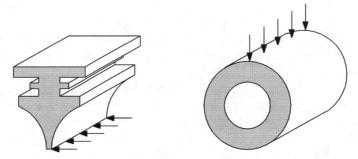

Figure 10.2 Examples of Plane Strain Problems

10.2 Axisymmetric Models in Workbench

Axisymmetric problems are those that can be generated by rotating a cross-section of the geometry plus loads and supports 360 degrees about the axis of symmetry. In the case of Workbench, the geometry is constructed on the XY plane and rotated about the Y axis. Example situations in which axisymmetric elements can be used to model actual physical parts include: pressure vessels, hose nozzles, circular plates subjected to axisymmetric loads, shafts subjected to axial loading, and centrifugal loading of a disc of constant cross section rotating about its axis of symmetry.

- Axisymmetric models are constructed on the XY plane and rotated 360 degrees about the Y axis. The geometry has to lie on the positive X axis. In these models, the hoop displacement is zero (or nearly zero) but hoop strains and stresses are significant. A typical example is a pressure vessel.

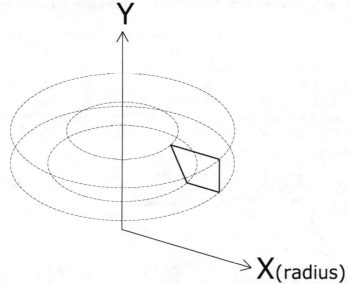

Figure 10.3 A single axisymmetric quadrilateral element

10.3 Plane Stress/Strain and Axisymmetric Element Capabilities and Limitations

Plane stress/strain elements are triangular or quadrilateral 2-dimensional elements that reside in the XY plane. The elements connect at common nodes and along common edges to form continuous structures. These elements have only two degrees of freedom (X and Y translation) and all the loading must be in the plane, because the element does not have any out of plane stiffness.

In the case of plane stress problems, the elements are free to expand or contract in the thickness (Z) direction depending on the stress in the XY plane due to the material's Poisson effect.

For plane strain problems, the loading is also on the XY plane and the part is assumed to have infinite (or in practical terms very long) length in the Z direction. In a plane strain model, only a unit thickness of the structure is considered in the analysis.

ANSYS Workbench uses quadratic plane elements to model plane stress, plane strain and axisymmetric problems. The elements have eight nodes or 6 nodes depending on whether they are four sided (quadrilateral) or three-sided (triangular).

Figure 10.4 below shows the quadrilateral and triangular elements. The mid-side nodes of these elements allow the sides to curve to match the boundary of the geometry being meshed.

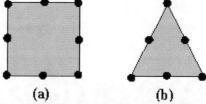

(a)   (b)

Figure 10.4 Quadratic (a) and Triangular (b) Plane Elements

10.4 Defining Plane Stress/Strain and Axisymmetric Models in Workbench

You can perform a 2-D analysis of the type plane stress/strain or axisymmetric, by linking to a surface body that was constructed in a CAD tool that supports surface bodies (Two dimensional wireframe bodies are not supported). As was stated previously, the model must be constructed on the XY plane. On the project page, you must choose **2-D** in the **Analysis Type** menu located under the **Advanced Geometry Defaults** as shown in figure 10.5. Once you have linked to the geometry file and started a new simulation, you can not change the analysis type from 2-D to 3-D or vice versa.

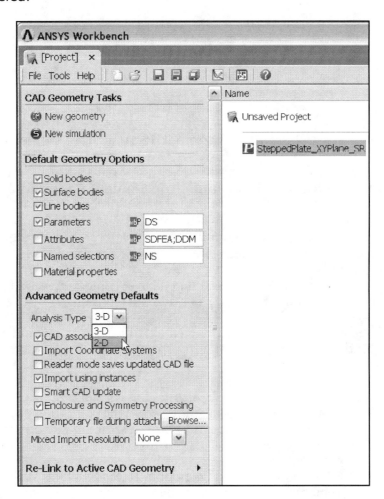

Figure 10.5 Selecting the Analysis Type on the Project Page

Note: If you are using DesignModeler to generate the surface body, draw the 2-D profile of your model on the XY plane and then use **Surfaces From Sketches** in the **Concept** menu.

Once you have started a new Simulation, select **Geometry** in the **Outline** window pane and specify the **2D behavior** under **Definition** as shown in figure 10.6.

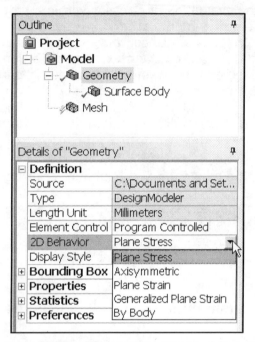

Figure 10.6 Specifying the 2D Problem Type

10.5 Loads and Boundary Conditions

When imposing loads and boundary conditions on plane stress and plane strain problems you will be limited to the components in the X and Y planes. Workbench automatically eliminates the Z components from the input fields of these quantities.

In the case of axisymmetric problems, care must be taken in the following cases:

Rigid Body Motion: In axisymmetric problems the elements are rotated 360 degrees about the Y axis and therefore no constraints are needed to prevent rigid body motion in the tangential direction. However, the part will be free to move in the Y direction. You must impose the appropriate constraints in the Y direction to prevent the part from moving in that direction.

Concentrated Loads: Since each node actually represents a circumferential line, concentrated loads applied at nodal points are actually line loads uniformly distributed around the node circle. Computations performed in Workbench evaluate only a one radian segment rather than the complete circumference. Therefore, the magnitude of any applied load should be the actual total load divided by 2π, since there are 2π radians within a circle.

10.6 Stress Results

Workbench provides output for several different types of stresses. The examples shown in chapters 6 and 8 used normal stress, because we were comparing our results with the beam bending stress formula Mc/I, which calculates stress normal to the beam's cross section.

For ductile materials, the evaluation of stresses within a part is usually based on either the maximum distortion energy criterion or the maximum shear stress criterion[1]. Workbench provides stress contour displays for both the von Mises equivalent stress (which is based on the maximum distortion energy criterion) and the Tresca (which is based on the maximum shear stress criterion). In most of the example problems in this book, we will be examining the von Mises equivalent stress and perhaps one or two of the other stress components. For plane stress problems, the von Mises equivalent stress is given by the following formula:

$$\sigma_e = \sqrt{\sigma_1^2 - \sigma_1\sigma_2 + \sigma_2^2}$$

where: σ_1 and σ_2 are the maximum and minimum principal stresses

Note that because of its mathematical definition, the value of the von Mises equivalent stress will always be positive, and therefore, does not give an indication of tensile or compressive stress. For this reason it is always a good idea to examine some of the other individual stress component displays.

10.7 Tutorial 10_1 A 1 mm thick Plate with hole under tension

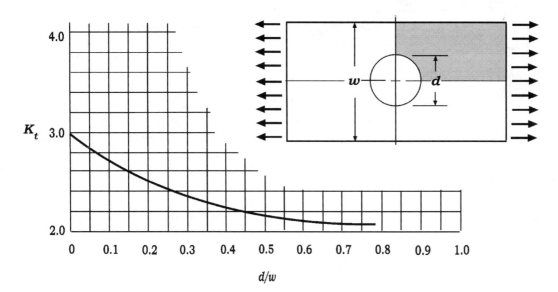

The dimensions of the plate are: width = 400 mm, dia = 200 mm, length = 1200 mm, thickness = 1 mm; and the applied load is a pressure of 1 MPa. The portion of the plate that will be modeled is shaded in gray.

Based on the stress concentration chart above, the estimated maximum stress in the plate is:

σ= K (P/A_net) = 2.18 ((1 MPa x 400 mm²) / 200 mm²) = 4.36 MPa

Step 1 – Start Workbench and create the geometry in DesignModeler by clicking on **Geometry** in the Start dialog box.

Geometry

Step 2 – Select millimeters as the working units.

Step 3 – Begin Sketching on the XY plane and draw the rectangle as shown below.

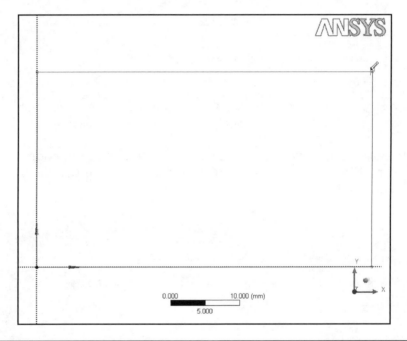

Step 4 – Draw an arc by using the **Arc by Center** option and following the prompts at the bottom left of the window.
   A. Click the corner of the rectangle.
   B. Drag the cursor on the horizontal axis and release the LMB to select one end of the arc.
   C. Move the cursor to the vertical axis and click to select the termination of the arc.

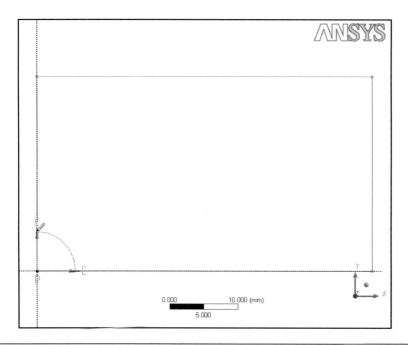

Step 5 – Trim the bottom left corner of the sketch. Use the **Trim** tool from the **Modify** toolbox of the sketcher to select the short line segments.

Step 6 – Dimension the Drawing. Dimension the top horizontal edge, the right vertical edge and the arc. Enter **600**, **200**, and **100** for the horizontal, vertical and radius dimensions in the **Details** window pane.

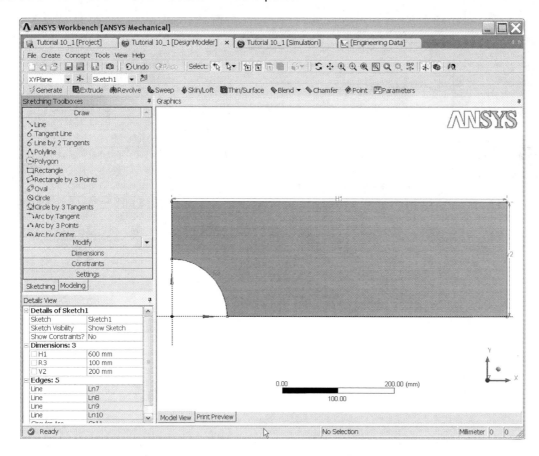

Step 7 – Create a surface body.
   A. Click on the Modeling tab.
   B. In the **Concept** menu select **Surfaces From Sketches**.
   C. Expand **XYPlane** and select **Sketch1**.
   D. In the **Details** window pane enter *1.0* for **Thickness (>=0)**.
   E. Click **Apply** in front of **Base Objects** in the **Details** window pane.
   F. Click **Generate**.

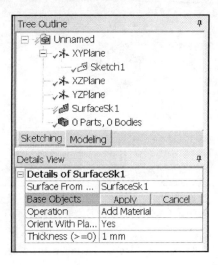

Step 7 (continued) – The surface model should appear as shown below.

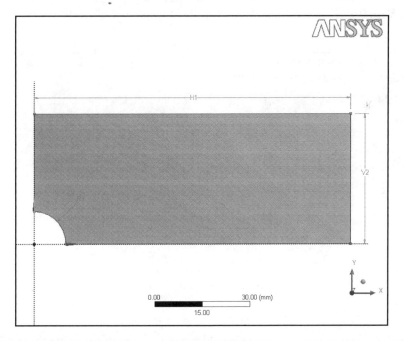

Step 8 – Save the geometry as Tutorial 10_1.agdb.

Step 9 – Start a new Simulation.
   A. On the project page click on **Advanced Geometry Defaults** to display the default settings.
   B. Select **2-D** from the **Analysis Type** drop down.
   C. Click on **New Simulation**.

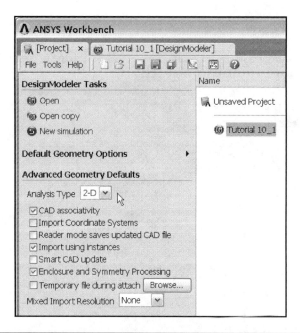

Step 10 – Check the bottom right corner of the Simulation window to ensure that the
unit system is set to **Metric (mm, kg, N, C, mV,...)**. Metric (mm, kg, N, °C, s, mV, n
If it is not, change the units from the **Units** pull-down menu.

Step 11 – Set the part material to Aluminum.
See Tutorial 9_1 for step-by-step instructions on how to change the material of a
part.

Step 12 – Insert a Coordinate Systems object.
Click on **Model** in the outline window.
Click on Coordinate Systems (⚡Coordinate Systems) in the toolbar.

Step 13 – Insert a Symmetry Regions object.
    A. Click on Model.
    B. Click on **Symmetry** in the toolbar (⬛Symmetry).
    C. Click on **Symmetry Region**.

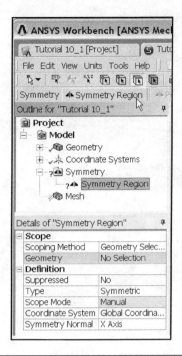

Step 13 (continued) – Insert a Symmetry Region for the vertical edge.
  D. Change the selection filter to Edge.
  E. Select the vertical line in the center of the plate.
  F. Make sure **Symmetry Normal** is set to **X Axis** in the **Detail** window.
  G. Click **Apply**.

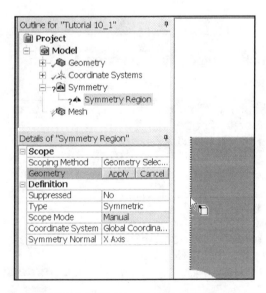

Step 13 (continued) – Insert a Symmetry Region for the horizontal edge.
  H. Click **Symmetry Region** in the toolbar.
  I. Select the bottom horizontal line.
  J. Change **Symmetry Normal** to **Y Axis**.
  K. Click **Apply**.

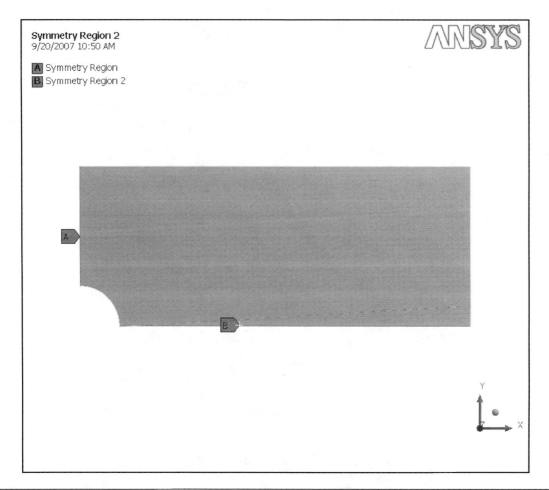

Step 14 – Select the analysis type. Click on **New Analysis** in the toolbar and select **Static Structural**.

Step 15 – Insert a pressure load on the right side of the plate.
   A. Select the right vertical edge
   B. From the **Loads** menu select **Pressure**.
   C. In the **Details** window pane change **Define By** to **Components**.
   D. Enter *1.0* for the **X Component** and press the Enter key.

Step 16 – Request results
   A. Select **Solution** in the **Outline**.
   B. In the Solution toolbar click on **Deformation** and select **Total**.
   C. Click on **Stress** and select **Normal**.
   D. In the **Details** window pane make sure that **Orientation** is set to **X Axis**.

Step 17 – Click on **Solve** to solve the problem.

Step 18 – Review the stress results.
   A. Click on **Normal Stress** to view the contour plot of the Normal Stress (σ_{xx})
   B. In the toolbar click on and select **Show Undeformed Wireframe**.

Step 18 (continued) – The Stress results are displayed below.

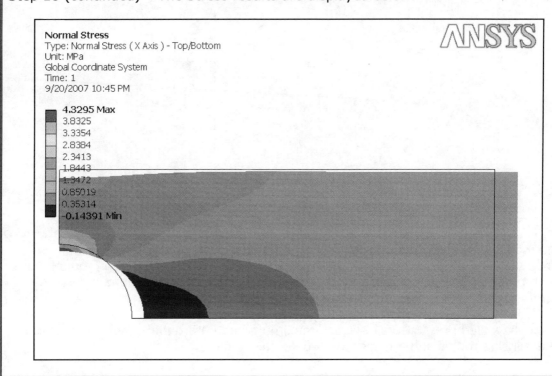

Summary of Results

As we can see from the above tutorial, the maximum stress shown in Step 18 was very close to the manually calculated value of 4.36Mpa.

Manually calculated maximum stress	4.36 MPa
Maximum (FEA) Stress shown in Step 18	4.33 MPa

10.8 Tutorial 10_2 – Thick-walled pressure vessel

In this tutorial we demonstrate how to perform an axisymmetric stress analysis.

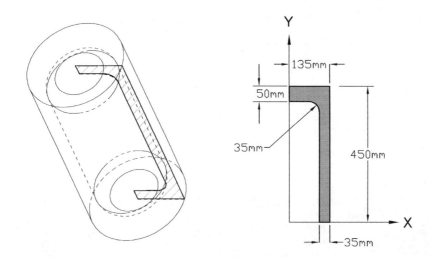

The model is a thick-walled cylindrical tank under an internal pressure of 100 MPa. Since the tank also exhibits symmetry in the axial (Y) direction, we can model only the top half of the cylinder. The closed form solution for this problem is given by Hamrock et al[2] which we can use to compare with our finite element results.

For thick walled pressure vessels, the maximum circumferential (hoop) stress occurs at the inside radius and for this case would be:

$$\sigma_{hoop} = p_i \left(\frac{r_o^2 + r_i^2}{r_o^2 - r_i^2} \right) = (100x10^6) \left(\frac{0.135^2 + 0.10^2}{0.135^2 - 0.10^2} \right) Pa = 343.2 MPa$$

and the axial (longitudinal) stress would be:

$$\sigma_{long} = \frac{\pi r_i^2 p_i}{\pi (r_o^2 - r_i^2)} = \frac{\pi (0.10)^2 (100x10^6)}{\pi (0.135^2 - 0.10^2)} Pa = 121.6 MPa$$

Step 1 – Start Workbench and select the Empty Project icon.

Step 2 – Link to the geometry file. Browse and select "Pressure Vessel.x_t" located in the "Student Files" directory.

Step 3 – Set the **Analysis Type** to 2-D.
In the project page expand **Advanced Geometry Defaults** and set the **Analysis Type** to **2-D**.

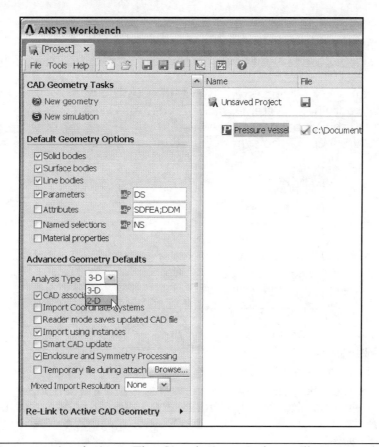

Step 4 – Start a new simulation. The Simulation window will open and the 2-D section of the pressure vessel is displayed.

Step 4 (continued) – Check the working units. The working units for the simulation are displayed at the bottom right corner of the simulation window status bar. The displayed units should be **Metric (mm,kg,N, °C,s,mv,mA)**.

Metric (mm, kg, N, °C, s, mV, mA)

If a different system is shown use the **Units** menu to change the working units.

Step 5 – Set the Part material to Structural Steel.

Step 6 – Set the 2-D Behavior to Axisymmetric.
   A. Select **Geometry** in the **Outline** window pane.
   B. In the **Details View**, set the **2D Behavior** to **Axisymmetric**.

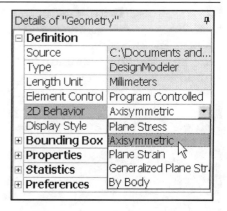

Step 7 – Add a coordinate system to the outline view.
   A. Select **Model** in the **Outline** window pane.
   B. Click on **Coordinate Systems** (⚹ Coordinate Systems) in the toolbar.

Symmetry boundary conditions (step 8) are imposed by referencing to either the global or a local coordinate system which you define. When you complete step B above, an icon for the global coordinate system is inserted into the project tree which can be referenced by the symmetry boundary condition.

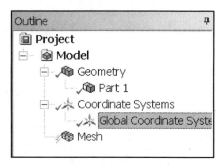

Step 8 – Insert a symmetry boundary condition.
   A. Select the **Model** folder in the **Outline** window pane.
   B. Click on **Symmetry** (⬛ Symmetry) in the toolbar.
   C. Click on **Symmetry Region** (⬥ Symmetry Region) in the toolbar.
   D. Set the selection filter to edge and select the bottom edge of the model.
   E. In the **Details** window pane click **No Selection** next to **Geometry** and then click **Apply**.

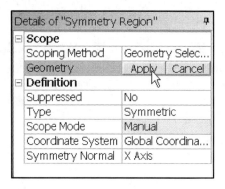

   F. In the **Details** window pane change **Symmetry Normal to Y Axis**.

Note: By imposing the symmetry condition on the bottom edge of the model, we are constraining that edge from moving in the axial (Y) direction. This is sufficient to prevent rigid body motion of the model in the only direction it could occur. No additional constraints are needed.

Step 9 – Set the analysis type. In the toolbar click on **New Analysis** and select **Static Structural**.

Step 10 – Impose an internal pressure. First select the inside edges of the vessel.
   A. Optional - Change the view to Wireframe from the View menu.
   B. Select the inside edges of pressure vessel. First set the selection filter to
       edge, next click on the inside horizontal edge, then while holding down the
       control key, click the other two edges.
   C. Select the **Static Structural** folder in the **Outline** window pane.
   D. Click on **Loads** and select **Pressure**.
   E. In the Details view enter *100* and press the Enter key.

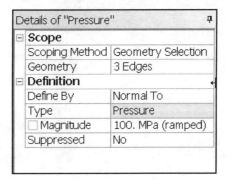

Step 11 – Request results.
   A. Select the **Solution** folder.
   B. Click on **Deformation** in the toolbar and select **Total**.
   C. Click on **Stress** in the toolbar and select **Normal**.
   D. In the **Details** view change the **Orientation** to **Z axis** (hoop stress) .
   E. Click on **Stress** in the toolbar and select **Normal**.
   F. In the **Details** view change the **Orientation** to **Y Axis**.

Step 12 – Solve. Click on **Solve** in the toolbar.

Sep 13 – Review results.
Select **Total Deformation** to view the deformed shape of the vessel and make sure
that loads and boundary conditions were imposed correctly.

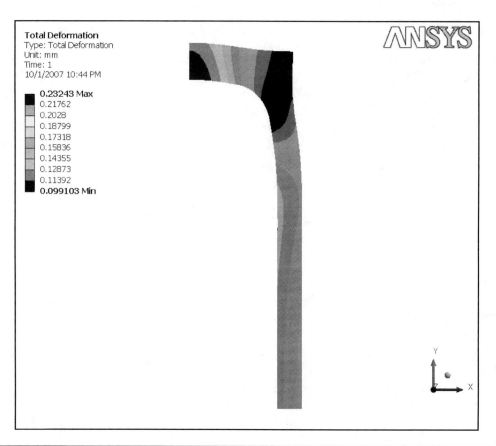

Step 13 (continued) – View the hoop stress.
   A. Select **Normal Stress** to view the hoop stress σ_{zz}
   B. Click on **Probe** and click on the lower inside corner of the model (you may
       need to zoom in to select the corner).

As you can see the finite element model has calculated a hoop stress of 342.3MPa
which compares very closely to the hand calculated value of 343.2MPa.

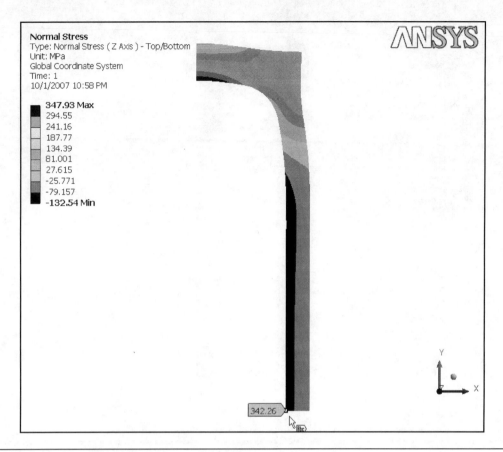

Step 13 (continued) – View the axial stress.
   C. Select **Normal Stress 2** to view the axial stress σ_{YY}
   D. While Probe is still selected, click on the lower edge of the model (you may need to zoom in to select the corner) .
   E. Click on **Probe** again to disable it.

The axial stress computed by the finite element model is 121.6MPa which is the same as our hand calculation!

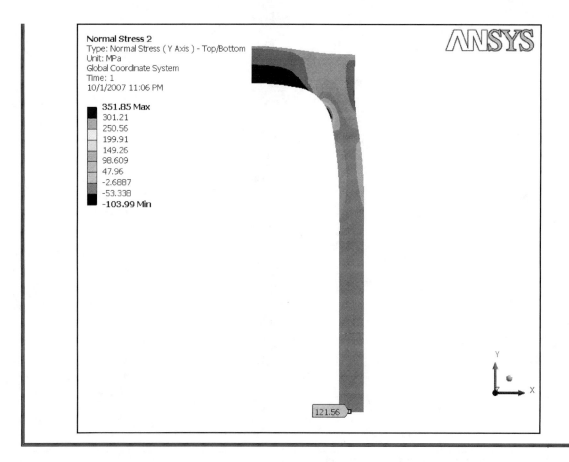

Summary

Tutorial 10_1 demonstrates the ease with which a simple two-dimensional model can be created in DesignModeler for use in a Plane Stress, Plain Strain or Axisymmetric analysis.

Tutorials 10_1 and 10_2 also show that by taking advantage of the two-dimensional nature of the problem, we can simplify the FEA problem greatly while at the same time achieve a very high level of accuracy. Needless to say, great care must be taken to ensure that the problem is truly two-dimensional before using this approach.

References

[1] Norton, R. L., Machine Design An Integrated Approach, Revised Printing, Prentice-Hall, 1998, Upper Saddle River, New Jersey.

[2] Hamrock, B.J., Jacobson, B. and Schmid, S. R., Fundamentals of Machine Elements, pp. 393-398, McGraw-Hill, 1999, New York, NY

[3] Pytel, A. and Singer, F.L., Strength of Materials, 4th Edition, pp. 485-486, Harper & Row, New York, NY, 1987

[4] Spotts, M.F. and Shoup, T.E., Design of Machine Elements, 7th Edition, pp. 680, Prentice-Hall, 1998, Upper Saddle River, New Jersey.

Exercises

1. Use ANSYS Workbench to determine the maximum stress, and the stress concentration factor for the rectangular steel plate with a center hole as shown in the figure below (all dimensions are in inches). Compare your results with those given in tables of stress concentration factors. Use convergence to insure that your results have converged. Use symmetry in your model wherever possible.

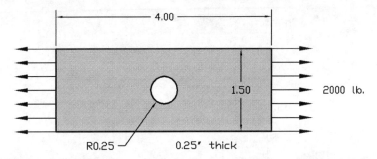

2. Use ANSYS Workbench to build a plane stress finite element model of the beam, that has a 20mm x 20mm cross section and is made from aluminum. Determine the maximum deflection and bending stress in the beam. Build at least three different models with a more refined mesh each time in order to show that your results have converged. Use symmetry in your model wherever possible.

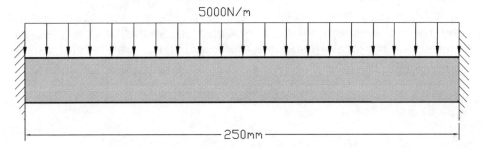

3. Use ANSYS Workbench to build a plane stress finite element model of the 50mm thick curved ring shown below. It is made from structural steel. Determine the value of the bending stress on the horizontal section at points **A** and **B**. Compare your results with the following values from Pytel and Singer[2]: σ_A = -127 MPa and σ_B = +62.9 MPa. Build at least two different models with a more refined mesh each time in order to show that your results have converged.

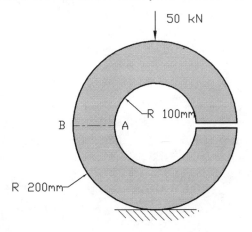

4. As the wall thickness of pressure vessels become less than $1/10^{th}$ of the inside radius, the pressure vessels are usually classified as "thin walled", and the hoop stress is calculated with the formula: $\sigma_{hoop} = pr_i/t$. Evaluate how well this formula agrees with a finite element analysis of a pressure vessel that has the top half dimensions shown below, and experiences an internal pressure of 5MPa.

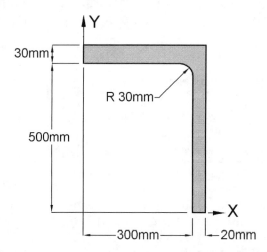

5. The below dimensioned figure is the top half of the cross section of a thick walled pressure vessel. The internal pressure is 5000psi. Use the formulas in this chapter to determine the hoop stress and longitudinal stress, and then evaluate how well these values agree with a finite element analysis of the pressure vessel. Also, determine the location and magnitude of the maximum von Mises stress.

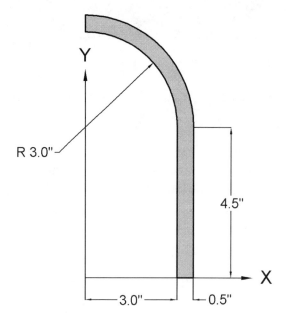

6. The Circular flat plate, diameter=24", thickness = 0.75", structural steel, simply supported around its outer edge, supports a uniform pressure of 100psi as shown below. Build an axisymmetric model of the plate, to determine the bending stress along the bottom edge of the plate close to its center. Compare your results with the following formula from Spotts and Shoup[4].

$$\sigma = \frac{3(3+\mu)qr^2}{8t^2}$$ where: μ= poisson's ratio (usually 0.3 for steel)

                        q = pressure
                        r= radius of the plate
                        t= thickness of the plate

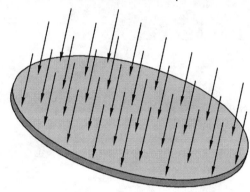

7. Determine the maximum von Mises stress and the stress concentration factor for the axially loaded notched shaft that has a large diameter of 1.5" and a small diameter at the inner radius of the notch of 1.0". Compare your results with those given in a stress concentration table of a machine design or mechanics of materials book. This part can be analyzed by building an axisymmetric model of the cross hatched region of the part.

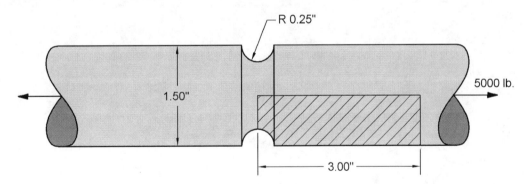

8. Build an axisymmetric model to determine the maximum von Mises stress and the stress concentration factor of a stepped shaft that has a large diameter of 1.5″ and a small diameter of 1.0″ with a 0.25″ radius notch. Compare your results with those given in a stress concentration table of a machine design or mechanics of materials book.

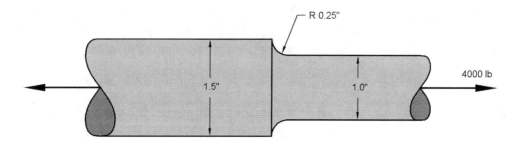

11

Plate and Shell Element Modeling

The element type that will be discussed in this chapter is generally used to model parts such as automobile body panels, ships' hulls, airplanes' skin, thin walled structural shapes or components made from sheet metal. Generally, any part that has a relatively small thickness as compared to its other dimensions (usually having a ratio if 1:10) is a good candidate to be modeled with plate/shell elements. Another guideline that can be used to determine if a part should be modeled with plate/shell elements is: when a zero thickness surface model be accurately recognized as the part. In structural analysis a plate is a flat structural member while a shell usually refers to a curved structure and different theories and formulations are used for analyzing them[1].

Plate/Shell elements are usually defined by triangular or quadrilateral elements located anywhere in three-dimensional space. Therefore, a plate/shell element is truly a 3-dimensional element. The element has the ability to resist both transverse loads as well as loads applied in the plane of the element. The mathematical formulation of the element is actually developed by using a combination of plate theory (bending) and shell theory (membrane), therefore, the name plate/shell.

ANSYS Workbench Simulation refers to the element used for modeling of thin parts as a shell element. Therefore, from this point on, we will simply refer to this element type as a shell element.

Formulation of the mathematical definition of shell elements has been one of the most difficult of all the different elements types used in the finite element method. There is not any one particular formulation that has met with broad acceptance in the analytical community. Although there have been a large number of proposed formulations, no one formulation stands out as an acceptable formulation which gives completely satisfactory results. In Simulation, ANSYS Workbench uses a 4 node general purpose element with six degrees of freedom at each node that can be used for modeling thin to moderately thick structures.

Due to the difficulty of arriving at an element that can accurately predict the response of a thin structure, it is paramount that the user proceeds with caution, and try to verify results to the best of his or her abilities – through correlation with experimental results or closely related solutions. One might argue that models should be build entirely of 3-dimensional solid elements, rather than even using shell elements. However, due to the very large number of 3-D solid elements that would be required to correctly model thin plate structures, this is often not economically feasible.   Whenever a mesh of solid elements is used to model a thin structure, the convergence feature of Simulation should be employed to ensure that the mesh is sufficiently refined for this purpose.

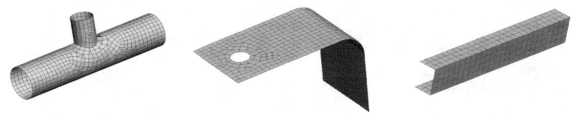

Figure 11.1 Typical finite element models using shell elements

11.1 Modeling Techniques

When building finite element models with shell elements, the elements should be defined at the part's mid-surface, and then assigned a thickness value that equals that of the part. The mesh should as always be finer in regions of high stress gradients. However, if detailed stress results are required in regions where plates are connected at welded joints, or rapid changes in radius or thickness occur, we may be better off creating a model that uses both 3-D solid elements combined with shell elements. Also, stress results at locations where two non co-planar shell elements are joined will not be accurate due to the "modeling gaps and overlaps" as illustrated in the below figure.

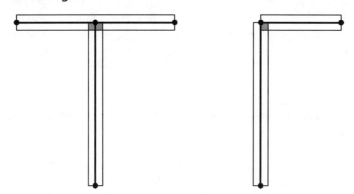

**Figure 11.2 Situations where shell elements
theoretically overlap or contain gaps**

Quadrilateral elements produce more accurate results than triangular elements. Since mesh generation in ANSYS Workbench Simulation is automatic, the user generally leaves the element selection to the program and you will notice that the triangular shell elements are usually used as transition and where the quadrilateral element is not possible.

During the building of the model, symmetry conditions should be exploited as much as possible to reduce the model size. In order to properly impose symmetry boundary conditions, a combination of translational and rotational D.O.F.'s must be employed, as was first discussed in section 8.11. As an example, consider the plate shown in Figure 11.3 that is supported along all edges. Due to symmetry of the geometry and the centrally applied load, a quarter section of the plate with appropriately designated boundary conditions is adequate for the model. The boundary conditions applied along the lines of symmetry should be such so that no in plane displacement occurs and the rotation of the plate about the line of symmetry is prevented. For the case shown, nodal points along the line x=5 should be restrained in X-translation and Y-rotation. The nodal points along the line y=5, should be restrained in Y-translation and X-rotation. The nodes along the outer edges of the plate (solid lines) should be restrained in Z-translation if it is simply supported or restrained in all D.O.F. if it is clamped.

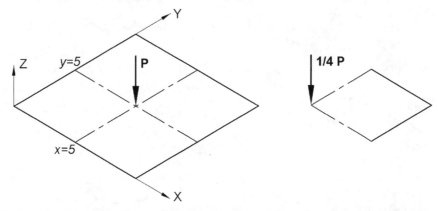

Figure 11.3 A 10" x 10" Square plate that is supported along its edges and has a concentrated load applied at its center and the corresponding quarter model of the plate based on applying symmetry boundary conditions.

11.2 Creating the finite element mesh

ANSYS Workbench automatically generates a mesh consisting of shell elements when the CAD model used is a surface body. Recall from chapter 5 that surface bodies are three dimensional bodies that have no volume associated with them and as such, they do not have a thickness which can be measured. Instead, since they represent a physical body that does have thickness, they have a thickness number associated with them. This thickness number can be assigned in some CAD tools and transferred to Simulation or it can be entered in Simulation itself.

A CAD model can contain both surface bodies and solid bodies at the same time. Therefore it is important to decide which type of geometry should be brought into Simulation for meshing. There are two important cases that you should keep in mind:

- The surface model is intended to represent the entire solid body. In this case you should use one or the other but not both types of geometry.

- The solid and surface bodies are different parts of an assembly which is made of thin and thick bodies. In this case both the surface and solid body should be used. In this book, we have chosen to work only with single parts (no assemblies) therefore; for the purpose of the examples and tutorials in this book you should always choose one type or the other.

The choice of which type of geometry is used must be made on the project page. Here you can direct ANSYS Workbench to attach to Line Bodies, Surface Bodies, Solids or all of the types present in the CAD model. Figure 11.4 shows where this selection is made. To link to a particular geometry type, check the box next it.

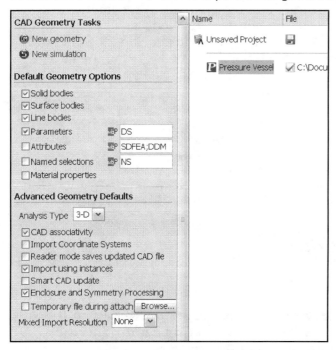

Figure 11.4 Selecting Solid, Surface or Line Bodies

11.3 Tutorial 11_1 Deflection of a Thin Bracket

This tutorial demonstrates: how to create a surface body that lies at the mid-surface of a 3-D solid CAD model; and then how to specify the element size of the mesh of shell elements that are then used in a stress analysis. The CAD model for this tutorial is supplied as an IGES file named "Tutorial 11_1.igs" and is located in the "Student Files" directory. The Geometry is a thin bracket which is supported and loaded as shown below. The bracket is made from ASTM A242 steel.

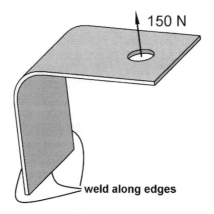

Recall that we must use a surface body in order for Workbench to generate the mesh of shell elements.

Our objective is to calculate the amount of deflection that will occur at the end of the bracket when the load of 150 N is applied at the bolt hole. Since there are no standard formulas available, a manual calculation will not be done.

Step 1 – Start a new geometry by clicking on Geometry in the Start dialog.

Step 2 – Select **millimeter** as the length unit.

Step 3 – Import the model into DesignModeler
   A. From the File menu select **Import External Geometry File...**
   B. Browse to "Student Files\models" directory and select **Tutorial 11_1.igs**.
   C. Click **Generate**.

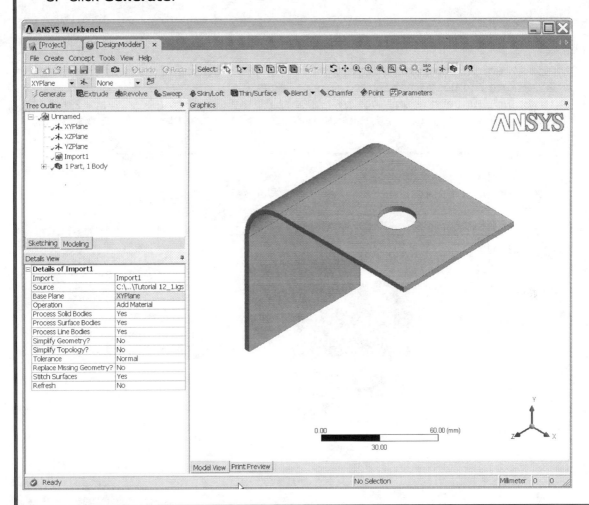

Step 4 – Measure the thickness of the bracket
   A. Click on the edge selection tool.
   B. Select one of the short corner edges.
   C. Read the thickness in the status bar.

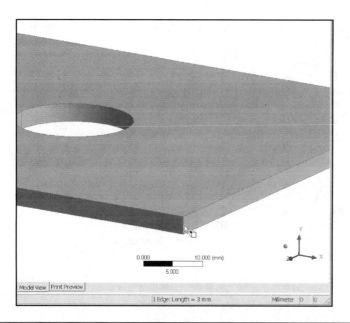

Step 5 – Create a thin surface representation of the bracket
  A. Rotate the body to show the outside faces.
  B. Select the outside surfaces by first setting the selection filter to face and then dragging the cursor on the outside faces so that the three faces are selected as shown.

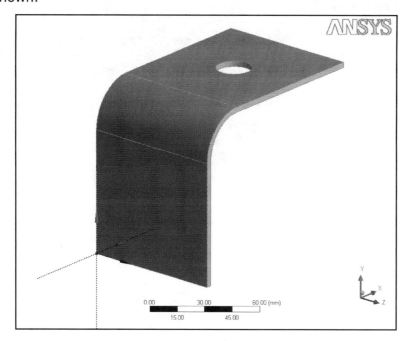

Step 5 (continued) –
  C. Click on **Thin/Surface** in the toolbar.
  D. In the Details window pane enter *0.* for **FD1, Thickness (>=0)** and press the enter key.
  E. In the Details window pane enter *1.5* for **FD2, Face Offset (>=0)** and press the enter key.
  F. Click on **Geometry** and then **Apply**.
  G. Click **Generate**.

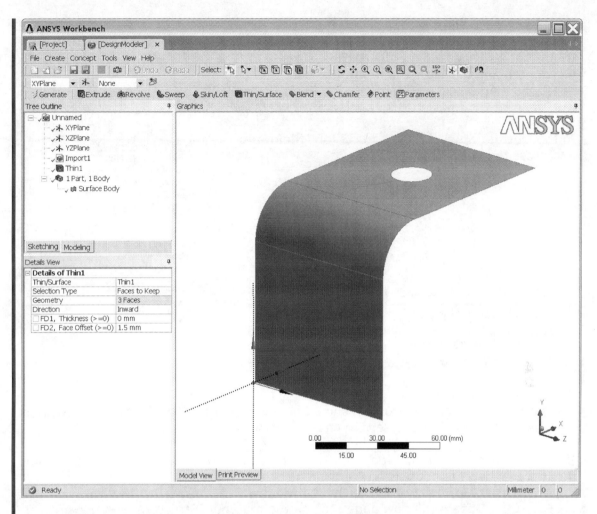

The result is a surface body which is offset by 1.5mm (half the thickness of the solid) from the selected faces towards the opposite faces of the original solid body. This locates the faces at the mid-surface of the solid.

Step 6 – Save the project
   A. Click on the project tab.
   B. Select **File** then **Save All**.
   C. Browse to a desired directory and save the geometry as ***Tutorial 11_1***.

Note: You will also be prompted to save the project with the same name. Click **OK** to accept the project name and location.

Step 7 – Start a new simulation.
   Click on **New simulation**.

Step 8 – Set the thickness of the part. The
Simulation window opens and the model is displayed.
In the Details window pane the thickness property is
highlighted and indicates 0.0 mm. Also note the
questions marks next to Geometry and Part 1 in the
Outline View window.

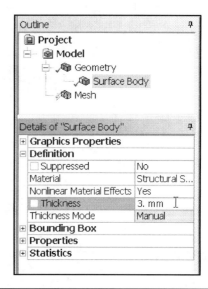

In the **Details** window pane enter *3* for **Thickness**
and press the enter key.

Step 9 – Rename the part
   A. Select **Surface Body** in the **Outline window**.
   B. Click the **RMB** and select **Rename**.
   C. Enter *Thin Bracket* and press the enter key.

Step 10 – Check the working units.
The working units for this problem should be **Metric (mm, Kg, N, °C, mV, mA)**.
Use the **Units** menu if necessary to change the working units.

Step 11 – Set the material type. You will import the properties for ASTM A242 from
the material database supplied with this book.
   A. Select **Thin Bracket** in the Outline window.
   B. In the **Details** window pane click on the material (Structural Steel) .
   C. Select **Import...**

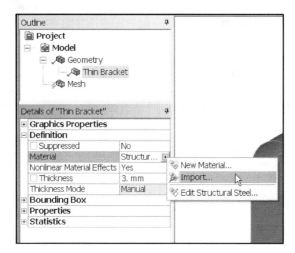

Step 11 (continued) –
   D. In the dialog box that appears, select **Tutorial Material Database**.
   E. In the bottom portion of the
      window click on the radio
      button next to **ASTM A242**.
   F. Click **OK**.

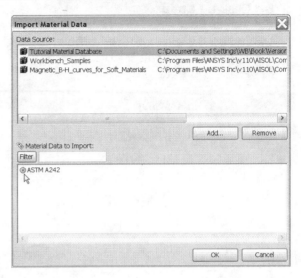

Step 12 – Set the analysis type.
   A. Click on **New Analysis** and select **Static Structural**.

Step 13 – Impose boundary conditions (supports).
   A. Select **Static Structural** in the **Outline** window pane (Wireframe view is
      selected for clarity).
   B. Select the three edges shown below.
   C. Click on **Supports** in the toolbar.
   D. Select **Fixed Support**.

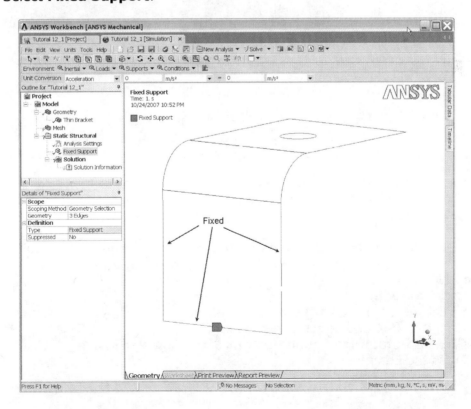

Step 14 – Impose Loads.
   A. Select the two arc segments that describe the hole.
   B. Click on **Loads**.
   C. Select **Force**.
   D. In the **Details** window pane change the **Define By** to **Components**.
   E. Type *150* for the **Y component**.
   F. Press the enter key.

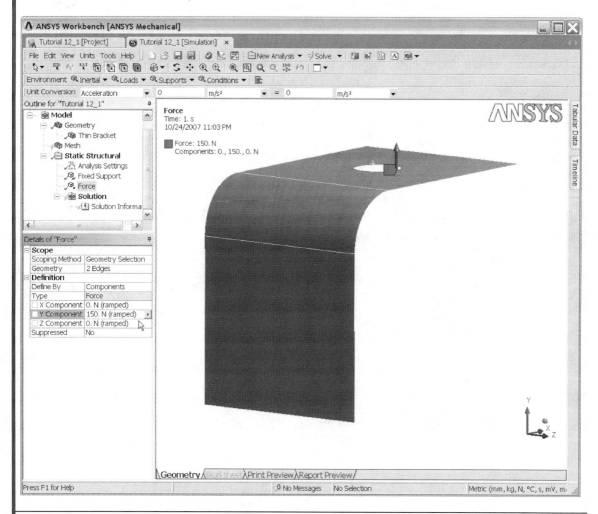

Step 15 – Request results
   A. Click on **Solution** in the **Outline**.
   B. Click on **Deformation** in the toolbar.
   C. Select **Total**.

Step 16 – Specify element size. Note that this step is not required to obtain a solution but allows us to demonstrate the procedure for specifying element size in Workbench.
   A. Click on **Mesh**.
   B. Select the edge shown in the figure below.
   C. Click the **RMB** and select **Insert Sizing**.
   D. Click on **Default** in front of **Element Size** and enter *5*.
   E. Press the Enter key.

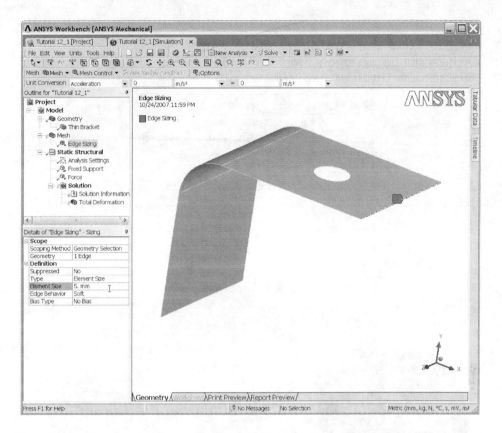

Note: The element size of 5mm will divide the selected edge into 16 divisions or 16 elements across the tip of the bracket. However, the **Edge Behavior** property is set to **Soft**, which allows the program to alter this value slightly if it can not generate elements that meet its internal quality standards. In order to force the exact element edge length entered, the **Edge Behavior** setting can be changed to **Hard**.

Step 17 – Generate the mesh
  A. Select **Mesh** in the **Outline** window pane.
  B. Click the **RMB** and select **Generate Mesh**.

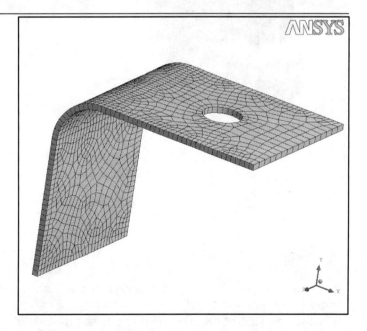

Step 18 – Solve. Click **Solve** in the toolbar.

Step 19 – Review the results.
  A. Click on **Total Deformation** in the Outline.
  B. Click on the Edge Options icon in the toolbar.
  C. Select **Show Undeformed Wireframe**.

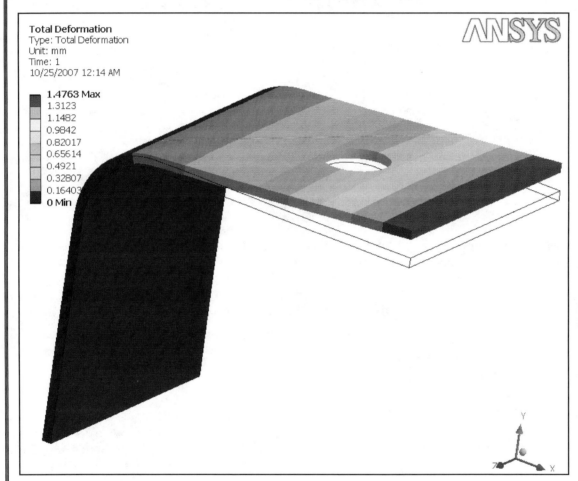

The results indicate that the edge of the bracket has moved approximately 1.5mm as a result of the 150N force.

Summary

Since we did not perform a manual calculation for this problem, the bracket should now be re-analyzed using a smaller element size. The results of this second analysis should then be compared with the first analysis in order to determine if the deflection values changed significantly, which would indicate that we should continue the analysis process.

Reference

[1] Hellen, Trevor, How to use Beam, Plate and Shell Elements, NAFEMS Ltd, 2007

Exercises

1. In an effort to stiffen the bracket analyzed in this chapter, it was redesigned to include folded over edges as shown below. The IGES file for this bracket (Exercise11_1.igs) is contained on the accompanying CD. Analyze this bracket using the same material, boundary conditions and load that were specified in the example problem, in order to determine the maximum deflection at the end of the bracket. Make sure to run various element sizes until you are satisfied that your results have converged.

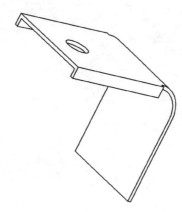

2. C-channels are often used in the construction of frames for various types of applications such as: trucks chassis, trailers frames and roofing systems. Due to the shear flow within the C-channel when it is loaded in bending, it is critical that the load is applied at a position where it will not introduce a twisting action. In order to illustrate this condition, analyze both of the C-channels shown below. They are 48" long and are made from 0.15" thick structural steel. The 6" and 4" dimensions are measured to the center of the thickness. Apply a load of 500 lbs. and constrain all of the nodal points on the opposite end in order to represent a cantilevered beam. In the case shown on the left, apply the load on the midline of the vertical flange. For the second case, add an endcap on which the load is applied. The distance $e = b / (2 + (h/3b)) = 1.6$" for our case of: $b=4$" and $h=6$".   Use DesignModeler to create surface models. Determine the angle through which the vertical portion of the C-channel twists.

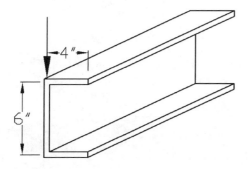
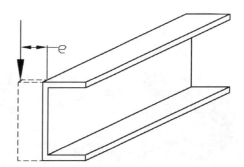

3. Determine the maximum deflection in the 15mm thick rectangular plate by
   modeling both the entire plate, and also by using symmetry conditions create a
   model of a quarter of the plate. The plate is made from ASTM-A242 steel and is
   considered to be clamped (fixed in all 6 *D.O.F.*) along all edges. Build both
   models by creating surface models using DesignModeler.

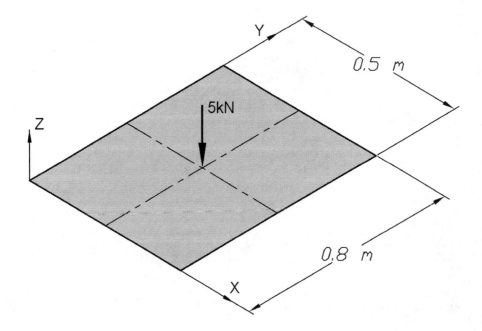

12

Natural Frequency and Mode Shapes Analysis

In the previous chapters of this book we have only considered the response of a structure to static loads. In this chapter we will introduce an analysis type called Modal Analysis that predicts a structure's vibration response to loads that cycle with time.

You have probably experienced some type of vibration effect in a car as it increases in speed from a stop up to cruising speed. As you first start to speed up, perhaps the back of the seat next to you begins to shake or perhaps it's the rear-view mirror or the steering wheel. Then as your speed increases even more the vibration may stop or becomes less. What has just happened is that you have introduced time varying loads to the various component of your car. When the rate at which the load is applied to a component corresponds to the component's natural frequency, we notice it vibrating. All components have natural frequencies. When the exciting force coincides with one of the natural frequencies a condition of *resonance* is encountered, which produces large amplitudes of displacement. It is usually important to design components so that their natural frequencies do not correspond to the rate at which cyclic loads are applied. However, there are some situations in which it is desirable for the structure to operate in a vibratory manner. Several examples of this would be: vibratory feeder bowls used for sorting, vibratory cleaning equipment, and ultrasonic cutting machines.

As we will find, Modal Analysis results in the calculation of a structure's natural frequencies and its corresponding mode shapes. It does not determine displacements and stresses. Modal Analysis is, nevertheless, an important step in the design process. Often the goal of an analysis is to insure that the structure's natural frequencies do not correspond to its operating frequency or driving force. For example, we would not want the natural frequencies of a support frame of a large motor to be close to the operating RPM of the motor.

12.1 Free Vibration, One degree of freedom system

We will begin by examining the one degree of freedom system shown below in figure 12.1. The motion is referred to as *free* vibration since there is no force applied after an initial displacement is imposed to start the system vibrating. It contains only one spring and a single mass. The spring has a spring constant of *k*. If the mass is vibrating without any forcing or damping (it is moving on a frictionless surface), then summing the forces acting on the mass yields:

$$F = -kx = ma \qquad\qquad\qquad \text{eq. 12.1}$$

where:

x = displacement of the mass

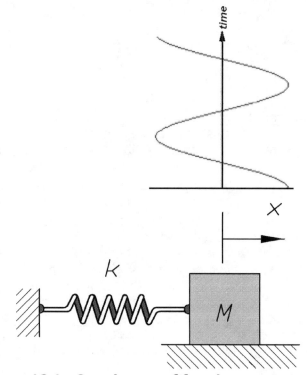

Figure 12.1. One degree of freedom system

Expressing the acceleration as the second derivative of *x* with respect to time as $\ddot{x}$ gives the linear differential equation of motion:

$$m\,\ddot{x} + kx = 0 \qquad\qquad\qquad \text{eq. 12.2}$$

setting: $\omega^2 = k/m$

We can then write eq. 12.2 as:

$$\ddot{x} + \omega^2 x = 0$$

which has a solution in the form of:

$$x = A \sin \omega t \qquad\qquad\qquad \text{eq. 12.3}$$

where **A** is a constant that indicates the amplitude of motion. Eq. 12.3 describes *simple harmonic motion.* ω is the natural frequency of vibration, which is also sometimes referred to as the *circular frequency*. It has units of radians per second. Cyclic frequency is defined as $\omega/2\pi$, and has units of hertz (Hz) or cycles per second. Therefore, to summarize:

$$\omega = \sqrt{\frac{k}{m}} \ \ radians/sec \qquad\qquad\qquad\qquad \text{eq. 12.4}$$

$$f = \omega / 2\pi \ \ cycles/sec \ \ or \ \ Hz \qquad\qquad\qquad \text{eq. 12.5}$$

EXAMPLE 12.1

The single degree of freedom system shown below has a 50-kg mass and a spring rate of 10,000 N/m. Determine the natural frequency of the system.

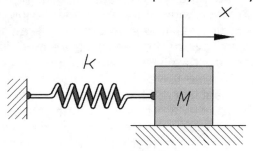

using eq. 12.4

$$\omega = \sqrt{\frac{10,000 \ \text{N/m}}{50 \ \text{kg}}} = 14.14 \ \ radians/sec$$

or, in terms of cycles per second:

$$f = 14.14/2\pi = 2.25 \ cycles/sec \ \ or \ 2.25 \ Hz$$

12.2 Multiple Degrees of Freedom

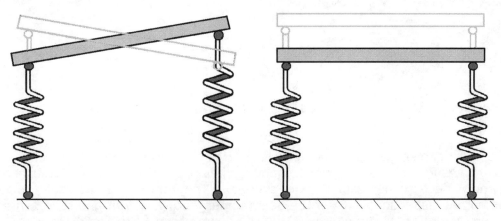

**Figure 12.2 A system with two degree of freedom,
illustrating its pitch and bounce modes of vibration**

The two degree of freedom system shown in figure 12.2 illustrates the concept of vibration modes. A vibration mode is simply the deformed shape that the structure takes on as it vibrates. Each of these different shapes is referred to as a *mode shape*. As we can see, because the rigid beam is attached to two springs, it will vibrate in two distinct modes. The pitching mode occurs when the springs move "out of phase" with one another. That is, one spring is being stretched while the other spring is being compressed. The bouncing mode occurs when both springs are moving in the same direction – "in phase". Each of these vibration modes occur at a different natural frequency. In fact, for any vibrating system, there are as many natural frequencies as there are degrees of freedom. Therefore, for a two degree of freedom system, there will be two distinct natural frequencies.

Unlike the single degree of freedom system shown in section 12.1 or the two degree of freedom system, real world structures have an infinite number of degrees of freedom. It can become a monumental analytical problem to solve for all the natural frequencies, because as stated above, for each degree of freedom that a structure contains, there is a corresponding natural frequency. However, for most practical purposes, a real world structure's lowest frequencies are usually the ones of greatest concern. This is because they are the ones that are most likely to correspond to the operating loads that the structure is subjected to.

Consider the case of the cantilevered beam that is mounted in the shaker shown below. By varying the rate at which the supporting structure vibrates we will be able to visually see the mode shape as the rate corresponds to a natural frequency of the beam. Figure 12.3 is a photograph that was taken when the shaker was vibrating at a rate that corresponded to the 2nd natural frequency of the beam. The deformed shape of the beam is referred to as the mode shape.

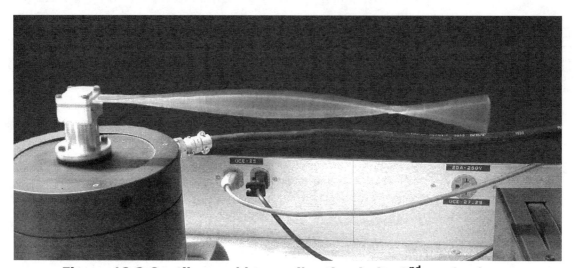

Figure 12.3 Cantilevered beam vibrating in its 2nd mode shape

A different mode shape will correspond to each of the natural frequencies of a structure. As figure 12.4 illustrates, mode shapes that correspond to higher natural frequencies become increasingly more complex. The first mode shape corresponds to the normal deflection shape of the beam under its own weight and represents the minimum amount of strain energy within the beam of any of the mode shapes. However, the magnitude of the displacements is meaningless in a modal analysis, and is usually normalized to one for display purposes. Figure 12.5 is an actual plot of the amplitude of displacement as the actuating force cycles through a spectrum of different frequencies.

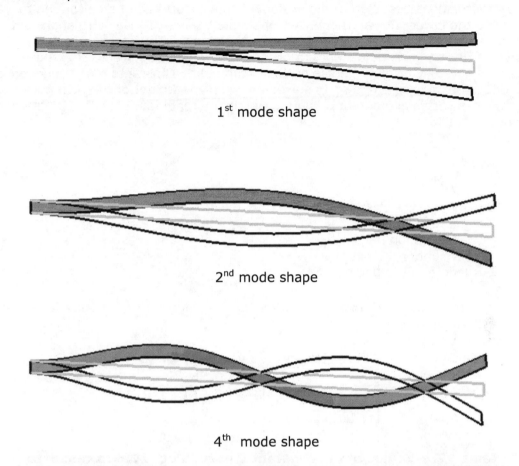

1st mode shape

2nd mode shape

4th mode shape

Figure 12.4 Finite Element Analysis Modes shapes of a cantilevered beam (the 3rd mode shape, not shown here, is a twisting mode shape)

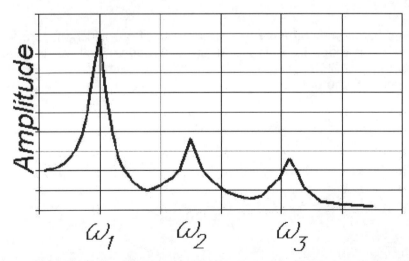

Figure 12.5 Amplitude of the displacement as the frequency of the actuating force corresponds to several natural frequencies

12.3 Manual calculations of beam vibrations

Manual calculations based on "2 dimensional beam theory" can be performed to determine the lower natural frequencies of simple beams. These calculations are limited to vibration modes that occur "within the plane". Therefore, modes that involve any twisting or movement out of the plane will not be predicted. These calculations usually involve the use of tables containing constants that are dependent on how the beam is attached to its surroundings[1]. The weight of the beam, its length, cross sectional moment of inertia, and its material modulus of elasticity are included in the formula as shown below.

$$f_n = C\sqrt{\frac{EIg}{WL^3}}$$
                                                                          eq. 12.6

where: E = modulus of elasticity
I = moment of inertia
g = acceleration of gravity
W = weight of the beam
L = length of the beam

For cantilevered beams: the values of C for the first four natural frequencies are given in the table below:

Frequency	Value of C
1	0.56
2	3.51
3	9.82
4	19.2

Table 12.1 Values of the constant C used in eq. 12.6 to calculate the first four natural frequencies of a cantilevered beam

---

EXAMPLE 12.2

The cantilevered beam shown below has a length of 18 in. width of 2 in. and is 0.0775 in. thick. It is made from an aluminum alloy, so we will use the Workbench supplied values: E = 10.298 x 10^6psi and density = 0.10015 lb./in^3. Determine the natural frequencies of the beam.

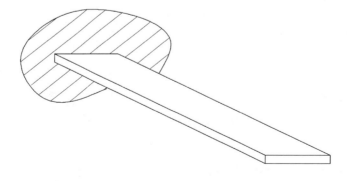

Using the given values for the beam, we can calculate:

$$I = \frac{(2in)(0.0775in)^3}{12} = 77.581x10^{-6}\,in^4$$

$$W = (0.10015lb/in^3)(18in)(2in)(0.0775in) = 0.27942\,lb.$$

and then substituting these values into eq. 12-6;

$$f_n = C\sqrt{\frac{(10.298x10^6\,lb./in^2)(77.581x10^{-6}\,in^4)(386in/\sec^2)}{(0.27942lb.)(18in)^3}} = C(13.76)$$

using the values of **C** in table 12.1, we have:

Frequency	Value of C	Natural Freq.
1st	0.56	7.706 Hz
2nd	3.51	48.30 Hz
3rd	9.82	135.1 Hz
4th	19.2	264.2 Hz

12.4 Finite Element Modal Analysis

The finite element method of solving for natural frequencies involves defining both mass and stiffness matrices that are based on the element type used, the geometry defined by the mesh and the boundary conditions. Since finite element models usually contain a large number of nodal points, the total number of natural frequencies is quite large. A number of different numerical procedures can be used to efficiently solve for the lowest natural frequencies and mode shapes. This is usually satisfactory because in most cases only the first five or ten natural frequencies will be of interest.

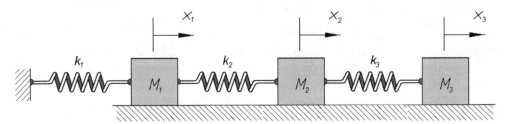

Figure 12.6 Mass-spring system with three degrees of freedom

The matrix form of equation 12.2 is shown below, where 'a' represents $\ddot{x}$;the second derivative of x with respect to time. The 3 x 3 matrices represent the 3 *dof* system show in figure 12.6, but also illustrate the general format that is used in finite element analysis solutions.

$$\begin{bmatrix} m_1 & 0 & 0 \\ 0 & m_2 & 0 \\ 0 & 0 & m_3 \end{bmatrix}\begin{bmatrix} a_1 \\ a_2 \\ a_3 \end{bmatrix} + \begin{bmatrix} k_1+k_2 & -k_2 & 0 \\ -k_2 & k_2+k_3 & -k_3 \\ 0 & -k_3 & k_3 \end{bmatrix}\begin{bmatrix} x_1 \\ x_2 \\ x_3 \end{bmatrix} = 0 \quad \text{eq. 12.7}$$

The solution for this set of equations is referred to as an eigenvalue/eigenvector problem. The above matrices are usually written in the compacted form shown below.

$$A\phi = \lambda\phi \quad \text{eq. 12.8}$$

Where λ is an eigenvalue that represents the set of natural frequencies, and ϕ represents the corresponding eigenvectors (mode shapes).

12.5 Modeling Techniques

Performing a modal analysis in ANSYS Workbench is similar to performing a static stress analysis. The same basic steps are required to prepare the model, except that no loads are applied and the type of analysis must be changed to a Modal analysis. Therefore, a model that was used for static stress analysis can be used in a modal analysis by removing the loads and changing the analysis type.

Since only the first few mode shapes are usually desired, the models generally do not have to have as fine of a mesh as a static analysis. Any of the element types can be used when performing a natural frequency analysis, however, the use a symmetry modeling is not recommended. This is because of the difficulty of predicting the deformed shape of the structure as it vibrates.

12.6 Tutorial 12_1 – Modal Analysis of a Cantilevered beam

We will analyze the same beam that was used in the previous numerical example

Step 1 – Start a new DesignModeler project, and select Inches as the desired length units.

Step 2 – Create the beam solid model
   Sketch a rectangle on the XY plane that is 2 in. x 0.0775 in., and then extrude it 18 in. and then select generate.

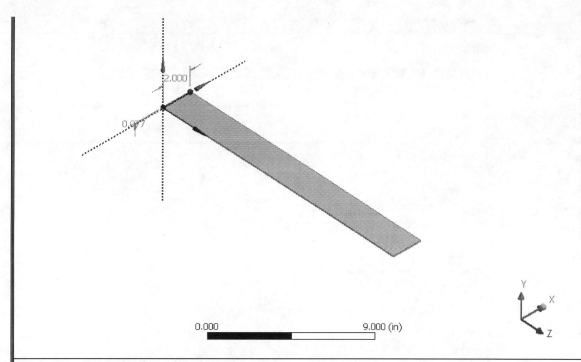

0.000   9.000 (in)

Step 3 – Start the simulation process
Click on the **Project tab**, followed by clicking on **New simulation** to start the simulation module.

Step 4 – Set the material to the Workbench supplied Aluminum Alloy.
Click on **Solid** in the Outline window.
Then click on **Structural Steel** in the Details window.
And select the **Import** option.

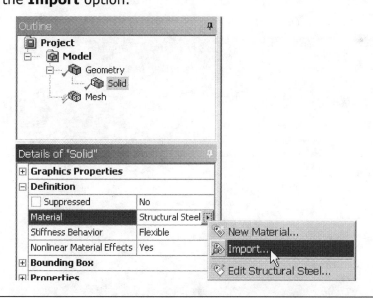

Step 4 (continued) – Make sure that Workbench Samples is selected at the top of the Import Material Data window, and then select the **Aluminum Alloy** radio button, followed by selecting the **OK** button.

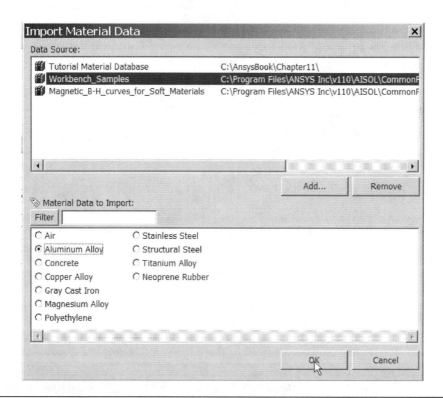

Step 5 – Set the Analysis type.
From the **New Analysis** pull down menu select **Modal**.

Step 6 – Define the Boundary Conditions.
Zoom-in of the end of the beam, then used the **Face** selection tool to select the end of the beam, followed by selecting the pull down menu options: **Supports – Fixed Support**.

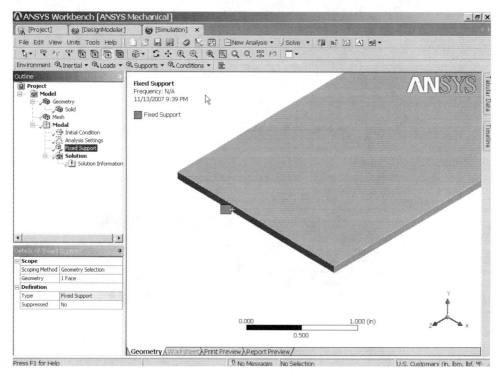

Step 7 – Define number of mode shapes.

Click on **Analysis Settings** in the Outline window, then in the Details window select the number next to **Max Modes to Find**, and change the value to **8**.

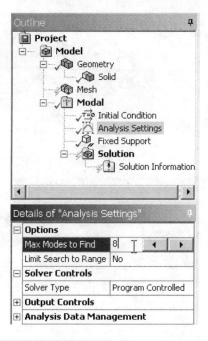

Step 8 – Request Results

Select **Solution** in the Outline window, then by select the pull down menu options: **Deformation – Total**. Make sure that **Mode** in the Details window is set to 1.

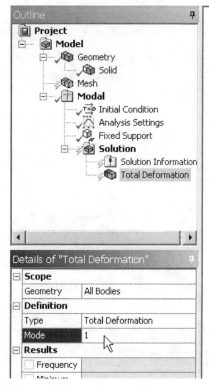

Step 8 (continued) – Request Results
    Repeat the process of inserting **Deformation – Total** so that eight items exist, while setting the corresponding **Mode** to agree with the Total Deformation number for all eight of the items.

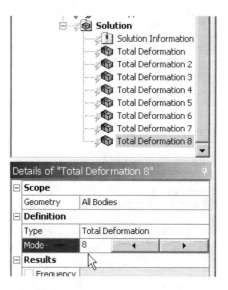

Step 9 – Solve the problem.
    Click on **Solve** in the toolbar.

Step 10 – Review the results.
    Select **Total Deformation** in the Outline window, and then select the **Show Undeformed Wireframe** option in the toolbar.

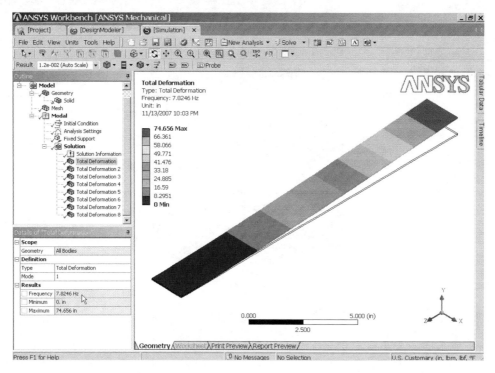

As we can see both on the graphic display and in the Details window the first natural frequency is 7.8246 Hz and the mode shape agrees with what we expected.

Step 11 – Animate the results

Click on the **Timeline tab,** and then click the **red arrow** next to **Animation,** in order to animate the beam deflecting with respect to time.

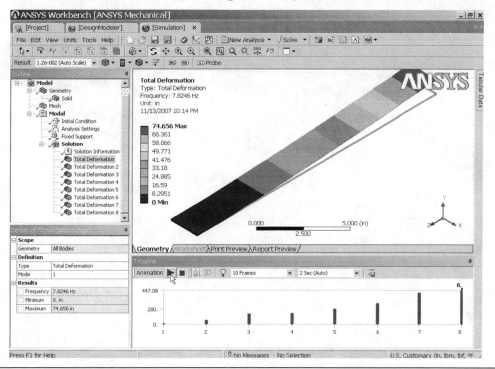

Step 12 – Continue to examine other mode shapes and their corresponding natural frequencies.

Summary of the tutorial results

The first six mode shapes of the cantilevered beam are shown below:

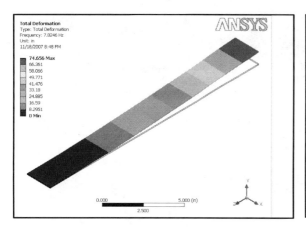

mode shape 1

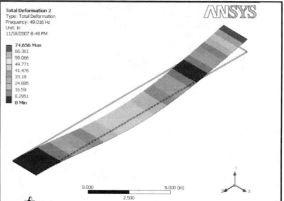

mode shape 2

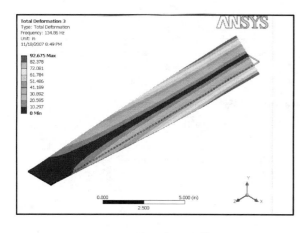

mode shape 3

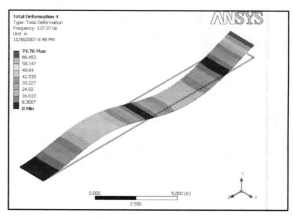

mode shape 4

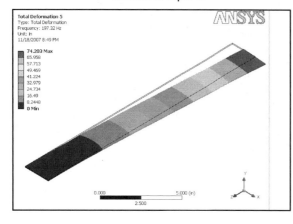

mode shape 5

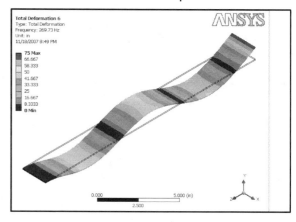

mode shape 6

The images above show that the movement of both mode shapes 3 and 5 are "out of the plane". They involve either a twisting motion (mode 3) or translation in the x-direction (mode 5). Therefore, in order to compare the FEA results with the manual calculations these two modes will not be considered.

The summary of the two analyses is shown in the table below.

Frequency Manual / ANSYS WB	Manual Natural Freq.	ANSYS WB Natural Freq.
1st / 1st	7.706 Hz	7.825 Hz
2nd / 2nd	48.30 Hz	49.02 Hz
3rd / 4th	135.1 Hz	137.4 Hz
4th / 6th	264.2 Hz	269.7 Hz

Reference

[1] Steinberg, D.S., Vibration Analysis for Electronic Equipment, 3rd Edition, pp 63, John Wiley & Sons, New York, NY, 2000

Exercises

1. A spring-mass system, similar to figure 12.1 has a natural frequency of 85 Hz and has a mass of 3 lbs. Determine the spring constant, k.

2. Determine the first four natural frequencies of a cantilevered beam that is made from structural steel and has the dimensions: 10 mm thick by 50 mm wide and 400 mm long. Do both manual calculations and FEA simulation.

3. Determine the effect of mesh density on the accuracy of the natural frequencies by repeating the tutorial in this chapter with 9 – 2"x2", 36- 1"x1", and 576 – ¼" x ¼" elements. Comment on the level of accuracy (assuming that the 576 element model is 100% accurate).

4. For an 8 inch by 12 inch by 0.5 inch thick steel plate, find all of the natural frequencies under 7500 Hz. The 12 inch long edges are fixed and the 8 inch edges are free.

5. Compare the first four manually calculated natural frequencies of the simply supported 18" long beam with an ANSYS Workbench simulation. For the manual calculations, use the values in the table below. The beam is made from aluminum and has a 1" x 1" square cross section.

Frequency	Value of C
1	1.57
2	6.28
3	14.1
4	25.2

NOTES:

13

Steady-State Heat Transfer

In the previous chapters we described how the finite element method can be used to perform stress and vibration analyses. FEA is also used extensively in performing both steady-state and transient heat transfer analysis as well as thermal analyses that include fluid flow. In this book however, we will limit our discussion to steady-state heat transfer in solids.

In this chapter it is assumed that the reader has some familiarity with the basic concepts of heat transfer, therefore, the material presented here can be considered a refresher and also used to introduce the FEA formulation of the heat conduction equation.

13.1 Fundamentals of Heat Transfer

Heat transfer is the flow of energy due to the existence of a temperature difference. Heat flows by three distinct mechanisms or modes; Conduction, Convection and Radiation.

- Conduction occurs inside a solid body from the high temperature region to the low temperature region
- Convection occurs when a solid body is in contact with a fluid such as air or water
- Radiation occurs between a body and its surroundings without the presence of a medium.

In the remainder of this section each of these heat transfer modes is discussed in more detail.

Conduction or heat flow in a solid body is governed by Fourier's law which states that "The rate of heat flow per unit area in a solid is proportional to the temperature gradient in the direction normal to the heat flow".

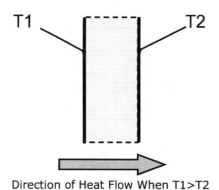

Direction of Heat Flow When T1>T2

Figure 13.1 - Conduction Heat Flow

Referring to Figure 13.1, Fourier's law can be expressed mathematically as shown in equation 13.1.

$$\dot{q} = -k\frac{dT}{dx} \quad \Rightarrow \quad q = -kA\frac{\Delta T}{\Delta x}$$ eq. 13.1

Where:

$\dot{q}$ = Heat flux [W/m^2]

q = Heat transfer rate [W]

k = Thermal conductivity [W/m.°C]

A = Surface area [m^2]

Convection is the exchange of heat between a surface and the surrounding fluid. Figure 13.2 shows a convection heat exchange where the fluid is at the temperature T_a and the surface is at T_w.

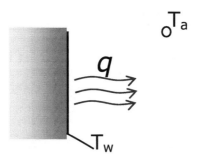

Figure 13.2 - Convection Heat Flow

Mathematically, the heat flow is given by equation 13.2

$$q = hA(T_w - T_a)$$ eq. 13.2

Where:

q = Heat transfer rate [W]
h = Convection heat transfer coefficient [W/m^{2}K]
A = Surface area [m^2]
T_w = Wall or surface temperature [°C]
T_a = Ambient (bulk) fluid temperature [°C]

In equation 13.2, T_a or bulk fluid temperature refers to the temperatures of the fluid measured at a distance sufficiently far from the wall so that it is not affected by the heat transfer process. The convection heat transfer coefficient is also referred to as film coefficient.

Convection heat transfer can occur as natural, also referred to as free convection, or forced convection. Natural convection occurs when the fluid is originally stationary and heat transferred to it causes it to expand and rise (If heat is removed from the fluid, the opposite situation occurs and removal of heat from the fluid results in its contraction and increase in density). The decrease in the density of the fluid adjacent to the surface where heat transfer occurs induces a natural motion whereby the heated fluid rises and is replaced by fluid initially unaffected by the heat transfer process. This process induces a motion in the fluid adjacent to a solid body called natural or free convection.

Forced convection refers to situations where a fan or other means is used to cause the fluid to flow over a solid surface. The fluid exchanges heat with the solid surface as it flows over it; lowering or increasing the temperature of the fluid.

Radiation heat exchange occurs between the surface of a body and the atmosphere and objects not in contact with the radiating body. The situation where a body with a surface temperature T_w is exchanging heat via radiation with the environment at T_a is shown in Figure 13.3.

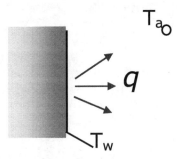

Figure 13.3 - Radiation Heat Flow

The formula for radiation heat flow is given in equation 13.3.

$$q = \varepsilon \sigma A (T_w^4 - T_a^4)$$

eq. 13.3

Where:

q = heat transfer rate [W]

ε = Emmisivity

σ = Stefan Boltzmann constant [W/m²K⁴]

A = Surface area [m²]

T = Temperatures must be in an absolute scale

Most real world heat transfer problems involve a combination of these mechanisms and the degree to which heat flows by each of these mechanisms is problem dependent. For example radiation heat transfer generally involves elevated temperatures and in many common engineering problems the amount of heat transfer by radiation is negligible and can be safely ignored.

For the purposes of this book, we are only concerned with conduction heat transfer and where convection plays a significant role we will limit the problem domain to the solid body and use boundary conditions to take into account the amount of heat that flows into or out of the body by convection.

13.2 Element Equations for One-Dimensional Conduction

In this section we develop the element equation for a one-dimensional heat conduction problem. Figure 13.4 shows the element e used in this formulation. The element has a cross-sectional area A, and is ΔX units long. The thermal conductivity of the material is *k* and the element is assumed to be at equilibrium.

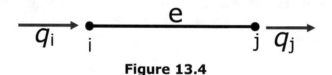

Figure 13.4

The principal of conservation of energy (from the first law of thermodynamics for a control volume) applies to this element as well as to any system that is undergoing heat or energy exchanges regardless of how many modes of energy exchange (or in our case modes of heat transfer) are acting on the system. This principal can be expressed as follows:

$$E_{in} + E_g - E_{out} = \Delta E_{sys}$$

Where:

E_{in} = Energy input to the system

E_g = Energy generated inside the system

E_{out} = Energy removed from the system

E_{sys} = Change in the internal energy of the system

In the case of the one-element model in figure 13.4, under steady-state conditions and no internal heat generation, this means

$$q_i = -q_j$$

We will now apply Fourier's law to element e and write the heat flow equation for each node.

For node i:

$$q_i = -\frac{kA}{\Delta x}\left[T_j - T_i\right]$$

or

$$q_i = \frac{kA}{\Delta x}\left[T_i - T_j\right]$$

And for node J:

$$-q_j = \frac{kA}{\Delta x}\left[-T_i + T_j\right]$$

In matrix notation, equations for nodes i and j can be combined and written as:

$$\frac{kA}{\Delta x}\begin{bmatrix} 1 & -1 \\ -1 & 1 \end{bmatrix}\begin{bmatrix} T_i \\ T_j \end{bmatrix} = \begin{Bmatrix} q_i \\ -q_j \end{Bmatrix}$$

or

$$\begin{bmatrix} k_e & -k_e \\ -k_e & k_e \end{bmatrix}\begin{bmatrix} T_i \\ T_j \end{bmatrix} = \begin{Bmatrix} q_i \\ -q_j \end{Bmatrix} \qquad \text{eq. 13.4}$$

Equation 13.4 is the element equation for element e. It can be written more concisely as equation 13.5 below.

$$[\mathbf{K}]\{T\} = \{Q\} \qquad \text{eq. 13.5}$$

Where:
   [K] = Thermal conductivity matrix
   {T} = Column vector of nodal temperatures
   {Q} = Column vector of nodal heat fluxes

Notice the similarity of equation 13.5 with the equation we developed for structural analysis in chapter 2. In structural analysis the matrix is referred to as the stiffness matrix and the vectors are nodal displacement and load vectors respectively.

Once the element equation has been developed, equations for the elements in the mesh must be assembled to produce a set of equations which describe the entire domain of the finite element problem [1]. The assembly process takes advantage of the compatibility condition which states that the value of the unknown variable being computed for all the elements that share a node must be the same at that node. In the one dimensional example we are using, each node can at most have two elements connected to it. The compatibility condition makes it necessary that the temperature calculated by both elements be the same at the node they share. In order to satisfy this requirement at all the nodes the nodal stiffness and the nodal forces (heat flows) are added together to calculate a net stiffness and net load at each node.

The assembly process can be described by the example of a mesh which has two elements as shown in Figure 13.5

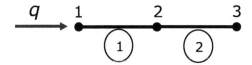

Figure 13.5 - Mesh Consisting of Two Elements

We assume that the two elements are made of the same material and have the same thermal conductivity k. We further assume that the elements are Δx units long and have the same cross-sectional area A.

Writing the heat flow equation for element 1 at nodes 1 and 2 we have:

$$q_1 = \frac{kA}{\Delta x}\left[T_1 - T_2\right]$$

and

$$q_2 = -\frac{kA}{\Delta x}\left[T_1 - T_2\right]$$

Similarly for element 2 at nodes 2 and 3 we can write:

$$q_2 = \frac{kA}{\Delta x}\left[T_2 - T_3\right]$$

and

$$q_3 = -\frac{kA}{\Delta x}\left[T_2 - T_3\right]$$

We will now denote the term $\dfrac{kA}{\Delta x}$ as **K** and write the previous four equations in matrix form:

$$\begin{bmatrix} K & -K & 0 \\ -K & K+K & -K \\ 0 & -K & K \end{bmatrix} \begin{bmatrix} T_1 \\ T_2 \\ T_3 \end{bmatrix} = \begin{bmatrix} q_1 \\ q_2 \\ q_3 \end{bmatrix} \qquad \text{eq. 13.6}$$

The previous discussion that resulted in equation 13.6 demonstrates the process of assembling the element matrices for a simple two element mesh. Once the matrix has been assembled, boundary conditions are introduced and the final set of simultaneous equations is solved for the unknown variable temperature. For a more detailed explanation of this process see references 1 and 2.

13.3 Modeling Considerations

In this section we will point out some important issues when modeling heat transfer problems.

Unlike stress analysis problems in which the finite element method is used to solve for an unknown vector quantity (displacement) which can have up to six degrees of freedom (three displacement and three rotation DOF), in heat transfer problems the unknown is temperature which is a scalar quantity and therefore only one DOF is involved. This fact reduces the complexity and size of most common heat transfer problems and allows us to use larger and more accurate meshes to formulate and solve the problem.

As with stress analysis problems, loads and boundary conditions play a very important role in simulating a heat transfer problem. Heat transfer loads and boundary conditions can be classified as follows:

- Known Temperature
- Convection
- Heat Flow
- Heat Flux
- Internal Heat Generation
- Radiation

Known Temperature: When solving real engineering problems, occasionally we know that a certain boundary is maintained at a fixed temperature and can use this fact as a boundary condition. In workbench you can apply a Known Temperature boundary condition to a vertex, an edge or a face. Just as in the case of a point load, applying a known temperature to a single vertex should be avoided.

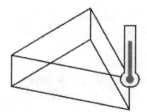 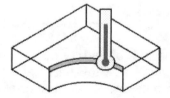 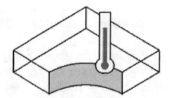

Convection: In many engineering problems heat removal is by means of either natural or forced convection. When specifying convection boundary conditions you must specify the convection heat transfer coefficient h as well as a bulk fluid temperature (see equation 13.2). The convection heat transfer coefficient, also called the film coefficient, is dependent on many variables including the type of fluid, the nature of the flow and specifically in the case of natural convection the orientation of the surface from which heat transfer occurs. Film coefficients are available in many engineering texts and handbooks as tables or empirical equations. Workbench provides a set of coefficients for air and water which can be used in the analysis. Alternatively, the user can enter new values using the Engineering Data application.

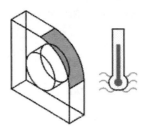

Heat Flow: Heat flow (energy per unit time) can be applied to vertices, edges and faces. A positive heat flow value indicates heat flowing into the selected entity. If you select multiple faces, edges or vertices when applying a heat flow boundary condition, the heat flow is divided among all the selected entities.

Heat Flux: Heat flux (heat flow per unit area) can be applied to vertices, edges and faces. A positive heat flux value indicates heat flowing into the selected entity. If you select multiple faces, edges or vertices when applying a heat flux boundary condition, the same heat flux value is applied to all the selected entities.

Internal Heat Generation: Internal heat generation specifies the amount of heat generated per unit volume for a body. It is applicable to solid bodies only. This type of loading is used when one or more of the bodies in the analysis generate heat as opposed having heat transferred to them. Two of the most common examples of this type of heat generation are electric heating elements and Integrated Circuits (ICs or chips) found in electronic equipment. If you select more than one body when applying heat generation, the same value (heat per unit volume) is applied to all the bodies.

Radiation: Radiation heat transfer requires an understanding of the mechanism and the nature of the radiating surfaces which is beyond the scope of this book. We recommend against using this boundary condition unless you are familiar with radiation heat transfer and its application in FEA.

13.4 Application of Thermal Loads and Boundary Conditions

In Workbench application of thermal boundary conditions and loads is done the same way as was shown for stress analysis. However, before any thermal loads can be applied, the analysis type has to be set to thermal analysis by clicking on **New Analysis** and selecting **Steady-State Thermal**.

Once the analysis type has been set, application of thermal load and boundary conditions can be accomplished by following the four step process below.

1. Select the **Steady-State Thermal** folder.
2. Select the geometric entity to which the load or support applies.
3. Select the desired load or boundary condition from the toolbar pull-down menu. Alternatively, click the **RMB** and from the pop-up menu select **Insert** and then the appropriate load or boundary condition.
4. In the **Details** pane enter the required values or adjust other settings as required.

A brief description of each of these steps follows:

Select the Steady-State Thermal folder – This step is necessary in order to activate the loads and boundary conditions toolbars and context (pop-up) menus.

Select the geometric entity – In this step you select the portion of the model where the load or boundary condition is to be applied.

Select the desired load or support – In this step you apply the actual load such as heat flow and heat flux or boundary conditions such as temperature or convection heat flow. You can select the appropriate quantity from the toolbar which is shown below or from the pop-up menu.

Details View – In this step you can enter the required input for the load or BC you are imposing. Examples are temperature, heat flow rate convection coefficient, etc.

Note: A question mark appearing in the **Outline** to the left of a load or boundary condition indicates an ambiguity that must be resolved before you can continue. In most cases, this means that the load or boundary condition is not associated with a geometric entity. To resolve this problem, select the ambiguous condition, select the geometry where it is to be applied and then click on the **Apply** button in the **Details** pane next to **Geometry** as shown below.

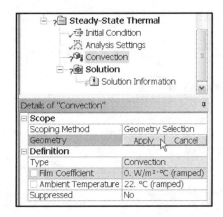

13.4 Tutorial 13_1 - Conduction through a plane wall with heat source

In this tutorial we will perform a thermal analysis on a wall with internal heat generation and temperature boundary conditions as described by Holman[3]. Examples of internal heat generation are nuclear reaction, electrical conductors and chemically reacting systems. The tutorial assumes that the height and depth of the wall are large enough so that heat transfer occurs in one dimension – through the thickness.

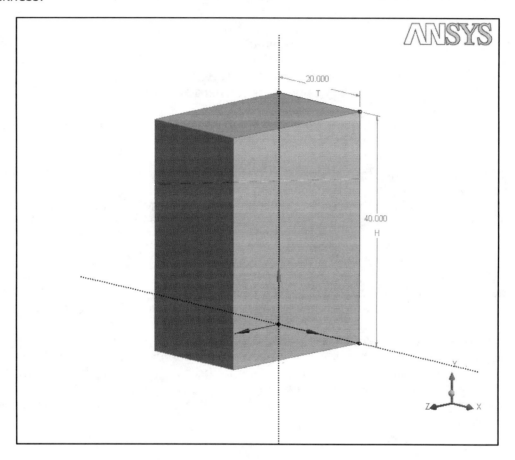

Step 1 – Start a new Simulation by clicking on **Simulation** in the **Start** dialog box.

Step 2 – Attach to the geometry file.
   A. Click on **Geometry** in the toolbar and select **From File...**
   B. Navigate to the "Student Files\Models" directory and select **Plane Wall.x_t**.

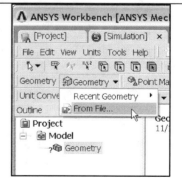

Step 3 – Check the units.

The working units for this problem are **Metric (mm, Kg, N, °C, mv, mA)**. To verify the units, check the status bar at the bottom right corner of the window or use the **Units** pull-down menu.

Step 4 – Set the part material to Polyethylene.
   A. Expand **Geometry** in the **Outline** and select **Part 1**.
   B. In the **Details** window pane select the material and click on **Import...**
   C. In the **Import Material Data** dialog box select **Tutorial Material Database** then **Wall Material for Tutorial 13_1**.

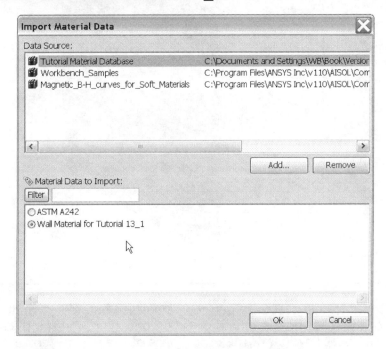

Step 5 – Set the analysis type to Steady-State Thermal.

Click on **New Analysis** in the toolbar and select **Steady-State Thermal**.

Step 6 – Set the outside surface temperatures.
   A. Select **Steady-State Thermal** in the **Outline window**.
   B. Select the two largest walls (with normals in the X direction) .
   C. In the **Environment** toolbar click on **Temperature**.
   D. In the **Details View** window pane enter **25** for **Magnitude** and press the enter key.

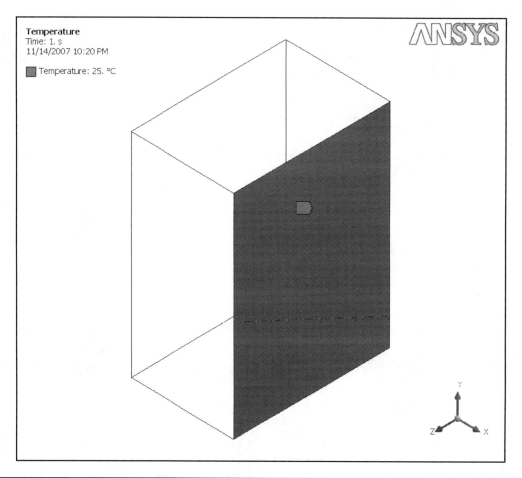

Temperature
Time: 1. s
11/14/2007 10:20 PM

Temperature: 25. °C

Step 7 – Set the remaining faces to perfectly insulated boundary conditions. In order to ensure that heat flow is in one direction only (through the thickness), we must specify that heat flow out of the other faces of the wall is zero.
    A. Select the other four faces.
    B. In the **Environment** toolbar click on **Heat** and then **Perfectly Insulated**.

Step 8 – Specify internal heat generation for the solid.
    A. Select the solid body and from the toolbar select **Heat**, and then **Internal Heat Generation**.
    B. In the **Details** window pane enter **0.0001** W/mm^3 and press the enter key.

Step 9 – Request results.
    A. Select **Solution** in the **Outline window**.
    B. Select the solid.
    C. In the **Solution** toolbar click on **Thermal** and select **Temperature**.
    D. Click on **Thermal** and select **Total Heat Flux**.

Step 9 (continued) – Request temperature results for one of the short edges. The reason for requesting this result quantity will become clear when we review the results.
    E. Click on **ISO** to orient the part.
    F. Select one of the short edges on the top portion of the wall.
    G. In the **Solution** toolbar click on **Thermal** and select **Temperature**.
    H. In the **Details** window pane verify that only one edge was selected.

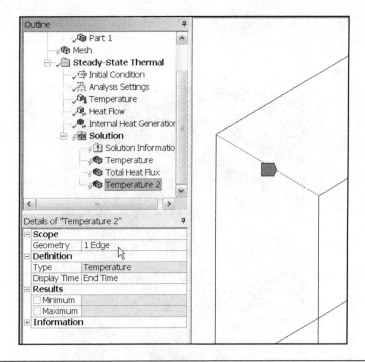

Step 9 (continued) – Use the solution probe to find the total heat flow out of the wall.

I. Click Solution.
J. From the Probe pull-down menu select Reaction.
K. In the Detail window pane, for Boundary Condition select Temperature from the pull-down menu.

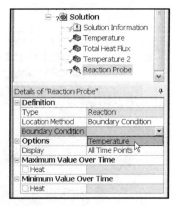

Step 10 – Save the project. In the **Project Page** select **Save All** from the **File** menu.

Step 11 – Solve the FEA problem by clicking on Solve.

Step 12 – Review the results. Click on Temperature to see the temperature distribution for the entire wall segment.

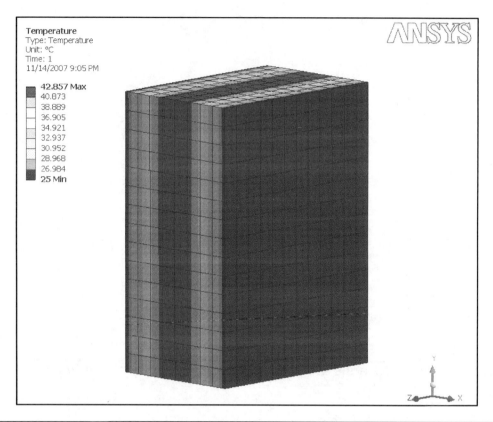

Step 12 (continued) – View the heat flux results.
   A. Click on **Total Heat Flux**.
   B. In the **Result** toolbar click on the horizontal arrows to switch to vector display. The vector style and magnitude can be adjusted from **Vector Display** toolbar.

   C. In the **Geometry** window, click the **RMB**, select **View** then **Front**.

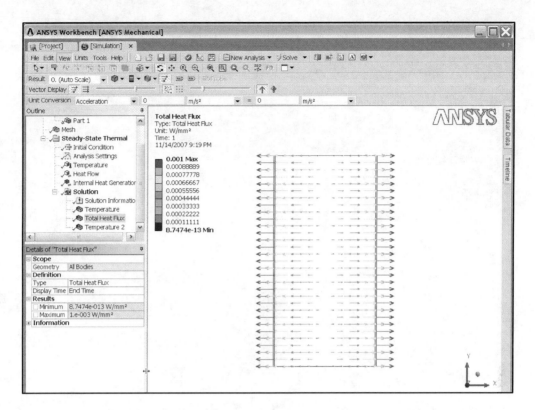

The vector display shows that heat flow is occurring only to the sides of the wall where the temperature BCs were imposed. Other views such as Top or Bottom can be used to verify that no heat is escaping the other sides of the wall.

Step 12 (continued) – Click on **Reaction Probe** and read the total heat flow out of the wall in the **Details** window pane. This value (2.4 W) can be verified by multiplying the heat generation rate by the volume of the wall segment in the model.

Step 12 (continued) – Click on **Temperature 2** to review the temperature distribution on the top edge. The resulting display shows the line plot of temperature along the selected edge. To view the graph without the associated geometry click on the Worksheet tab in the bottom of the window.

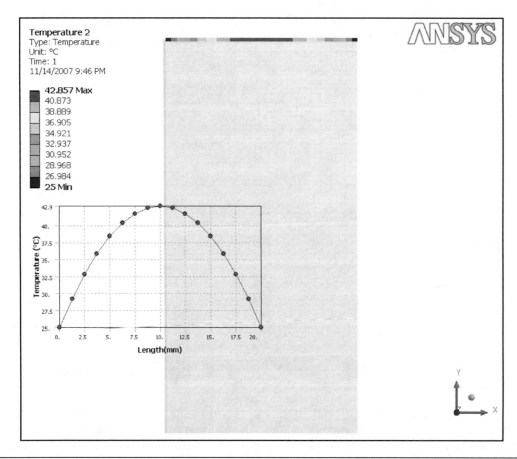

Step 13 – Comparison with closed form solution. The temperature distribution in the wall as derived by Holman[3] is given by the following equation:

$$\frac{T - T_0}{T_w - T_0} = \left(\frac{x}{L}\right)^2$$

Where:

T_0 = Centerline temperature
T_w = Wall surface temperature
L = Wall thickness/2
x = distance from the centerline

The temperature distribution is therefore parabolic which is verified by the edge plot from our Workbench results. By using the probe tool you can find the temperature at various locations in the wall and verify the accuracy of the finite element solution by comparing to the analytical solution given above.

This tutorial demonstrates how a thermal problem can be solved in Workbench. The tutorial also shows the use of vector heat flux displays as a means of verifying the correct setup of the problem. As shown in Step 12, the heat generated within the wall flows only in the thickness direction which is important in achieving the parabolic distribution indicated by the analytical solution.

13.5 Tutorial 13_2 – Air Cooled Heat Sink

In this tutorial we will perform a thermal analysis on an Aluminum heat sink. The heat sink which has three fins is attached to a heat generating object at its base and is cooled by free convection of air.

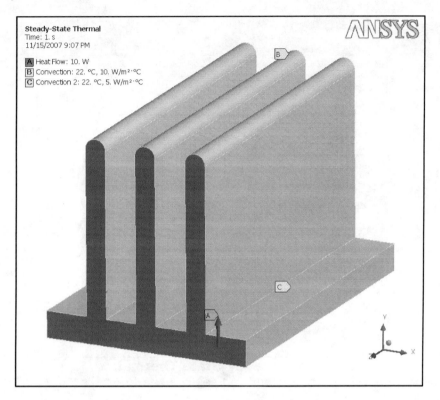

Step 1 – Start a new Simulation by clicking on **Simulation** in the **Start** dialog box.

Step 2 – Attach to the geometry file.
    A. Click on **Geometry** in the toolbar and select **From File...**

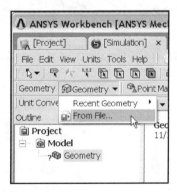

    B. Navigate to the "Student Files\Models" directory and select "**Heat Sink.x_t**".

Step 3 – Check the units. The working units for this problem are **Metric (mm, Kg, N, °C, mv, mA)**. To verify the units, check the status bar at the bottom right corner of the window or use the **Units** pull-down menu.

Step 4 – Set the part material to Aluminum Alloy.
  A. Expand **Geometry** in the **Outline** and select **Part 1**.
  B. In the **Details** window pane select the material and click on **Import...**
  C. In the **Import Material Data** dialog box select. **Workbench_Samples** and then **Aluminum Alloy**.

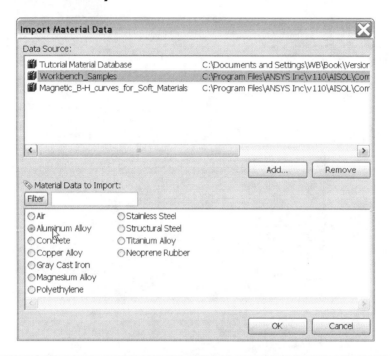

Step 5 – Set the analysis type to **Steady-State Thermal**.
Click on **New Analysis** in the toolbar and select **Steady-State Thermal**.

Step 6 – Set the amount of heat input into the heat sink.
  A. Select the bottom face.
  B. In the **Environment** toolbar click on **Heat** and select **Heat Flow**.
  C. In the **Details** window pane enter *10.0* W and press the enter key.

Step 7 – Impose a film coefficient of 5e-6 W/mm^2 °C on the horizontal surfaces of the heat sink.
  A. Select the four horizontal faces on the top side of the base.
  B. In the **Environment** toolbar click on **Convection**.
  C. In the **Details** window pane enter *5e-6* W/mm^2 °C for film coefficient and press the enter key.

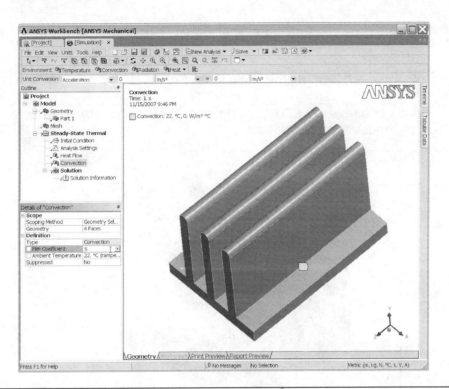

Step 8 – Impose a film coefficient of 10.e-6 W/mm² °C on the vertical faces of the heat sink and the top of the fins.

    A. Select the 13 vertical and top curved faces of the heat sink.

    B. In the **Environment** toolbar click on **Convection**.

    C. In the **Details** window pane enter *10e-6* W/mm² °C for film coefficient and press the enter key.

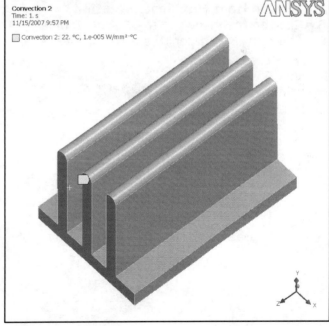

Step 9 – Request results

    A. Select **Solution** in the **Outline** window pane.

    B. In the **Solution** toolbar click on **Thermal** and select **Temperature**.

    C. In the **Solution** toolbar click on **Thermal** and select **Total Heat Flux**.

Step 10 – Save the project. In the **Project Page** select **Save All** from the **File** menu.

Step 11 – Solve the FEA problem by clicking on **Solve**.

Step 12 – Review the results. Click on **Temperature** under **Solution** to view the temperature distribution in the heat sink.

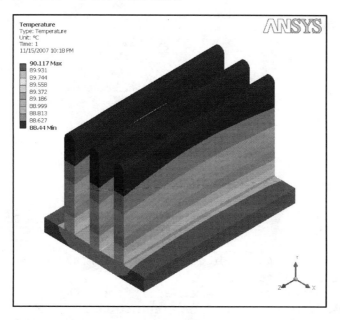

Step 12 (Continued) – View the Heat Flux results
   A. Click on **Heat Flux** under **Solution**.
   B. Click on the Arrows in the **Result** toolbar.
   C. Adjust the arrow lengths by using the slider in the **Vector Display** toolbar.

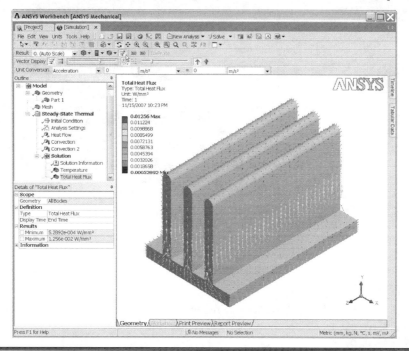

Tutorial 13_2 demonstrates how to perform a thermal analysis which includes convection boundary conditions. In this tutorial two different values of film coefficient were imposed; One value on the horizontal surfaces and a higher value on the vertical surfaces. This is due to the fact that free convection heat transfer coefficients (film coefficients) are higher from vertical surfaces since buoyancy plays a very important role in this type of heat transfer.

This type of heat sink is very commonly used for cooling electronic components by attaching the heat generating device to the base of the heat sink. In some cases such as in personal computers, a fan may be used to direct air flow over the fins to improve the heat removal rate. In that case, the convection heat transfer is called Forced Convection and the heat transfer coefficient is much higher than that achieved by free convection.

References

[1] Huebner, K.H., Thornton, E.A., The Finite Element Method for Engineers, Second Edition, John Wiley & Sons 1982.

[2] Ransing, R.S., Hardy, S.J., Gethin, D.T., How To- Undertake Finite Element Based Thermal Analysis, NAFEMS Ltd 1999.

[3] Holman, J.P., Heat Transfer, 4th Edition, pp 31, McGraw-Hill Book Company 1976.

Exercises

1. A wire 1 meter long has a diameter of 3mm carries a 200A current resulting in internal heat generation equal to 5MW/m^3. The wire is submerged in a liquid which is maintained at 110 °C resulting in a convection heat transfer coefficient (film coefficient) of 4 Kw/m^2°C. The wire is made of stainless steel and has a thermal conductivity K=19 W/m°C. Build the solid model as a cylinder in DesignModeler and use it to computer the center temperature of the wire.

2. A heat rail designed to remove heat from electronic devices is constructed as an L-shaped bracket whose base is maintained at 85 °C. Six heat generating devices, each generating 3 Watts of power are attached to one of the vertical faces and the remaining vertical surfaces of the bracket (with normal vectors in the X and Z directions) are exposed to ambient air at 55 °C resulting in an effective film coefficient of 10 W/m^2°C. Convection from the horizontal faces can be ignored in this problem. Set up the finite element problem and solve for temperature distribution and total heat flux.

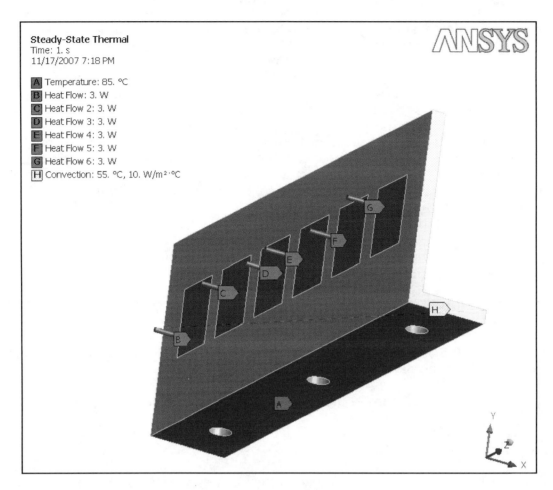

The solid model for this exercise is called "Heat Rail.x_t" and is supplied in the "Student Files\Models" directory.

3. A pipe carrying a liquid at 200 C is exposed to air at 20 C resulting in a film coefficient h=3.0 W/m² °C. The pipe is to be insulated with a material which has a thermal conductivity k=0.17 W/m°C. The pipe is at thermal equilibrium therefore, the outside surface temperature of the pipe is the same as the liquid. The Critical Insulation Thickness is given by [2] as

$$r_o = \frac{k}{h}$$

Where r_o is the outside radius of insulation required to impede heat flow. Until this value is reached, adding insulation material actually increases heat flow.

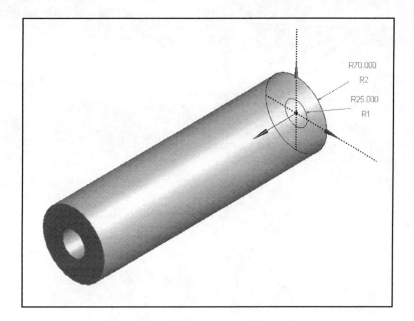

a) Using equation13.2 calculate the heat transfer per unit length of pipe if no insulation is used.

b) Use the supplied DesignModeler file "Pipe Insulation.agdb" to perform a thermal analysis and determine the heat transfer through a 31.7mm thick layer of insulation. Solve for the maximum temperature and total heat flow. Use the Probe Reaction to calculate heat flow on the outer surface of the insulation. Calculate the heat flow per unit length.

c) Using DesignModeler, increase the thickness of the insulation to 35mm and repeat the analysis in b.

d) Compare the results.

NOTES:

14

Finite Element Analysis For Engineers

Finite Element Analysis has gradually become an indispensable part of the design process in many companies around the world. In this role, FEA is now employed by product engineers as one of their many computational tools rather than being used only by a specialist whose main activity is to do FEA evaluations. In this chapter, we will provide some historical background as well as practical considerations that should be made by these engineers.

As recently as the late 1990's, Finite Element Analysis was used only by specialists who spent all of their time learning the mathematics behind FEA and how to use FEA tools that were available at the time. As the power and potential benefits of using FEA to help design better and more reliable products became clear, and as the cost of maintaining a highly skilled group of specialists to perform FEA rose, a few companies sought to enable their product engineers to integrate this powerful tool in the product design process.

One challenge for these product engineers is to develop an understanding of how this method of analysis is formulated and how it can be used to solve their engineering problems. The second challenge is to learn how to use a particular FEA program to perform an accurate analysis. While it is reasonable to expect that engineers should know the mathematical basis for the analysis techniques that they use, the second requirement is less justifiable. This is because finite element programs that were available prior to the late 1990s required that the user become specialized in using one specific FEA program to perform a relatively simple analysis while they would be unable to perform the same analysis in another FEA program. This situation practically put FEA out of the reach of non-specialists and in the domain of those who performed FEA as their main task on a daily basis. Consequently, companies that wanted to use FEA had to devote considerable resources to employ and train a group of highly specialized individuals whose only job was to perform finite element analysis for product engineers. These factors created a situation in which FEA was not being used as efficiently or effectively as it could be.

During the past decade, a whole new class of software has been introduced, which has allowed many more to incorporated FEA into their design process. ANSYS, Inc.

was one of the first software companies to recognize the potential benefits of creating an FEA tool that could be used by product engineers. The challenge was, and remains, to create a tool that is easy to use without leading the user to erroneous results. The program initially introduced by ANSYS as a stand alone tool was called DesignSpace. Currently, the DesignSpace functionality is incorporated into Workbench as the Simulation application. DesignSpace was designed to be used by product engineers who would only use it occasionally as part of their job.

In order to ensure proper use of this powerful tool, careful consideration must be given to those who uses it and how it is used. Contrary to the mistaken belief by some, FEA is not the same as CAD software. Furthermore, FEA software should only be used by individuals who have been taught how to correctly prepare FEA models and how to correctly interpret the results. In order to eliminate errors and maintain a high quality final product from the analysis effort, some companies have developed in-house rules and standards while others rely on guidelines produced by outside organizations[1].

In the remainder of this chapter, some of the recurring and important issues that product engineers face when using finite element analysis is discussed. The discussion includes both high level concepts such as interpretation of the results as well as specific modeling considerations.

14.1 Interpreting your results

Needless to say, interpreting FEA results and determining the accuracy of those results is the most important part of an analysis. Given the fastest computer hardware and the best software, a user can still misinterpret the results and arrive at an incorrect conclusion. In this section we will examine some of the common reasons for misinterpreting the results of an analysis and in the following sections we will look at some of the ways to minimize the chances of this occurring. It should be noted that the issues, problems and suggested solutions that are highlighted here are aimed at the product engineer who will be performing finite element analysis occasionally and as part of their work rather than the full time FEA analyst.

Although there is no clear and concise answer to the question "How do I interpret the results", we can point out some key issues that are sometimes overlooked where FEA is concerned and are critically important in correctly interpreting the results of an analysis.

Physics of the problem

First and foremost, the engineer must understand the physics of the problem he or she is trying to solve. This means understanding the system being analyzed and its surroundings. External influences on the system must be known to a reasonable level of certainty and translated into loads and boundary conditions carefully. The dominant external influences must be identified and taken into account. Examples of external influences in stress analysis problems are: forces, pressures, body forces and in thermal analysis temperatures, heat flows and radiation. Boundary conditions and supports play an equally important role; for example, in many stress analysis problems, the choice of which degrees of freedom are constrained and which are left free are critically important to the outcome of the solution. Likewise, in a modal analysis, replacing simply-supported boundary conditions on an edge with a fixed support will, in most cases drastically change the results. When there are ambiguities and unknowns, these should be documented and included as part of any report produced for the project.

Goals of the analysis

Once the physics of the problem is known, a clear goal should be established for the analysis. Finite element analysis is used in all phases of product development; from concept evaluation to postmortem analyses that seek to understand what went wrong. Therefore, it is very important to clearly state the goals of an analysis before it begins. During concept evaluation, FEA can be used to establish the feasibility of a design concept by identifying the limits beyond which the design will not work. Using reasonable assumptions, this can be done relatively easily. For example if the modal analysis of a system indicates that the first mode is at 300 Hz and the design guidelines call for a first mode of 100 or above, the FEA results can be used with high confidence. However, when a system has unexpectedly failed and FEA is being used to determine or verify the cause of failure, much more precise input to the FEA model is required. In most cases, this type of analysis falls beyond the scope of this book which focused only on linear, steady-state analyses.

Failure modes and Solution result quantities

Failure modes and determining which solution result quantities are used to determine failure are closely related to the previous two subjects: Physics of the problem and Goals of the analysis. First we must define what is meant by failure in the context of the problem we are solving. We know in general that a part or system is said to have failed if it can not perform the functions for which it was designed. But to correctly use FEA, we have to be more specific. Does failure mean stress values beyond yield point of the material have been reached? Does it mean strains beyond the acceptable limits for the material? Does it mean deflection exceeding as specified value? Does failure mean temperatures beyond a certain limit? This should be clearly understood before proceeding with the analysis. Clarifying what failure means goes a long way in establishing which solution result quantities to use.

14.2 Theories of failure

In the previous section we discussed the importance of establishing the meaning of failure in the context of the analysis being performed. In this section we will briefly discuss the theories of failure that have been developed to predict yielding in ductile materials. In most stress analysis problems that involve static loads, the part is said to have failed if the stress in the part reaches or exceeds the elastic limit of the material. Recall that stresses and the associated deformations that are below the elastic limit are reversible and the material returns to its original shape and size once the load is removed. Limiting our discussion to this type of material behavior is consistent with the previous chapters of this book.

Behavior of materials that are subjected to the standard uniaxial normal or shearing loads is readily available in the form of stress-strain diagrams. In real-world problems, however, parts experience a combined state of stress in which both normal and shearing stresses are present. Theories of failure have been developed in order to predict the onset of yield in materials which are experiencing a combined state of stress. Unfortunately, no single theory accurately predicts failure under different loading conditions; therefore, several have been developed with varying degrees of success[2]. Some of the common theories of failure are the Maximum Principal Stress Theory, the Maximum Shear Stress Theory, and the Maximum Distortion Energy Theory. ANSYS Workbench Simulation supports four common theories (two for ductile materials and two for brittle materials) in the form of Stress Tools which are available when a stress analysis is performed.

For Ductile materials, the most commonly used failure theory is the von Mises-Hencky theory also referred to as the Maximum Distortion Energy theory. This theory states that failure due to yielding occurs when at any point in the body the distortion energy per unit volume exceeds the yield stress of the material measured in a tensile test. When expressed in equation form, we arrive at the familiar von Mises or equivalent stress formula:

$$\sigma_e = \sqrt{\frac{(\sigma_1 - \sigma_2)^2 + (\sigma_2 - \sigma_3)^2 + (\sigma_1 - \sigma_3)^2}{2}}$$

Where σ_1 and σ_2 and σ_3 are the maximum, intermediate and minimum principal stresses. To use this theory, we simply compute the maximum equivalent stress and compare with the yield stress of the material under tensile loading. Despite its simplicity and ease of use, this failure criterion should be applied with care and only to problem areas where it was intended to be used. For example many materials that are classified as ductile at room temperature conditions, behave marginally brittle at low temperatures. Therefore, while we would apply the von Mises criterion to these materials at room temperature, we can not use the same criterion at low temperature conditions.

In practice, selection of a failure theory depends heavily on the experience and engineering judgment of the analyst, as well as his or her knowledge of the problem and the materials involved.

14.3 Absolute versus comparative answers

As we have discussed before, finite element analysis is an extremely powerful and versatile tool which is used in a variety of situations during the entire product life cycle. Another area of application of FEA is in comparing designs where exact input data may not be available. In this type of usage, FEA is used to compare two situations where only the relative difference between the two situations is more important than the exact results.

As an example, consider the bracket analyzed in Tutorial 11_1 in chapter 11 and the follow up exercise 1 at the end of the chapter. The bracket was first analyzed in its original form and its deformation due to the applied load was observed. Exercise 1 included a modification of the geometry (by adding the "wings") in order to stiffen the bracket. The modified bracket was to be analyzed using the same load, boundary conditions and material properties to see if the addition of the wings actually helped to stiffen the bracket and reduce the deformation. If the results of the modified design are favorable, we can retain it as a possible solution to our goal of reducing the deflection of the bracket. Other options in this type of comparative analysis may include using a thicker bracket or using a different material if these options are allowed by our design constraints.

When performing this type of comparative analysis, it is very important to minimize or eliminate unintended changes in other variables. For example, we must be sure to use the same quality mesh in both cases. Comparing the results obtained from a coarse mesh to those from a much finer mesh would invalidate the comparison. This is particularly important because the automatic mesh generation provided by Workbench Simulation may necessitate that manual mesh controls, such as sizing, be used to enforce nearly identical meshes.

14.4 Rules to live by

Despite the fact that there is no simple answer to the interpretation of FEA results, there are certain things that can be done that reduce the chances of producing erroneous results or misinterpretation of the results.

Establish a clear goal for the analysis

Before performing a finite element analysis, it should be clearly understood, what the results of the analysis are to be used for. The purpose of an analysis can be to evaluate a design concept, or to evaluate a design change, or to determine the cause of failure of a design. These are generally performed at different times during a product's life cycle, and correspondingly, determines how much data is available and what level of precision must be used.

Model loads and boundary conditions accurately

The loads and boundary conditions for the analysis should be based on the best information available regarding the operation and use of the product or system you are analyzing. There are generally two reasons why error may be introduced in this part of the FEA data: (1) - external influences are not well understood, or (2) - external influences are not accurately translated to loads and boundary conditions. In the first case incorrect assumptions have to be made to quantify these influences. These assumptions should not be made in isolation. In many corporations, detailed technical knowledge about a certain product may be spread across many organizations and even divisions. It is well worth the analyst's effort to seek out this information before doing the analysis. Once the data is obtained or assumed, it must be carefully translated into loads and boundary conditions to reproduce the physical situation as closely as possible.

Use all the resources at your disposal

By using all the resources you have access to, be they internal or external to your company, you increase the chances of performing a successful analysis and interpreting the results correctly. Internally, your engineering organization may have design guidelines, lessons learned or similar documents which can help you better formulate and understand the product and its use. Another very useful source of information are other engineers who may have done similar work in the past. Before the use of FEA became common in product design, engineers had to rely on testing to validate their designs. Validation reports can often times provide useful information in the form of failure data, operating conditions, etc., or in some cases, they may be used as benchmarks to build confidence in the Finite Element model. As we did in many of the previous chapters, make use of closed form solutions to verify results whenever possible.

Modeling specifics
Throughout the book we have discussed ways to improve the accuracy of finite element models and the results obtained from them. Below is a summary of these points.

- **Simplification**
  o Use symmetry when possible
  o Take advantage of two dimensional models of the problem (plane strain/stress or axisymmetry) when possible

- **Mesh**
  o Use the best mesh that your computing resources can handle. In Workbench Simulation, usually the most efficient means to do this is to use the Convergence feature.

- **Loads and boundary conditions**
  o Avoid artificial loading and support conditions such as point loads and supports
  o Verify that the free and constrained degrees of freedom in the problem accurately represent the physical situation

- **Material properties**
  o Verify the accuracy of the material properties by using multiple sources when possible. Be as specific as possible in the material designation when looking up properties.
  o If the materials in your model exhibit temperature dependent properties, match the properties to the condition of the analysis. If the properties vary significantly as a function of temperature, a nonlinear analysis maybe required.

14.5 Summary

In this chapter we have tried to highlight some of the practices that determine the success or failure of a finite element analysis project. Despite the importance placed on these practices, it has to be kept in mind that in the final analysis, the engineering judgment and experience of the user is the most important factor in insuring the success of an analysis project. It is hoped that by following these guidelines, a new practitioner can begin to build the experience and knowledge that will help them use this powerful tool to its full potential.

References

[1] Adams, V., How to Manage Finite Element Analysis in the Design Process, NAFEMS Ltd.,2007

[2] A.C. Ugural, S.K. Fenster, Advanced Strength and applied Elasticity, 1981 Elsevier North Holland.

Appendix A

Matrices and Simultaneous Equations

A matrix is an *m by n* array of numbers that contains *m* rows and *n* columns. The equation below, illustrates a matrix with *m* rows and *n* columns.

$$[a] = \begin{bmatrix} a_{11} & a_{12} & a_{13} & a_{14} & \cdots & a_{1n} \\ a_{21} & a_{22} & a_{23} & a_{24} & \cdots & a_{2n} \\ a_{31} & a_{32} & a_{33} & & \cdots & a_{3n} \\ & \vdots & & \vdots & & \\ a_{m1} & a_{m2} & \cdots & & & a_{mn} \end{bmatrix}$$

If *m* is not equal to *n* in a matrix, the matrix is referred to as a rectangular matrix. If the elements form a single row, the matrix is called a row matrix (also, sometimes called a row vector). If the elements form a single column, the matrix is called a column matrix (also, sometimes called a column vector). If the number of rows and columns are equal, the matrix is called a square matrix. The force and displacement matrices used in finite element analysis are column matrices, whereas the stiffness matrix is a square matrix (see chapter 2).

To designate an individual element of matrix [*a*], the notation a_{ij} is used; where the subscripts *i* and *j* specify the row number and the column number, respectively.

In finite element analysis, matrices are used to express the simultaneous algebraic equations. This is because matrix operations are employed in order to solve the system of equations.

A.1 MULTIPLICATION of MATRICES

In order to multiply two matrices [a] and [b] in the order shown below, the number of columns in matrix [a] must equal the number of rows in matrix [b]. For example, consider

$$[c] = [a] \bullet [b]$$

If [a] is an *m* x *n* matrix, then [b] must have *n* rows. Using subscript notation, we can write the product of matrices [a] and [b] as

$$[c_{ij}] = \sum [a_{il}] [b_{lj}]$$

where *l* goes from 1 to the total number of columns in [a] or rows in [b].

EXAMPLE:

The process of matrix multiplication is often referred to as the multiplication of rows into columns as illustrated in the following example.

$$[c]=[a]\bullet[b]=\begin{bmatrix}3&2&-1\\0&4&6\end{bmatrix}\bullet\begin{bmatrix}1&0&2\\5&3&1\\6&4&2\end{bmatrix}=\begin{bmatrix}(1\bullet3)+(5\bullet2)+(6\bullet-1)&(0\bullet3)+(3\bullet2)+(4\bullet-1)&(2\bullet3)+(1\bullet2)+(2\bullet-1)\\(1\bullet0)+(5\bullet4)+(6\bullet6)&(0\bullet0)+(3\bullet4)+(4\bullet6)&(2\bullet0)+(1\bullet4)+(2\bullet6)\end{bmatrix}$$

therefore,

$$[c]=\begin{bmatrix}7&2&6\\56&36&16\end{bmatrix}$$

Matrix multiplication is not generally commutative; that is,

$$[a]\bullet[b]\neq[b]\bullet[a]$$

and often times cannot be performed because of a mismatch in the number of columns and rows.

A.2 UNIT (or IDENTITY) MATRICES

A unit (or also called identity) matrix, denoted as $[I]$, is a square matrix that contains 1's along the principal diagonal and zeros at all other locations. It has the property that if it is multiplied by any other square matrix of the same order, it does not change the value of any of the elements in the matrix. That is:

$$[I]\bullet[a]=[a]$$

The unit matrix is always a square matrix. An example of a 3 x 3 unit matrix is shown below:

$$\begin{bmatrix}1&0&0\\0&1&0\\0&0&1\end{bmatrix}$$

A.3 SYMMETRIC MATRICES

A symmetric matrix is a square matrix that has the property that each element of the matrix:

$$a_{ij}=a_{ji}$$

for all elements of the matrix.

The following matrix is an example of a symmetric matrix:

$$\begin{bmatrix} 12 & 5 & 8 & 4 \\ 5 & 9 & 7 & 5 \\ 8 & 7 & 5 & 3 \\ 4 & 5 & 3 & 1 \end{bmatrix}$$

As illustrated in chapter 2, stiffness matrices are symmetric matrices. This condition is taken advantage of in most finite element programs during the storage of the structure's stiffness matrix. This is done by storing only the diagonal elements plus the upper right elements of the matrix.

A.4 INVERSE of a MATRIX

The inverse of a matrix is denoted with a superscript -1, and it exhibits the property that:

$$[a]^{-1} \bullet [a] = [I]$$

If the determinant of a matrix is equal to zero, then the matrix is said to be singular. A singular matrix does not have an inverse. Stiffness matrices used in the finite element method are initially singular until sufficient boundary conditions (support conditions) are applied. This characteristic of the stiffness matrix is discussed in chapter 2.

By solving for the inverse of the coefficients matrix of a set of simultaneous equations, the set of equations can be solved by using matrix multiplication techniques as illustrated below. First, we will express the following simultaneous equations:

$$\begin{aligned} 2x + y + z &= 7 \\ 4x + 4y + 3z &= 21 \\ 6x + 7y + 4z &= 32 \end{aligned}$$

in matrix form as shown below:

$$\begin{bmatrix} 2 & 1 & 1 \\ 4 & 4 & 3 \\ 6 & 7 & 4 \end{bmatrix} \begin{Bmatrix} x \\ y \\ z \end{Bmatrix} = \begin{Bmatrix} 7 \\ 21 \\ 32 \end{Bmatrix}$$

Next, the inverse of the coefficients matrix can be found, by using a program such as Excel™ or MATLAB™ or some calculators to be:

$$\begin{bmatrix} 2 & 1 & 1 \\ 4 & 4 & 3 \\ 6 & 7 & 4 \end{bmatrix}^{-1} = \begin{bmatrix} 1.25 & -0.75 & 0.25 \\ -0.5 & -0.5 & 0.5 \\ -1.0 & 2.0 & -1.0 \end{bmatrix}$$

Now premultiply both sides of the original matrix equation by the inverse:

$$\begin{bmatrix} 1.25 & -0.75 & 0.25 \\ -0.5 & -0.5 & 0.5 \\ -1.0 & 2.0 & -1.0 \end{bmatrix} \begin{bmatrix} 2 & 1 & 1 \\ 4 & 4 & 3 \\ 6 & 7 & 4 \end{bmatrix} \begin{Bmatrix} x \\ y \\ z \end{Bmatrix} = \begin{bmatrix} 1.25 & -0.75 & 0.25 \\ -0.5 & -0.5 & 0.5 \\ -1.0 & 2.0 & -1.0 \end{bmatrix} \begin{Bmatrix} 7 \\ 21 \\ 32 \end{Bmatrix}$$

yields:

$$\begin{bmatrix} 1 & 0 & 0 \\ 0 & 1 & 0 \\ 0 & 0 & 1 \end{bmatrix} \begin{Bmatrix} x \\ y \\ z \end{Bmatrix} = \begin{Bmatrix} 1 \\ 2 \\ 3 \end{Bmatrix}$$

Therefore: $x=1$; $y=2$; and $z=3$.

A.5 SIMULTANEOUS EQUATIONS

During the solution process of a finite element program many simultaneous equations must be solved. This process is by far the most computationally intensive portion of the analysis. Much research has been done on perfecting solution algorithms, which use far more sophisticated techniques than those presented here. Since this book is aimed at the user of a finite element program rather than the developer, we will not delve into these details, but leave these to the interested reader [1,2].

Reference

[1] Bathe, K. J. and Wilson, E. L., <u>Numerical Methods in Finite Element Analysis</u>, Prentice-Hall, Englewood Cliffs, N.J., 1976.

[2] James, M. L., Smith, G. M., and Wolford, J. C., <u>Applied Numerical Methods for Digital Computation</u>, 3rd ed., Harper & Row, New York, 1985.

Exercises

1. Find the product ([a]•[b]) of the matrices, [a] and [b] shown below.

$$[a] = \begin{bmatrix} 2 & -1 & 0 \\ 0 & -2 & 1 \\ 1 & 0 & 1 \end{bmatrix} \quad [b] = \begin{bmatrix} -2 & 1 & -1 \\ 1 & 2 & -2 \\ 2 & -1 & -4 \end{bmatrix}$$

$$[a] = \begin{bmatrix} 3 & 4 & 2 \\ 6 & 0 & -1 \\ -5 & -2 & 1 \end{bmatrix} \quad [b] = \begin{bmatrix} 1 \\ 3 \\ 2 \end{bmatrix}$$

2. A 3x3 matrix **[a]** is shown below. Determine which of the other two matrices **[b]** or **[c]**, is the inverse of **[a]** by multiplying each of them by **[a]**.

$$[a] = \begin{bmatrix} 3 & -1 & 1 \\ -15 & 6 & -5 \\ 5 & -2 & 2 \end{bmatrix} \quad [b] = \begin{bmatrix} 2 & 0 & -1 \\ 3 & 1 & 0 \\ 0 & 1 & 5 \end{bmatrix} \quad [c] = \begin{bmatrix} 2 & 0 & -1 \\ 5 & 1 & 0 \\ 0 & 1 & 3 \end{bmatrix}$$

3. There are special cases of square matrices that are commutative. Determine which of the three sets of matrices shown below are commutative by calculating the product ([a]•[b]) and ([b]•[a]).

set 1)

$$[a] = \begin{bmatrix} 1 & 2 & 3 \\ 3 & 2 & 0 \\ -1 & -1 & -1 \end{bmatrix} \quad [b] = \begin{bmatrix} -2 & -1 & -6 \\ 3 & 2 & 9 \\ -1 & -1 & -4 \end{bmatrix}$$

set 2)

$$[a] = \begin{bmatrix} 4 & 1 & 3 \\ 3 & 5 & 0 \\ -1 & 1 & -1 \end{bmatrix} \quad [b] = \begin{bmatrix} 4 & -1 & -4 \\ 3 & 8 & 9 \\ -1 & 7 & -4 \end{bmatrix}$$

set 3)

$$[a] = \begin{bmatrix} 1 & 1 & 2 \\ 2 & 3 & 1 \\ -1 & 2 & 4 \end{bmatrix} \quad [b] = \begin{bmatrix} 2/3 & 0 & -1/3 \\ -3/5 & 2/5 & 1/5 \\ 7/15 & -1/5 & 1/15 \end{bmatrix}$$

4. Determine the inverse of the two matrices shown below, and then multiply the inverse by the original matrix and show the product.

$$[a] = \begin{bmatrix} 3 & -2 & -1 \\ -4 & 1 & -1 \\ 2 & 0 & 1 \end{bmatrix} \qquad [b] = \begin{bmatrix} 1 & 0 & 0 & 0 \\ -2 & 1 & 0 & 0 \\ 0 & -2 & 1 & 0 \\ 8 & -1 & -1 & 1 \end{bmatrix}$$

5. For the three simultaneous equations shown below, find the inverse of the coefficient matrix and then use matrix multiplication to solve for the variables X, Y, and Z. If your calculator does not have the capability to find the inverse of a matrix, use a program such as Excel, or MATLAB.

$$5x + 2y - 5z = 21$$
$$-7x + 5y + 10z = 0$$
$$x - 5y + 8z = 6$$

Appendix B

Matrix Operations Using Excel

Excel can be used to carry out operations on matrices. Following are examples of how to perform several common matrix operations in Excel:

Matrix Addition

To add two matrices A + B = C:

A Matrix:			B Matrix:			(manually) C Matrix	
3	1		3	-5		6	-4
4	3		1	0		5	3

In Excel:
1. Enter the matrix A into the Excel sheet: by keying in values A1:B2, followed by highlighting this region of the spreadsheet and selecting **Insert>Name>Define** (or in Excel 2007: **Formulas>Define Name**): and keying in '**A**'

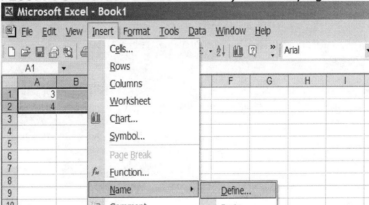

2. Repeat this process for matrix B

3. Highlight the region of the sheet that you want the resulting matrix C to be placed. In this case we know C will be 2 x 2 so we highlight some 2 x 2 area, and then key the following formula into the formula bar:
$$= A + B$$
4. When the expression has been entered and the cursor is still next to expression, simultaneously hold down the control Ctrl key, the Shift key and press the Enter key. This indicates to Excel that this is a matrix operation, and it will automatically place brackets around the expression: {=A + B} and display the results in the spreadsheet.

Matrix Multiplication

Excel has a built in command for matrix multiplication. The form of the command has the form:

$$=MMULT(array1,array2)$$

For example: (manually)
    AA matrix: BB Matrix: CC Matrix:
    1   -2   -5   6   -19   22
    3   -4   7   -8   -43   50

1. If the matrix **AA** is in cells C10:D11 and the matrix **BB** is in Cells G10:H11, we first highlight these cells and name the matrices as we did in the matrix addition example.

2. Now highlight a 2 x 2 area in this case (because the result will have as many rows as matrix AA and as many columns as matrix BB and then key in on the formula line:

$$=MMULT(AA,BB)$$

followed by holding down the Ctrl and Shift key while pressing the Enter key. This indicates to Excel that this is a matrix operation. The resulting equation becomes:

$$\{=MMULT(AA,BB)\}$$

3. The resulting C matrix will be in the highlighted cells.

Matrix Inversion
Excel also has a built in command for finding the inverse of a matrix. The command has the form:
$$=MINVERSE(array)$$

After the command has been typed in, hold down both the Ctrl and Shift keys while pressing the Enter key.

For example:
    A matrix: A^{-1} Matrix
    2   3   +1/6   +1/6
    4   -3   +2/9   -1/9

Index